THE "ACTUAL" NORMAL
A GUIDE TO RECLAIMING YOUR SELF AND YOUR LIFE IN CHALLENGING, CHANGING TIMES

PETRA PAIGE

BUSHKA BOOKS

Published by Bushka Books in 2022.

Petra Paige copyright 2022.

Cover and internal layout by Petra Paige.

All Rights Reserved. No part of this book may be reproduced by any mechanical, photographic, or electronic processes, or in the form of a phonographic recording. Nor may it be stored in a retrieval system, transmitted or otherwise be copied for public or private use — other than for 'fair use' as brief quotations embodied in articles and reviews — without prior written permission of the Author.

A catalogue record for this book is available from the National Library of Australia.

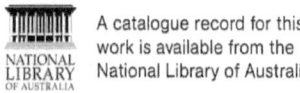
A catalogue record for this work is available from the National Library of Australia

ISBN: 978-0-6452254-7-1

Disclaimer

The Author of this book offers information of a general nature to help you in your quest for personal success and peace. This information is not meant to be used, nor should it be used, to diagnose or treat any medical condition. The information, concepts and exercises contained within this publication are designed to provide helpful information only on the subjects discussed, and are not designed to be a definitive guide or to take the place of advice from a qualified professional. Owing to the variable natures of individuals, there is no guarantee that the methods suggested in this book will be successful. If any individual or organisation does wish to implement the ideas discussed herein, it is recommended that they obtain their own independent advice specific to their circumstances. The author does not take any responsibility for any choices or actions that any individual or organisation may make relating to this information in the business, personal, financial, familial or other areas of life. The author is not liable for any damages, negative consequences or losses resulting from reading or taking action on the information contained in this book, and any such liability is expressly disclaimed. Any opinions expressed in this work are exclusively those of the author and are not necessarily the views held or endorsed by others quoted throughout.

This book is available in print, and eBook formats.

REVIEWS ON THE ACTUAL NORMAL

"As our Western way of life unravels in one of the most volatile periods in Human history, we need a new understanding of the place we find ourselves in at this unique moment in human history. The 'Actual' Normal offers information and insights into what's actually going on and gives you an understanding of our Human experience from a new perspective, while helping you to figure out what to do about yours."

"Grief travels with any kind of loss. In the aftermath of the pandemic (and even before then), many of us have been grieving the loss of feeling safe, and the freedom of lifestyle we've been used to! 'The Actual Normal''s particular take on things enables readers to begin creating powerfully healing responses to loss and change that returns us to living in hope — despite the current massive pressures on our way of life in Western cultures."

Petra shares the lessons's she learned in the trenches of Western middle class pain, and shows that there is a way out of struggle, grief and feelings of hopelessness. You will find a roadmap set with guideposts in 'The Actual Normal' — that move you effectively through personal suffering, to arrive resourced on the other side, despite all.

"Offering proven ways to liberate your untried Human potentials and reclaim the power of your true Self — no matter what may come at you — Petra teaches that YOU truly are a force on this planet! Combining personal anecdotes with proven wisdoms, Petra offers deep insights to inspire new ideas and actions, along with practical strategies to find and leverage your personal power.

More than that, Petra succeeds in showing that there has never been more opportunity to address the problems of our world, than by managing and changing ourselves. This book will show you the way."

TO RIC, NADIA AND KAI
The gleams in my tufted grove.

Thank you for the privilege of walking this road with you.

It's my mission...
to inspire hope in you,
to encourage you to believe in yourself, in Life
— and in other Human Beings.

∽

And to keep trying, *no matter what may come*.

∽

"The most authentic thing about us
is our capacity to create,
to overcome,
to endure,
to transform,
to love,
and to be greater
than our suffering."[1]

—Ben Okri

CONTENTS

Part I
INTRODUCTIONS

1. Is This You?   3
   Who This Book Speaks To
2. Why This Book Was Written   7
   Struggle And Suffering Is Rising In Modern Western Culture
3. The Powerful Message Of This Book   13
   And Why You Should Read It
4. Searching For A Way Forwards   16
   "Self-Help" That Actually Helps
5. How To Use This Book   24
6. Checking My Privilege   28
   ...And A Little About Me

Part II
FALLING INTO SUFFERING
What Suffering Is And Why It Happens

7. Things Fall Apart   35
   My Journey Into This Particular Pain
8. A 'First-World' Problem   43
   The Reality Of Inner Experience
9. The School Of The Soft Touch   52
   Our Ideas About Difficulty
10. The Beginnings   57
    A Struggle With Powerlessness
11. Components Of Suffering   64
    Painful Emotions Pile On...
12. Fear   72
    What If.....?
13. Who Am I If I Can't...?   79
    Our Sense Of Identity Under Siege
14. Diary Entry...   85

Part III
THE SCHOOL OF HARD KNOCKS
What's Going On In Our World?

15. The Stage Is Set 89
    The "Experience" Of Life
16. Our Western Cultural Context 93
    A 'Set-Up' Of Expectations
17. A Shifting Context 98
    How The "Rules" Changed
18. The Greatest Risk In Our Future 107
    The Anguish Of The Middle Classes
19. "Real" Victims 117
    Our "First World Problem"
20. Cultural Myths 124
    Trapped By Our "Stories"
21. A Word On "Mental Health" 136
    Labelled Into "Illness"
22. Grieving The Losses 148
    How To Process Grief

Part IV
THE 'ACTUAL' NORMAL
How Things Truly Are

23. A New Orientation To Life 157
    Finding A New Way Forward
24. The Superpower Of Human Beings 167
    The Gifts Of Thought And Thinking
25. The Kryptonite Of Human Beings 177
    Spectacular Illusions
26. Taking Charge Of Ourselves 187
    Owning And Sculpting Our Experience
27. This Is The Water 194
    Fundamental Realities of Human Life
28. Swimmers 205
    What Propels Us Through 'The Water'
29. Grappling With Change 212
    The Transformative Opportunity
30. Choice 224
    The Fundamental Power Of Human Beings

31. Activating Our Personal Power   234
Widening Our Existential Circumference

32. Goggles And Snorkel   245
Stopping Up Our Power Leaks

Part V
YOUR TURNING POINT
Igniting Our Own Empowerment: Reclaiming Ourselves And The Future

33. How I Became Empowered   261
My Reclamation Story

34. The Vital Pivot   275
Nothing Changes, Until You Do

35. Your Empowerment Path   284
Putting Personal Power Into Practise

36. Embracing Your Road   296
Live, While You Are Alive

37. Go Forth Inspired   308
Step Into The Future — Empowered Being That You Are

38. Closing Verse   319

Glossary Of Terms   321
Acknowledgments   329
Sources   333

PART I
INTRODUCTIONS

IS THIS YOU?

WHO THIS BOOK SPEAKS TO

The best part of my day?

Going to bed.

Knowing that I will not have to tread the path of life for a few hours. That I will be unconscious and unaware for a few blissful hours, and therefore, not suffering.

For while I sleep, I don't really know or understand that I exist and have a life and Self I must deal with minute by minute.

The worst part?

Waking in the morning.

There is that blissful, brief moment before consciousness reasserts itself —where I have a moment of peace in being me, as I come-to.

Then reality crashes in.

I must get up and face another day in the light. A day where I will be confronted by my life, which I've come to loathe. A life which has not worked out at all as I imagined, and which seems impossible to reshape, no matter what I try. Another day where I must wrestle with my thoughts, my fears, my anger, and my feelings of lack and dissatisfaction."

DO YOU FEEL THIS WAY, TOO?

You've suffered losses, your personal circumstances are difficult, and you're regularly enveloped by uncertainty—and even occasional terror. Rather than the sense of opportunity, hope and joy which you've SO yearned for, the hand of (Life) cards you're holding at the moment are 'powerlessness', 'impotence' and 'disconnection'—from your plans, hopes, motivation, and even your loved ones.

You bought the story. And looks as though it's never going to come true.

Your aspirations lie in tatters. As you've failed to find 'purchase', your dreams for your life and Self have been slipping away. You're grieving the loss of the life you hoped and worked for. You don't know how to get things back on track so you can make the kinds of choices that expand you, and your life.

You've come to a frightening realisation that there is nothing you can practically do to turn things around. You're miserable, angry and despairing—and often feel hopeless.

- You're stuck. —Not through falling off the confidence cliff or because of a personal "skill or discipline deficit", but stuck in an unresolvable situation.
- Opportunity (and luck) doesn't hang around your neighbourhood —or anywhere where you are.
- Maybe you've lost your job and can't get another one. Your career may have imploded. Perhaps you've even lost your home.
- You're miserable in a key relationship and can't resolve the problems, yet can't just walk away.

- Someone you love or cared about left you, maybe even died, and you just can't get past it.
- Maybe you've had a health diagnosis that changes everything for you. You're ill, or disabled in some way, with no end in sight.
- You're feeling poorer by the year no matter how hard you work or try. You're getting behind, things are slipping away, and you're deeply afraid.
- You're disconnected from your own power.

NOTHING YOU DO SEEMS TO WORK OUT

What to do with what you have been landed with—and with yourself? Day after day you wake to the same reality: you—standing on the sidelines of your life, with no idea of how to shape it back into something you want, or of how to rediscover the joy that you long for.

—This isn't about the minor disappointments; the every day stuff of life that you can contextualise and then bow to the hand of fate with grace (even if only eventually). Rather, things have truly fallen over—seemingly irretrievably, with high impacts on your life and on you personally. A sense of ongoing failure becomes coupled with despair, and washes over you regularly in waves of anxiety.

Perhaps you've been through a cycle of shock and anger at what caused the problem. Perhaps you've fought back to change the situation and/or outcomes, with everything you have: to take it on, to rally, to be positive, to try harder, to be different, to take responsibility. Yet nothing much has changed. No action you've taken has brought you closer to your objectives. Stuck in 'fight or flight' with no way of acting on either of them, you feel powerless.

Things feel outside of your control now. Sustained 'stuck-ness' is exhausting and life-sapping, and you've become drained and miserable. You don't know how to be with how hard and painful things are for you, and you're resentful at Life itself for forcing bad luck and hard times on you. Your relationships have become tricky—and the one you have with yourself is hard work.

YOU'RE GRADUALLY UNRAVELLING

In fact, you're experiencing inner chaos. Negative thoughts dominate your mind, constantly circling; spirals that pull you down and drain you of your vitality, your enthusiasm, your sense of possibility, your belief in yourself, and your hope. You're gradually becoming traumatised—particularly since it seems that there will be no end to what you're going through.

In this terrible place, you feel fear, along with loss and grief. To keep on hoping and trying into what seems to be an endless future of 'nothing changes'—especially on your own—is increasingly difficult.

You're tempted to stop trying. You often go inwards these days, blaming yourself for the choices that got you here and blaming yourself for being useless. You're giving up on yourself, turning on yourself. Doing self-hate.

Is this you? Then please read on.

WHY THIS BOOK WAS WRITTEN

STRUGGLE AND SUFFERING IS RISING IN MODERN WESTERN CULTURE

*I*f you're living in Western culture, you're probably looking for new answers (and even asking new questions)—about Life, about yourself, about the future, and about your power in all of it: for yourself, for your Life, and for the future. Because you're struggling in this "new normal"—and suffering in it. Feeling powerless (and understandably anxious about that), you're disorientated and outraged about the dwindling of both opportunity and possibility, the sullying of our planet, and the muddying of the future.

In fact there is nothing "new" about it. It's just that the veil that modern Western society had pulled over what *really* goes on in Life, has been flung aside.

What has been revealed?

—That despite the modern age of innovation, opportunity, enlightenment and facility, Life is full of more struggle, pain, ugliness and suffering than we either allow for, or admit to.

And we're *all* subject to it.

—That Change (and particularly the kind of seismic change we've been experiencing across the world since the early 2000's) has actually *changed our world,* impacting our possibilities, our responsibilities and our overall way of life.

—That despite what we impose on it in our tidy minds and modern lives, we are *all* affected by this changed, greater Context. (Unless we're gazillionaires, perhaps, but even then…) Life is increasingly challenging for millions of people, and now, especially, for growing numbers of middle class people.

—That there is no going back. That we need a new practical way forward. All of us.

SUFFERING IS RISING IN WESTERN CULTURES

More and more of us are finding ourselves in lives that don't work any more, in jobs and relationships that are unsatisfying.

More and more of us are afraid, and desperate in this vast, now alienating Context, finding that "success" has fallen beyond our reach, as the edifice of a civilisation that we've constructed over decades begins to fall over.

We're aching; carrying unbearable pain.

When my middle-class-Western-culture-life fell over, I strove to restore it. I could not. For five long years, mired in mental anguish and trapped in a sense of powerlessness, I sought a way out of pain, but could find nothing useful or sustaining to turn to.

I was dismissed everywhere I turned for help and explanations; left simply struggling—with this unhelpful message:

 Your suffering is a 'First World Problem'. *(Shrug).*

With my pain seen as illegitimate, *I* became diminished. Eventually, I fell into despair.

For much of that time I didn't really understand why I felt the way I did. I certainly didn't know what I was up against. And I had no idea of what I could do about it.

But over time I came to understand that my experience was reflective of a new, rising reality in the Western world, that was revealing truths that I, steeped in our cultural myths as I was, had never seen or known before.

Huge and unusual shifts in our world and societies over the last two decades or so have 'changed reality' for millions of us, shrinking opportunity, and eroding usual possibilities in middle class lives. The infrastructure we've grown up in—long established systems—has been quietly falling over: the economic system, social systems, political systems. Around us increasingly, wages have been stagnating while the cost of living (including house prices) has soared. Many people are struggling to get jobs and are very often underemployed, if not unemployed. The planet's delicate ecosystems are under existential threat, foreshadowing further disasters, and irretrievable losses.

These disintegrations seem to mirror so many people's descent into inner anarchy and desperate confusion.

Increasingly, people are feeling disquieted and apprehensive—if not actually afraid. Relationships are under terrible pressure. Millions of people are grieving losses; millions currently are struggling with anxiety and depression.

Men, and the younger generation in particular, are gripped with fear and hopelessness in the "new normal". Suicides in these groups are at record highs.

Never before, in the whole history of mankind, have so many decided that the only way to cope with the pain and the fear is to simply opt out.

Yet it's not just these shifts that have caused us to be struggling as we are in this "new normal".

WE HAVE LOST OUR BEARINGS

The fact is—*Life is not fair.* And what on earth are we thinking—expecting it to be? Life is not constrained by the "rules" we project onto it!

Yet, caught up in our Culturescape of "happiness and success" as we are, in large part we no longer know that suffering is a normal part of Life.

And somewhere, along that "happiness-and-success" road we've been walking since the end of the Second World War, we've lost the valuable tools we Humans once knew how to deploy in challenging time —in order to carry suffering, to process it, and rise intact from it.

This is a crucial oversight in a Human life where suffering in one form or another is inevitable.

Because we're not just on 'pause' as we work to overcome Covid-19 and it's after-effects, such as the ongoing global supply chain failures; or the impacts (as yet unknown) of Russia's war on Ukraine—or the massive economic adjustments still to come from both of these. We're not waiting for 'business-as-usual' to return.

The balance of everything, is shifting, and shifting out of balance. Massive, ongoing change has us grappling, while caught in uncertainty. Ongoingly, we're dealing with the resultant losses, pain and fears. At this turning point in Human existence, this is unlikely to diminish in incidence or intensity any time soon.

We need a new, practical way forward. All of us. Because suffering diminishes us: disconnects us from our personal power, from others, and from hope itself.

Millions of us now, are living "lives of quiet desperation" (as Henry David Thoreau put it)—falling into the crack between being delegitimised in our anguish and receiving skilled support. We need help, but don't know how to define that help. And certainly we don't know how to get it.

We're told that we're just down, or depressed, and are genuinely expected to rise up and change the things not working in our lives out of an inner determination.

> **Yet we cannot hope to restore anything in our own lives (much less our rapidly changing world) when we're coming out of our most broken Selves, instead of our best ones.**

We need to be heard and understood. We need to know it's not just us.

We need a way out of pain. We need to get some traction; to become enabled by doing simple things that will quickly bring us the outcomes we're desperate for.

AN ANTIDOTE TO POWERLESSNESS, AND DESPAIR

After recognising that my particular malaise was widespread across the Western World (and finding a path to overcome my suffering in it), I was impelled to give voice to it—to normalise and bring some comfort to a shared and devastating experience.

And crucially, by doing so, to shift as many people as I can out of disempowerment and despair, and towards hope, re-engagement and healing. Because…

> **There isn't just something to grieve here. There's also something to powerfully and passionately fight for.**

Our Lives. Our healing. Our empowerment. And—Possibility, as we go onward.

The insights I gleaned through my own experience of suffering in change, loss, grief and powerlessness, distilled into a powerful new "philosophy" that changed me, and turned my life around. I share this with you now as a true resource in this time of great change, uncertainty and pain in the world.

Packed with my deepest insights and ideas and the practices I believe to be most supportive of You in meaningfully re-engaging with the building of a thriving, peaceful and joyful life—I offer this book as an antidote to powerlessness, and feelings of despair:—ideas and insights not just for coping, but for living powerfully, no matter what life throws at us.

THE POWERFUL MESSAGE OF THIS BOOK

AND WHY YOU SHOULD READ IT

It's very likely that the reason you have picked up this book is because you have reached rock bottom.

Even when the most beautiful of days has dawned—when you're walking in nature, talking with your healthy family, reading a great book, or laughing and reminiscing with old friends—your fear and loneliness in your terrifying situation is always with you, in you, consuming you from the inside.

This is no way to live.

You need to know that someone gets what you're going through, and how difficult this burden is to carry.

And you need to know that you're not broken.

I know that when we don't believe in Life and ourselves anymore and have lost hope, we begin to experience inertia, and to withdraw. Anger and bitterness replace the hope and the trying that we used to do, silencing the internal voice that reminds us that Life matters; that asks us to give the best of ourselves.

Our personality changes, goes inward; slumps in misery. We accomplish less and less, and we value and respect ourselves less and less.

We project all this out on the world, and believe that we are receiving this message from *it*, rather than understanding that we're generating that from within ourselves.

Yet now, more than ever, we all need to step forward as our best selves, so that we can generate something life-affirming and healing, something future-proof: a way of being that is so much more healthy, sustainable and hopeful for our futures and the world as a whole.

I want you to find answers to your questions. And I want you to find them quickly. I hope to **translate** for you what you're experiencing—giving you words and concepts that you can work powerfully with. Because once we understand something, we can form a response, and importantly, one that's coherent.

I hope to **normalise** what you're experiencing, and to empower you to move forward into it rather than feel victim to it, or take it personally—becoming diminished by it.

I want you to thrive again. I want you to feel hopeful. I want you to engage with your incredible capacities and effort deliberately—and purposefully.

Because all we really have—against the elements, the unpredictability of life, the mess we've made in the world, and others, who may wound and even desert us—is ourselves.

And that's no small thing.

You are much more powerful than you realise.

While it may feel that you can have no impact—not even on your own life, let alone on bigger issues—know that what you generate in yourself does ripple out into the world, creating effects.

I want *you* to reclaim both your place and your power, in our great community of Humanity.

You can begin here, with this guide, to re-activate your personal power and re-shape your life.

And once you start engaging with ideas of your own power and how it works, and what you can do to leverage it and actually get what you really want, it becomes both interesting and wonderful!

Your future is in the making—right now. You do have all the tools you need to shape it, and to move the needle in your own life.

This is the powerful message at the heart of this book.

SEARCHING FOR A WAY FORWARDS

"SELF-HELP" THAT ACTUALLY HELPS

My disorientating, disempowering experiences had me searching, questing for years trying to make sense of what had happened to my power to create my life, and to find a place to land that could work for me, with options that, crucially, could return to me the ability to make choices.

All of those things did come to me eventually, but by the long route.

PAIN RELIEF: SELF-HELP RESOURCES

There is plenty of help for "sufferers" of course, for 'stuck' and 'lost' people.

Free information on the internet, organisations we can join (from alcohol addiction, to raw grief), Self-help books, professional therapists and Life Coaches—and a dazzling array of medications designed to suppress pain and stimulate dopamine and endorphins. They all combine to form an amazing modern smorgasbord of pain relief.

Many wonderful teachers and leaders with amazing ideas and strategies are also offering help, writing in the public space about finding success (and therefore happiness) within the arena of self-improvement. Their books and websites detail the unbelievable turnarounds they have made in their own lives through their discoveries and resulting wisdom. They offer help with how to move from A to B. All we need to do is to subscribe to their email list, watch their webinar, buy their book or course, or attend their three (or five, or nine) day seminar stacked with other luminaries like themselves, proffering hours of useful information.

'Change your life!' they say. *'We can show you how."*

"Unleash the power within! Control your thoughts, and find emotional mastery..."

"Organise your day. Plan massively and then follow through. Achieve your goals!"

"Find Purpose! Pursue results... Things will be great!"

After struggling for so long and feeling so much like a fish flopping about out of water, these were incredibly seductive messages. And they sounded easy! Apparently we need only a structure that facilitates a set number of key actions to be followed, and an attitude shift, to become enabled to power on through to success. And at the touch of my 'return' key, these would be made visible—and accessible—to me!

Blown away by the intelligence, insight, wisdom and practicality of so many of these individuals, on so many occasions I pictured myself walking *their* success path. *'Create a life I love?'* If I followed the advice, surely *I* could turn things around for myself too, and finally grasp success?

LOOKING FOR LEVERAGE

Much was out of my financial reach. But some things were free or financially accessible, and so—hopeful—I enrolled in several of them, over a period of time.

With self-help programmes, we're assured that we can go at our own pace. Believing this, we sign up, telling ourselves that it's *our* thing, we're on a track to getting back, and will get to it later on, if not now. After all… it's been set up for us to ultimately succeed!

This time I will, I'd promise myself.

I'd set to, full of hope and resolve. I'd follow the advice (mostly)—for weeks.

But I'd run into difficulties, often sooner, rather than later.

The first problem was the deluge of information arriving relentlessly in my inbox—as though I had nothing else to do in my day: no other tasks, nothing unexpected throwing my schedule off, like appointments or other arrangements that might derail me—let alone any disasters!

—Because that's Life, isn't it? Just as you've resolved to go on that detox program, four or more 'eating' invitations come in at once! Lunch at a friend's house, a celebration dinner somewhere else with a four course meal and alcohol included; or family coming to stay for a week—requiring you to provide breakfasts and cook big meals, and bringing all sorts of tempting foods into the house every day…

Webinars and YouTube things to watch sequentially would continue to arrive. Articles to read, actions to take, forms to fill in, things to consider—were required daily as the programme unfolded itself willy nilly in my email feeds.

Very quickly I'd fall behind. Usually the time-frames for turn-around were too short for me specifically, given that I seem to be the lynchpin around which our family's practical lives rotate. Perhaps for another person—who simply wants to move themselves to the next level in an ordered life—this issue wouldn't arise.

But soon, knowing I couldn't do this piecemeal and still be able to achieve the real changes I sought, I'd put it temporarily on the back burner. For when things calmed down somewhat.

Only, they wouldn't.

And in the meantime, encouraging emails and more material would continue to arrive in my inbox on the front end of the programme—as though I was still there and ready for it. Adding to the pile…

BECOMING OVERWHELMED

I'd wanted to be out there with all the other happy programme participants who'd started with me. I needed the group momentum! Yet there I was, lagging at the back of the class, still busy with the basics.

And when life did return to 'normal' (does it ever?) I'd start again, yet be travelling alone.

Then, I'd find all of the demands of the course or programme exhausting, rather than self-improving—because I was so low that I couldn't find the way into half of those actions! Massive self-reviews were required along with list-making and goal setting with a clear mind and clean diet. I'd start, and very soon be confronted by myself and then by my reality, and end up feeling demoralised. And pretty useless.

I'd quit soon after.

DIMINISHED (AND DIMINISHING) SELF-BELIEF

The practicalities I've just described may resonate with you!

I've given my failures here a lot of thought, and, with a few exceptions, I don't really blame the programmes or the way they are run. There was one key reason that the stuff didn't work for me.

I no longer had the inner resilience to take up the particular advice that was being offered.

That had fallen away after year 2.

I'd lost my belief in myself and my abilities, and the confidence to try turning things around.

And I'd reached a point of powerlessness that almost certainly guaranteed I'd quit when the going got too tough—because I couldn't bear the feeling of failing any more.

You may be a sufferer who feels a victim of circumstance. I felt *responsible* for my situation, believing I'd somehow been the architect of my own fall—and so I was also culpable in failing to 'relaunch.'

I couldn't understand how I'd got it so wrong given my vision and work ethic. Eventually I concluded that my difficulties must be the result of hidden (and thus irreversible) personal flaws in me. Clearly it was my choices—wrong choices, choices not made (which were choices in themselves)—that were now washing up on the shores of my life. In short, I was at fault, and must be unreliable and damaging.

Struck by disappointment, bitten every day by its offspring, I no longer had confidence in my ability to be effective.

With my self-esteem at an all-time low, my sense of possibility gone, it became almost impossible to hope, and to strive to create something new; to care enough about myself and my life to actually *want* to save myself and salvage something—rather than jump off a bridge.

And outside of not trusting myself, I'd stopped trusting *Life* itself. I felt more powerless than a legless ant at an anteater convention.

SO, WHAT IS THE WAY FORWARD?

Cynics, take heart.

This book does not offer instant miracles, with the promise that your first million dollars is easily within your grasp if only you...

Nor is this a practical guide claiming to lead to the 'change' and 'success' (and by implication consequent joy and healing) that are now missing in your life.

This approach also doesn't start with 'love yourself', 'be kind to yourself', 'repeat affirmations'—or any of that wonderful stuff. (Although, if you're already doing that, that is absolutely fantastic!)

In fact, I'm not even going to ask you to stop feeling the way you do about yourself and your life.

All I *am* going to ask is that you focus on some other things—*for now*.

Because I'm going to punch some holes in some of our commonly accepted notions about Life, Self and Culture that in themselves cause suffering—even before anything 'bad' has happened to us!

And I'll be going to work on stimulating your thinking and broadening your *awareness,* so that you see things differently from how you're seeing them now.

- I'll show you the key causes of First World suffering, bringing you to a new understanding of how you're finding yourself disempowered and despairing in our modern Context. And you'll find a certain peace, even just in that!
- You'll be brought to new insights in what to *really* expect from Life and—significantly—from yourself.
- I'll share ideas about what it means to be a Human Being (as different to being an animal species) and how this enables us uniquely, to rise powerfully in our lives.
- **And you'll discover what you can practically do**. Even at rock bottom, there is much that we can address to begin to move the needle in our lives, to restore hope and possibility to us. I'll show you new levers that you can pull to live expansively and luminously, no matter what comes at you while you are alive.

CARRYING SUFFERING, YET LIVING WELL

Equally—and significantly—there will be much that we *can't* change; certainly can't change without massive collaborative effort (I'm working on that…) There will inevitably be outcomes *outside* of the effects of our own individual lives and choices that ripple Suffering into our lives.

The fact is, no-one can make suffering go away completely—and no-one who is not selling drugs can claim to do that for us. (And I am not promising that here!) The only thing to do with suffering is to learn to deal with it, effectively, and sometimes that means simply learning how to carry it.

This alone is worth leaning about.

The truth is that it is only through our efforts with suffering – opening ourselves up to it, learning to carry it, and working to digest it—that it diminishes, and disappears.

It's an inside job. We each have to find our own way back to meaning and possibility.

So I'll present ideas for you to consider that will enable you to retrieve your sense of yourself as whole and well *despite circumstances,* so that you don't feel broken every day.

And I'll show you how to function despite suffering—and even how to carry your suffering in a state of something close to grace.

From those will come (surely?) increased inner resilience and courage, and new determinations to look forward again.

You'll find reconnection with your Self, and Your power in Life.

That's a bold promise. But I stand by it.

I said earlier that it's no small thing that we have ourselves against the elements, and the effects of our choices,and I meant that.

YOU—are the answer.

You will be invited into new perspectives and insights that enable you to deal with what is unfolding in your world (and *the* world) from a place within you that is both centred and empowered, no matter what comes at you.

Working with this inner game will change everything for you.

Get to the other side of this successfully—and you will—and you can dive deeper if you so wish with any guru of your choice. *But first get on track with me.*

This book *will* help you cope with circumstances that might not change much externally despite your efforts and your hope and your attitude. Most importantly, there will be the sense when you close its covers that there *is* meaning in Life and living it, regardless of the difficulties it presents: that every day, you do actually wake up to something worthwhile, rather than only to fear and despair.

HOW TO USE THIS BOOK

Our understandings build via the small details, as our lives unfold: 'glimpses' that gradually resolve themselves into the forms, parts and wholes of the world, of Life, of others, and of our Selves. As the bigger picture is revealed, we stand in it with ever deepening awareness, understanding , knowledge and insights—ultimately achieving wisdom.

I have wanted to bring you along a similar journey here. So I've structured this book in four sections, that build understandings from the ground up.

THE FIRST SECTION

"Falling into Suffering" explains what suffering really is, how we fall into it, why it hurts so badly, and why it's so damaging.

Suffering decimates us because, feeling both alone and powerless in it, we come to believe that it has something to do with us personally.

Devastatingly, we 'lose' ourselves.

HOW TO USE THIS BOOK | 25

Understanding both our experience and our feelings is the first step to dealing with them, reconnecting with ourselves, and moving out of pain.

THE NEXT SECTION

In *"The School Of Hard Knocks"* I show how we've been set up to suffer by our cultural values, ideas and myths—exposing the 'lies' we've been living in, and the *actual* realities and 'rules' of Life that underpin our existence. I shine a light on how, despite our comparatively safe, modern lives of opportunity, modern Western suffering is dominant in the middle classes, *and why this matters so much.*

THE THIRD SECTION

In *"The Actual Normal"*, I teach how we Humans function, including what 'generates' for us, what empowers us, and how we become diminished. I'll not only show you how we become disempowered, but also what to do about that.

THE LAST SECTION

—*"A "Turning Point"* invites you to journey out of your pain and disempowerment on the back of (hopefully) the shifts that the insights in this book may have wrought in you—so that you can go forward stronger, wiser, more peaceful and more personally empowered than you have ever been.

The practical path, showing exactly how to do it, is laid down here.

EASY ACCESS TO MASSIVE INSIGHT

I hope that you will find it both interesting to discover new ways of looking at things, and an enjoyable read.

I know the power of our thoughts.

> The way we see our world is how we see ourselves, and interpret possibility. This really matters, because our choices and actions come out of this thinking—and create our lives.

If I can shift your thinking at all as you make your way through this book, I will have succeeded beyond my wildest dreams — and, I believe, I will have given you an immeasurable gift in the process.

Shifting your thinking is thus the work of this book.

I hope that you'll find you can open the book almost anywhere and immediately pick up something useful. I have laid it out with the intention that you get value wherever you find yourself in the information, rather than being confronted with reams of print that make little sense if you haven't read everything else on the page!

(Yet of course, there is great value in doing just that... 😊)

I do know that when we're down and under-resourced, in an irritable, despairing 'everything-is-pointless' frame of mind, it can be difficult to show up to the page. And I want to make sure you're helped regardless, so if it does become hard-going for any reason, the key insights from each chapter are summarised into a 'cliff notes' version of the book, in which I've made it easy to see what the truly important takeaways are. Drop me a line on the 'Contact' page of my website, and I'll send it on to you. You can find me at www.petraspaige.com.

CAPITALISATION

My philosophy is a combination of Truths and concepts that stand together to create both Insight and personal empowerment. I've therefore capitalised certain words throughout the text to emphasise them as more than simple descriptors.

I know that this is grammatically unusual, but I hope that, as you make your way through the book, you'll forgive this, and understand it as a way of highlighting these as significant.

GLOSSARY OF TERMS

The specific 'meanings' I intend these 'concept' words to convey are to be found in the Glossary of Terms at the end of the book. Our use of and understandings of words varies widely across the English language and the cultures that speak it; it's important that these meanings are accurately understood, regardless of our own interpretations of language.

CHECKING MY PRIVILEGE

...AND A LITTLE ABOUT ME

*J*t may seem unusual for someone like me to write about 'suffering'—even to be creating such a dialogue around middle-class pain when there have been (and are) so many others who can much more 'legitimately' lay claim to the term in their experience of life.

So I want to say at the outset that I recognise that whatever I've suffered *pales* in comparison to the struggles of so many others in this world.

I know I'm counted as fortunate to have been born into certain opportunities, because I was:

1. living in the developed Western world

2. educated

3. middle class

4. Caucasian

5. in good health

6. loved and cared for

7. supported and enabled

8. fed and watered

9. had good access to sleep, and a comfortable mattress

9. not abused

Yet, as a Human being, I *have* suffered on my journey in Life in my own way—and it hurt so badly that it put me on my knees and made me pray to die. You may roll your eyes at this, and say I'm entitled and spoiled. Perhaps you'd be right. But at the time my suffering disorientated and weakened me, and even became destructive: it hurt to the point where I came very close to jumping off the planet.

And on the way there, I made my family—who were going through enough thank you very much—very unhappy indeed.

That was one of my legacies. I have to live with the scars they each carry as a result.

I do recognise that while much of the insight that is in this book was being born, I was 'being' a privileged person. And I'm grateful for the privilege that has enabled me the space to review my suffering, so that I might offer the insights I gained, here—in the hope that it might practically help you, to carry yours.

The result I created out of it has relevance to you, because it is actually about being a Human Being living an Earthly life. And that we do have in common.

HERITAGE

I carry two badges front and centre. They have been nailed to my forehead since the day I was born, and were the beginning of my suffering.

I am German. I am South African. The arrogance, aggression and cruelty of both of those are in my biographical line. These nationalities are also the reason I was always defined from the outside-in. Legacies of my forebears. The worst are the burdens of the Holocaust, and Apartheid: the ability to inflict suffering on others; to turn away from tolerance and inclusion; from compassion—indeed, from one's own humanity. To diminish Human value to the point of the most absolute dismissal.

Yet often it's the things we're given to carry that cause us to become clear. We notice the nuances in them: the foulness, or the sweetness. Awareness dawns.

What do we *Choose* once we become conscious?

We claim what is brilliant in those things and hold them close. We *choose* who to be, and how to be—and who we will *not* be, what we will *not* stand for. Anything but that...

These legacies were the beginning of a great distillation in me, the start of an ongoing refinement: I *am* this, I am *not* this. I *will* be that. Much later on, this particular propensity in me was given the opportunity to come to the full as I chose how I personally would respond to my painful, difficult circumstances.

German quality, high standards, leadership, courage—and (since the Second World War)—humility. I claim those as *values* that define my effort and the brightness of the polish on the work I try to put forth.

South African warmth, humour, forgiveness, collaboration—and forthrightness—I own too. I hope that all of these shine through these pages I've written for you, my fellow Human.

Like all of us, I've been forged in the flames of my significant relationships—with others, with my habitats, and, not least, by the one with myself! I've been so broken by them; broken open. Had so much hubris burned away. I have had to find not only who I was, but who I was not. This journey of Identity has been one of *defining myself from the inside out*—and forging myself into who I needed to be to carry my burdens, and into who I wanted to be, to help others to carry theirs.

All of this has marked me indelibly. Each moment of pain brought insight, every experience brought new resources that helped me strive forward—to live more consciously, and wiser, moving all the while away from unconscious blindness and assumption.

And only for the good! For this book could not have been born without all of it in my life, just as it was.

LEGACY

Nelson Mandela's legacy shines so brightly across the world that his name is known everywhere. A fellow South African, I have been deeply affected by it.

It's commonly held that his legacy was bringing an end to Apartheid with his public stance against it, yet I believe that his true legacy was the character qualities he held to and demonstrated to us all throughout that time, and afterwards: *grace* in particular. What it looks like, lived. —Not on the surface, but bone deep.

It has brought Mandela iconic status across the world. He had every reason to emerge militant and bitter from an experience that was designed to break him; that stole twenty seven of his best years from him and deprived him of the experiences he should have had as a worthwhile husband, father, friend, son and citizen.

Yet he managed to bring grace to the table, all the same. Kindness, forgiveness, compassion and collaboration—all wrapped up in a great appreciation of the miracle of Life. I have been in awe of that quality that he so admirably and consistently demonstrated from the time he was returned to society in 1994 and became visible again.

I believe that there is no legacy more enduring or regenerative than grace.

I've been inspired to bring that quality into my own life, no matter how crappy things have got, both at home, and in our world. To strive to handle my problems with grace. To be graceful in the face of difficulty. To stay in grace, even in the face of others' ignorance and unkindness.

This book is *my* 'sculpted' legacy to my family, to my friends, to the world—and to you specifically. I walked this road, and I learned something valuable. And I share it with you as an offering from my soul—and an affirmation of what is both possible and necessary to live well in this world.

I wish for it to nourish and comfort you in the hardest of times, to inspire you into your finest Self at all other times, and to remind you that what we do really does matter—even the smallest of things. We leave a trace.

And if I succeed in leading you into any worthwhile insights in these pages as you battle dissolution, disconnection, desperation, despondency and despair in our changing world, let it be these two things:

- Becoming self-aware enough to reach relentlessly for personal transformation. It's the most important thing you could ever do.
- And while you do this, to strive to live your life, with grace.

May this book give you the inspiration, energy and tools with which to engage with that purpose.

PART II
FALLING INTO SUFFERING

WHAT SUFFERING IS AND WHY IT HAPPENS

THINGS FALL APART

MY JOURNEY INTO THIS PARTICULAR PAIN

I am an ordinary, middle class girl, who held the usual expectations of Self and life in a First World country in the modern age.

I tried to be great. I tried for the dream.

I was hard working, co-operative; pushed myself, educated myself, took on jobs that gave me more money and opportunity every time; changed countries to up-skill and broaden my experience — believing always that if I was visionary, responsible and... myself—I could carve my way through life and step into its opportunities to create my Big Picture.

Like anyone else, I made a series of choices along the way. And I was successful. Up to a point.

On the surface, I married a man I adore. We could talk endlessly about everything, and our hearts were full of hope for a successful, full and happy future. Standing in the embrace of Western civilisation, we saw ourselves at the doorway of possibility. Yes, there were "rules"—but we could leverage them to make the most of Life and the opportunities before us! It wasn't so much what *could* we do — as what *would* we do!

With full trust in ourselves and our ability to be resourceful, we emigrated to London, England, where we both worked hard to add massive value in our jobs. I worked in senior Human Resources roles, progressing soon enough into Consultancy, our company specialising in "people solutions", and specifically in those leadership and teamwork behaviours that enable Organisations' to truly realise their potentials. Saving hard, we eventually bought our own home, which we renovated and improved over time—even learning to lay tiling ourselves! We spent more than a decade in the UK, and enjoyed a freedom of lifestyle, and wonderful, uplifting friendships with other interesting, resourceful, and similarly starry-eyed people. Often we'd be found cycling or riding horses in the countryside, and even more often, scuba-diving in the English Channel. We loved libraries and bookshops; music, movies and theatre; drinks in the pub, dining out on occasion, and entertaining friends at home. Most years we manage to ski the French or Italian Alps at Christmas time. And after seventeen years together, our daughter joined us.

We'd built a relationship and life that worked, and that we loved. What could we do next? What *would* we do next?

STEPPING INTO POSSIBILITY

As a new little family we emigrated again—this time, to Australia, arriving there just before the 911 attacks in the USA, in 2001. And in the aftermath of that horrific objection to Western civilisation, as thousands of Australians streamed back to the familiarity and safety of home, we found ourselves in a much smaller economy on the far reaches of the world, where competition for good jobs was now stiff, prices were rising and salaries were soon to grind into stagnation.

Instead of stepping into new opportunity as we'd expected, we found ourselves able to maintain the status quo at best.

We were experiencing (without knowing it) the beginnings of massive (invisible) change in the world that would unfold (and continues to roll out to this very day) .

Still, my amazing husband stepped up (as he always does) and after two years of freelancing and the stressful reality of impermanence, he won his way into a senior role in a large company. And, after welcoming our baby son, we were able to build a new lifestyle around home and family —but with beaches in abundant supply, instead of rain! We discovered new family hobbies and made many new friends, and enjoyed another decade of (relative) peace and adventure together.

FISSURES IN THE FUNDAMENT

When my husband was promoted into the CEO role in his company (based fifty kilometres outside Sydney), we decided to relocate our family nearby—to better facilitate the bigger role and additional responsibility that came with it. And so it was that several months later, we found ourselves living in our new home in a village in the Blue Mountains.

Finally—it felt as though we'd 'made it'!

Yet, of course, behind the scenes, Life continued to unfold itself. Long before we knew it, factors outside our control or sphere of influence were rippling towards our lives, soon to change everything.

DISASTER

The first thing to arrive (less than a year later) was a diagnosis: my husband was found to have Stage Four cancer from a melanoma. He had only a 20% chance of surviving it.

Then, hot on the heels of the shock of the diagnosis, the operations and a couple of weeks of recovery time from those, my husband's employer—concerned he would die—terminated his employment.

It was as though Life said, *"Enough. All that rushing here and there and changing lanes? You've made your last unseeing choice. We're taking over from now on."* And, just like that, we were redirected away from a way of living where we'd been able to impose our intentions and will on what we valued, desired and thought important: *doing, getting, having, going, choosing, producing,* and even pleasing and conforming.

"Life"—dis-abled us.

My husband was fighting for his life, his career had been destroyed at a stroke, and our livelihood was gone. We had no safety net of family, insurance policies, or savings. And we were very alone. Just the two of us with our two young kids (nine and twelve years old), far from home and family. Far even from our Sydney community of friends. Our life as we knew it, as we'd worked for, planned for, hoped for—had been annihilated.

Yet what *was* there to do but deal with what was before us, as best we could?

In the back of my mind somewhere, I imagined that we'd deal practically with our immediate situation. I had no current employment as I'd been caring full-time for our children, but I believed I'd get a job, we'd deal with my husband's recovery, and then at some point we'd be able to start working towards 'restoration' over time—whatever that might look like.

Yet my career break—spanning a change in countries—soon proved that I was now 'unemployable'. I wasn't able to get a job.

And, after he'd recovered from his surgeries, neither was my husband.

Over the next year or three, this unfolded as a new and additional disaster that became a cul-de-sac with no exit.

Disaster's friends began to arrive over the course of the next year. Fear. My panic was still off the charts—the terror that the man I'd been with since I was seventeen years old might die. The idea of my husband losing his life and us losing each other was unbearable. And alongside that was Anxiety: what else would be taken away? Then there was a sense of

Lack. And the Fear that comes with *that*. And then Grief over the losses of certainty, and possibility.

What if we (and specifically *me* now that my husband was ill) ultimately couldn't provide for ourselves—even just the basics, like food, and a roof over our heads? Would we enter the terrible treadmill of homelessness and poverty? Which raised the awful question of what would happen to our kids? How could we let them down like this?

Being trapped in a state of grief and fear became an ongoing, and unrelenting reality.

Over the next years, ripples from other choices and mistakes we'd made in our past—like personal issues we hadn't resolved—began to reach us too, coming on gradually; making themselves felt. We'd each insisted on things that we shouldn't have; not spoken up on things we should have; often hadn't acted where we could have.

Like the proverbial Boiled Frog, the water of Life had been heating up around us, unnoticed, and now, under the umbrella of disaster, it all came together. Suddenly it was all too hot. The story we'd bought into growing up, that we were going to create and live—that was going to be possible because we'd followed all the rules—was over.

Grappling with my difficulties, carrying disappointments and heartbreak, and frustrated by my failed efforts, I struggled with the situation, bewildered not only by what had unfolded, but by the fact that it just wouldn't go away. I was disorientated, and felt I'd flown into a cage instead of the clear air Australia had promised—with the door being shut behind me. I had never felt caged before; had never been so disempowered, or thrown to the sidelines of my own decision making and control.

THE ACTUAL NORMAL

I remember clearly the day the illusion the story—finally crashed away and 'reality' stood starkly before me: this daily agony wasn't going to be temporary. And I said to my husband, *"What I thought was Life—was* normal *in life*—isn't. *The* actual *normal is struggle and disappointment and pain and suffering.*"

I felt cheated, blindsided and devastated.

Unbelievably, it had been there all along. I'd just been lucky enough to be able to float above it for a time, buoyed into place by a level of upbringing and opportunity secured by my family of origin and ancestors, my chances in the specific culture and society I grew up in, and my place in time.

Change had been diluting the structures that had propped us up for so long, and we were falling through…

Many of us have been 'sold a story' about what life is for and about, and what we specifically are in it: an experience of happiness and success if we can grasp opportunity, with an upward trajectory by which we'd get to fulfil all our ambitions. All we need to do is wisely layer achievements and assets one over another—paints on a palette—to paint our 'Big Pictures'. Just follow 'the rules'. They may have been unspoken but they were well understood: get an education, get a job, work hard, be responsible, up-level your skillsets as you travel the road. Buy the house, have the children, aim for leadership roles at work; buy insurance, save… All would naturally unfold from there.

When I discovered through harsh personal experience that I had in fact bought into a lie, I lost myself for a time, because my values and aims—indeed my very Identity—were pinned on the story's successful enactment.

MY DARK NIGHT OF THE SOUL

Years of effort followed. Again and again I failed to make my practical circumstances fit my vision and support my values. The Big Pictures that I painted refused to materialise.

Or perhaps there was a form of them, but I couldn't see it because the narrative in my ears was too loud. The narrative was what I told myself 'should' have happened: that I'd followed the rules and what had resulted was unfair...

Without my picture of 'success', I was left with just 'me'—and I didn't connect with or really like what I saw. *I* wasn't 'enough'. Succumbing to the realisation of my own 'powerlessness', the shattered pieces of myself fell to the floor.

> "At the midpoint on the journey of life, I found myself in a dark forest, for the clear path was lost." **—Dante**

This was my "dark night of the soul"—and I was stuck there for a very long time.

I endured my existence, my relationships, and my days. Sleep was intermittent.

I felt dark emotions I didn't know I had in me—even jealousy simply at other people's ability to work, to make choices, to feel safe, and to take things for granted.

Gripped by frustration and a sense of powerlessness, I lived with loss and grief and the anxiety these wrought, bowed eventually by the understanding that I wasn't going to be able to fix what was broken, or even trade my life in for a new one—though I longed to.

During my darkest hours, I wondered why I was putting myself through existence. One day after another. What was it for? What was the point of it? What difference did it make if I was here on Earth alive—or not? What difference did *I* make? —Apart of course from the completion of chores at home that everybody needed me to perform, and not upsetting people who would feel bad if I ended the struggle... really—what was I doing here every day? It seemed that all I was really doing was feeling miserable and useless.

And making my family miserable to boot.

Not finding good answers to my questions—ones that made sense to me—brought me to despair, and I began to make myself 'invisible' to the world and to others.

RETREATING

I stayed home, and disengaged. I stopped trying for anything anymore.

Devastated that I couldn't fulfil my potential, carry out my ideas, or even carry my load in the way I wanted to, I chastised myself, over and over again. *"I Am A Pointless Waste Of Space."*

Self-blame became self-loathing.

I began to seriously contemplate removing myself from the equation altogether. If only I could die, I could stop inflicting myself upon my family and friends. Leaving seemed to be an easy, no-effort solution to end the suffering—and there seemed to be no other way out of the trap I was stuck in.

The actual act though, was beyond me. (I couldn't even get that done!)

What was I going to do to rescue myself from the disaster that had become my internal experience and the realities of my practical life?

Where *was* I to turn?

∼

A 'FIRST-WORLD' PROBLEM

THE REALITY OF INNER EXPERIENCE

I have reflected deeply on what happened then, how I reacted to difficulty on this scale—and particularly why and how I suffered as I did.

Because during that time, friends and family constantly reminded me (accurately) that I was in fact very lucky! My husband was fighting his illness with everything he had. We were managing to hang onto our house. And there were others out there who had far more reason to suffer than I did.

Perspective is all, I was told. *Accept. Be grateful.*

There seems to be only one view on grief and loss in our modern Western societies, and that is that 'real' grief is the domain of the bereaved. In other words, someone has to have died. *My* suffering wasn't really grief because I hadn't been 'bereaved' in this sense. And I am Caucasian. I wasn't living in poverty, or in a war zone; I wasn't homeless (yet) or abandoned. And clearly I wasn't suffering PTSD as war veterans, sexual abuse survivors and domestic violence victims might be. No. I was apparently "just miserable". Probably 'just depressed'.

I would fall silent. And then I would go and punch a pillow. Or break down in the bathroom, where no-one could see me cry.

Anguish is not depression. But it can lead there, and on from there— to other worse things. Why should it be diminished and dismissed until it can wear one of the labels currently in play? This question is particularly pertinent now when more people than ever are grieving the loss of the lives they'd constructed and worked for, along with their hopes for their future.

> *I felt guilty for suffering at all. But suffer I did. I was grieving, and afraid. I was angry, and impotent. I was terribly, terribly stressed. And really it wasn't about degrees—someone else's suffering being worse (or more legitimate) than mine. My pain was as real as anyone's.*
>
> **And awfully — it was mine.**

WE USED TO KNOW THAT LIFE WAS OFTEN HARD

Isn't suffering and grief just a part of life... *so just get on with it?*

In the past, suffering was ubiquitous. When people suffered or were unhappy, it was seen as a *natural* part of life rather than something unusual. Values of courage, stoicism, grace and grit came to the fore, were encouraged—and admirable. We knew that Life was hard.

People you love, people you know—may have told you stories of what life was like during the wars or the Great Depression. That people suffered and went without. Hardly anyone had fancy clothes or even cars —let alone fancy homes.

How, if you fell on hard times, there wasn't help from the government, or charitable agencies (there were none of those!). People were neglected and categorised and abused: at the mercy of the 'system.' Kids died of treatable illnesses, and sometimes with their mothers in childbirth. Charles Dickens' books are full of stories like these.

There was little access to information, or choice for most people.

You've probably read stories set in times even before then that describe life as often a grind, and little more than a fight for survival. People were treated callously and cruelly in a time when Human life was of little value and often hard to hold onto. They suffered through famine and cold; hungry, and with festering wounds and fatal illnesses (that we have well under control today)—and with little purpose beyond trying to survive it all—for centuries. Nothing was easy, especially for the underclasses and they died young.

People have endured all sorts of things. Because bad things happen all the time and have done all through the ages of Man. They really have.

So why do we no longer know and accept that a part of Life—of everyone's life—is suffering? That it happens to us all, in one way or another, and is simply unavoidable?

People in the modern, Western world today generally, are quite disconnected from the understanding that suffering and hardship are integral to Life, and barely know of the character strengths that people brought to bear on their circumstances, in times past.

What changed?

OUR OPPORTUNITIES AND VALUES HAVE SHIFTED EXPONENTIALLY

- The kind of suffering we used to experience has generally diminished in Western culture. As recently as one hundred years ago or so, one 'cataclysmic' event after another (the Spanish Flu, the two World Wars (sandwiching the Great Depression) and the scourge of polio for example) meant that people were still having to grow up in the 'School Of Hard Knocks'.

  Since then we've been living in the richest (and most peaceful) time in Human history generally—and in Western civilisation in particular. We've made incredible improvements; made so much possible for so many (that previously was restricted to just the lucky few)—that quality of life has improved dramatically for all.

—And not just in Western culture. Generally, Humans have never been so widely well off as we've been since the Second World War. Across the globe there have been improvements in health, in education, and in a reduction in poverty for those in Third World countries too. Though people still struggle with adversity, generally much has improved, both in quality of life and longevity. Across the world social hierarchies are flatter, more 'rights' are recognised, there is more opportunity and generally, more democracy. Information is more accessible, to absolutely everyone.

If we know or even remember that life was very harsh on Humankind generally until the end of the Second World War, we believe that we've moved on from it and will never see it again.

- We pursue (and have) ultimate power over the environment, over resources, and over others. We believe that there is very little we can't have or do—from creating Life itself here (without need for uterus, egg and sperm), to leaving the planet and setting up somewhere else in the galaxy. We believe that all we need do is meddle in the external world to keep hardship away; that we can keep all we don't like or agree with at bay (with nuclear weapons if necessary)—even if that means destroying the planet on which we depend for life! We have total 'power over', and confidence in our ability to maintain this. *Nothing will stand in our way!*

Consequently, we've found little use for 'wisdom' or character strengths, like stoicism, perseverance and grace, that previously held us up during times of hardship and personal struggle.

- Our values now are for an easy life and self-gratification. There is generally no shortage of anything: all around us we see abundance, opportunity, and people crossing barriers that would have been unthinkable just one hundred years ago. We expect things to be good, to be possible, and to work out well. Today we're looking for lots of disposable income, pre-prepared meals!

This has helped us along in a belief that we're 'owed' something purely by virtue of the fact that we were born, and created expectations that Life should be fair.

Few of us nowadays can imagine what it was like to try to scrape a living in the aftermath of war with all the death and destruction it wrought, or during a deep recession (though we may soon find out for ourselves…)

OUR OUTLOOK HAS SHIFTED EXPONENTIALLY INWARDS

An offshoot of having so successfully moved away from a focus on questions of survival is that we've found the time and inner space to shift our focus inwards (consciously or not). Now, we're questing for more existential answers.

> *"Why did that thing happen?"*
> *"Why did we (or someone else) behave as we did?"*
> *"What does that mean?" (right down to the very meaning of Life.)*
> *"What am I doing here, putting up with this?"*
> *"Can I choose something else?"*
> *"Do I matter? Do I have any power?"*

These are the kinds of questions we probably never really considered in past ages, before we questioned the existence of God or some higher authority.

The result is that we see ourselves differently now, from the way that Human Beings saw themselves in the past. We certainly have a different consciousness in us now, that is much expanded: much more aware of Self, much more self-directed.

It's given us the rise of the Individual.

We're no longer just trying to survive: now we're trying to personally thrive.

- We're looking for our Power now in things like how much influence we have in our various Contexts and relationships, and in the expectations we hold (of ourselves and from others).
- We're questing for Identity and Meaning: in the ideas we hold about ourselves, in the labels we wear and assign, and the weight we give to them.
- We're trying to discover Who we *can* Be by understanding ourselves and others, and how we can find joy.

The upshot of this is that we're living in and with a new inner awareness of ourselves and our experiences, and of our greater empowerment in the world. And alongside, we have the sense that the realities of disempowerment, pain, disconnection, and inner dis-equilibrium are something 'unusual', in our milieu.

This has awakened 'discernment' in us, of what we're *prepared* to experience, (particularly as we project forwards to what we hope for...)

Discernment is underpinned by expectations (and even entitlements) of our environments, relationships, of ourselves, and of Life itself. *Including that it* should *be fair.*

And so, our tolerance for suffering in general has lessened.

SUFFERING NOW DISLODGES US, INTERNALLY

It begins with some kind of loss, or fear. We may then find ourselves 'stuck' with a problem or situation, and grapple with it.

But things begin to feel 'out of our control' if we fail to regain traction. Ultimately this inability to control dislodges us from our inner Power, and then from our sense of ourselves as 'okay'. Of course, we feel the urgent need to rectify it, so we'll put everything we have into doing so!

But if, over time, we find that we can't over time, we begin to struggle.

We become anxious, and uncertain, sensing that we're 'falling behind', that our dreams for our lives are slipping out of reach. Our thoughts about our worries constantly circle in negative spirals, pulling us down, draining us of vitality and enthusiasm—and belief in ourselves and in possibility.

In the struggle, we begin to wonder what the *point* of the struggle and all the suffering is. And we suffer more, when we don't find answers to our questions—or when we find answers we don't like.

Now, rather than suffering because we're struggling to survive—much of our suffering is internally generated.

We begin to crumble from the inside out.

People who have not experienced losses, traumas or disabilities don't realise how one's entire world changes. *All* the plans for our life are changed (and even gone), including friendships, opportunities for work, hopes and dreams; a sense of possibility and the potential to manifest what we *need*—let alone what we might want!

Most of all, the fears we have to confront are phenomenal, beginning with, 'How will I survive?'

WHY IS SUFFERING AND GRIEF A 'PROBLEM'?

The fact is—Life is *not* easy. So many people are suffering, and stuck in suffering: grieving and lost.

But suffering is not only ubiquitous generally. These days (more than in a very long time), it's increasingly common among the previously 'privileged, middle class'. This massive group of people has worked really hard to shape so much of our modern world in excellent, life-enhancing ways for all, yet is becoming increasingly disempowered in rapidly changing times. Just when Humanity desperately needs to find a new and sustainable way forward, too many of these 'shapers' have begun spiralling down, practically and psychologically.

THE SHAME

This suffering has not been properly recognised for what it is, even by those in it! Middle-class people don't talk about their pain because they feel shame categorising it as "suffering"—knowing that there are truly tragic experiences of loss and grief out there, that are *surely* more deserving of the description.

So, too often we *don't* express our pain, and delay seeking help. We put extraordinary effort trying to get away from suffering instead: running from it, trying to find weapons to use against it, lying to ourselves (and others) about it, losing an inordinate amount of emotional energy to it—until we become depleted.

Alone, we sink further into powerlessness and anguish daily, and begin to experience hopelessness and despair. Some do jump off the planet—and in increasing numbers these days…

SUFFERING HURTS REGARDLESSLY

Outside of being actually physically tortured, your suffering and feeling stuck is *qualitatively* no different to that experienced by millions of people who wake up to difficult days, weeks, months and years, regardless of the reasons. Even those living what seems from the outside to be a wonderful, easy life, with no financial or emotional hardship are often dealing with awful, debilitating situations and feelings in their private space—be it abuse, grief, humiliation, loss of health or function, the early end of their career, or a hundred other reasons!

Suffering is suffering. It feels terrible. It's debilitating and constricting. It's personally diminishing—regardless of its cause.

When my life reached a never-before-contemplated low, in my chasm of despair I would have found it so valuable just to feel *understood*.

Yet there is no real understanding from those who haven't experienced this—of how painful and even terrifying it is to be trapped in it. And there is little support for people in these situations—who need to be heard, comforted, and helped to rediscover hope in their life—and re-empowered in themselves to deal with it effectively.

> **Being bereaved of our sense of safety, of our constructs, of our opportunities, of our sense of empowerment, of our belief in ourselves and in Life, and of our hope, becomes a bereavement of—'Self'.**
>
> **And that's almost worse than losing someone else whom we love.**

No bereavement is more 'worthy' or more terrible than another one. When it comes down to it, we suffer, and we suffer alone in a place where no-one can really reach us.

And from there we become less and less able to reach out for vital help.

THE SCHOOL OF THE SOFT TOUCH

OUR IDEAS ABOUT DIFFICULTY

Modern day parents, raised in today's easier times, are more deeply attuned to this 'inner experience', and also have access to new information about it that was previously unavailable or hard to obtain (only found in libraries!)

For example, from studies in psychology and behaviour, we now know that many of the difficulties people experience in coping with challenges in life and relationships result from the way they're raised ('nurture'). Consequently, when it comes to their children, many modern day parents (who may be much more 'enlightened' than their elders were) taking this to heart, have tried to ensure that their children don't *suffer* growing up, in the ways they did.

OUR PARENTING VALUES AND OUTLOOK HAVE SHIFTED EXPONENTIALLY

So it is that today, generally speaking, few children in Western culture have been schooled in the School of Hard Knocks—and *really* schooled there.

Instead, parents hover over them, worry about them, try (lovingly) to prevent them from catching any illnesses or injuring themselves in play, or from being hurt by failure and disappointment—and clear (so far as they are able) all obstacles and challenges from their offspring's path to smooth the way to 'success' and 'happiness'.

It's become such a feature of our culture these days, that tough love has become abuse or harassment, losing has become 'participation' (with an award for doing so); 'distressing' or confronting information to be delivered to adult students in a lecture at university is heralded with a warning at the hall doors, and teachers are more worried about what low marks allocated will do to self esteem than what mediocre effort will do to someone's future.

It's as if these caregivers believe that children today have no inner metal to deal with anything outside of an easy life and heaps of praise.

As if what's necessary for a Human Being to thrive is simply that they be protected, and get to assert their Rights.

WHIPLASH

New, modern day psychological wounds have arisen with this well-meaning behaviour.

Many of us today are products of the School of the Soft Touch, in which we feel *entitled* to a certain standard and kind of life, and are offended when we have to put in huge effort to attain it.

Then, when Life does take away our certainty and our comfort, we become resentful—and, feeling disempowered, tend to turn negative. We often don't see our difficult or painful experiences—the job that didn't work out, the friendship that failed, the relationship that hurts, the car that doesn't start, the person that death took from us—as a normal part of all life.

Instead we take the suffering personally, as if we've been singled out, and our tragedies are unique, to us.

Obstacles leave a bad taste in our mouths, jading our attitude and our self-esteem. We lash out at the world and the others who we feel played a part in setting our lives onto such a wobbly axis—and externalise blame to them.

> **We see our experience as 'unfair'; as something that has happened *to* us (and shouldn't have).**

And if we don't blame others, we label ourselves as a 'failure'.

We hurt ourselves with this approach. And we disable ourselves with this idea!

We *should* have been taught that suffering is a normal part of life—and even necessary for personal growth!

Now, we no longer know how to find resilience in the face of it, or know how to soldier on (ongoingly if necessary!) through difficulties when they arrive in our lives. The effects of well-meaning modern parenting practises, our sense of our entitlements, and our focus on our external environments have only complicated and exacerbated natural struggle.

What is incredibly painful and extremely uncomfortable then becomes even more so, simply because we've not been taught to expect it, and we've never been asked to find the depths within us with which to meet it: grit, resourcefulness, and grace.

We expect simply to be able to assert our rights and believe that the solutions to rid us of our pain should come from the system, or others.

And this is where our troubles really begin.

LEARNED HELPLESSNESS

In a life where we're often defined by our assets and results, and where what looks good from the outside counts more than 'Who We Are', it doesn't occur to us to turn inwards and strengthen what we find there: to face the world from *that* place of Identity in our lives.

We haven't been taught that this is either normal or desirable.

Manage that situation? That's never been asked of us! Our elders have always come along and sucked up all the crap that's ever stood in our way to clean up the situation we find ourselves in.

Yet Life never was and is never *ever* going to be an undiminished series of successful steps for anyone—even if it looks that way from the outside.

Things happen to us when we leave education for the world of working that are often unexpected and even simply not fair: companies merge, economies crash, strategies change—and a person can find themselves, through no fault of their own, out on the street.

After all, who gets it right all the time—really?

No-one!

Even those who seem never to put a foot wrong have their share of difficulty. And their pain might be that they can't turn to anyone and really reveal the mess that they are, because there is so much sunk into the appearance of all being well. (Which is something we all do. We make it all appear to be well, even when it damn well isn't).

Yet we only truly understand this when we're there, caught up in the rapids and totally unprepared—having bought into the myth that hard work and following the rules will get us to success and happiness.

The fact is that there is only so much influence we can have 'out there'.

Yet when we experience repeated failed attempts, many of us become discouraged and give up. We become indignant at being forced to bear aversive, painful or otherwise unpleasant situations and experiences—beyond what we feel to be our endurance.

We suffer from a 'learned helplessness'. We become unable or unwilling to try because we believe that we can't impact or control anything—even when opportunities for change do arise.

56 | THE "ACTUAL" NORMAL

Our external powerlessness becomes fatal to our sense of ourselves.

We lose perspective, and even lose meaning in Life. Then we lose ourselves, and lose hope. And so we make unhelpful choices, that further disempower us.

∼

THE BEGINNINGS

A STRUGGLE WITH POWERLESSNESS

Believe it or not, this inner turmoil begins with the simple experience of 'disappointment.'

When we take action to bring our idea or ambition to life, we anticipate a payoff. If it works out, we're elated and affirmed. We have a sense of things opening up, with opportunity and reward presenting themselves, to enrich our life. *The Vision is on track. Our hopes (and expectations) may be realised!*

But when it doesn't work out, we experience is disappointment.

Most of us are familiar with the feeling. None of us likes the reality that we didn't get and now don't have whatever it is that we wanted: a particular outcome, a sense of wellbeing from our endeavour; comfort and hope. Uncomfortable feelings, like inner tension, stress and anxiety—and even sadness, regret and dismay are present instead.

ORDINARILY, DISAPPOINTMENT IS A MOTIVATOR

Disappointment shows that we care. It highlights that there are things that really matter to us. The feeling pushes us into remedial action (and even into taking some risks) as we try to rectify the problem and put discomfort at a distance. We look at our outcomes, review the part we've played in creating those, and resolve to improve — reclaiming our sense of ease.

When we don't do well or succeed, when we lose a game, or fail to get a certain job, or house, or relationship for example, we'll go back to the drawing board and try again: a new tack, improving our strategies or process, demanding more of ourselves—and perhaps of others!

- We may tamper with the details of our environments, get a new job or even a new line of work, a new relationship, or a new wardrobe, for example. Perhaps we'll diet and exercise, try conventional or alternative therapies; self-help books, online courses and videos.
- Or we go inward, setting goals, clearing out the clutter, up-levelling our skills, and trying to be purposeful and positive. We may work on developing new positive attitudes and affirmations, take up meditation or therapy!

Depending on the strength of our desire, we do whatever it takes to succeed with our endeavour after all. Disappointment can drive us to think deeply: to create and choose, to improve, refine, and be inventive. Repeated experiences can even stimulate our resolve and our inner grit, developing resilience and determination in life. It can keep us working out how to be better versions of ourselves in the circumstances, rather than bowing to them. We hang onto hope and we go again.

It's a wonderful faculty to have, working on our behalf as it does.

DISAPPOINTMENT'S SHADOW

From this description, disappointment sounds like a 'minor' emotion. And of course, disappointment will be greater and less bearable depending on what did or didn't happen, on how vested we are in the result, and on the weight that the outcome carries in our lives!

But when it's sustained, it ceases to be the simple psychological reaction that spurs us on to try again to try harder or improve. Instead it becomes the gateway for devastating self-doubt.

Often the people in our lives witnessing our struggles with ongoing disappointments don't understand why they're so upsetting: they can't see past 'simple disappointment' as a spur-to-action! So I want to examine disappointment a little more closely now, in the context of Suffering.

Because disappointment is the first port of call for questions about our Personal Power.

Our Personal Power asks,

> *"How much agency do I have in my world, over my life, and over Life itself? How 'significant' am I, really?"*

PERSONAL POWER

Whenever we ask—'Why me?' or 'How can I *create* an outcome, or *change* one?'—we're trying to establish where our power is and how to use it. Because in this strange Context in which we find ourselves, here on Planet Earth and in our individual lives—we want (and need) to know that we *can make things happen* to meet our needs, and shape our journeys.

Everything that happens to us in our life is an encounter with our personal power—raising the question of how much of it we really have!

Meeting our needs gives us a sense of power. Fulfilling our desires gives us even more. We constantly experiment, test and negotiate with it in our relationship to other people, situations, environment, relationships and circumstances—to see how much of it we have, have lost, or have accrued.

A disappointing blow puts us in direct contact with this question—spawning discouraging feelings like stress, anxiety and sorrow.

Often, we'll often override those feelings (at first)—motivated to assert our power over the defeat. But if, over time, our remedial actions and motivated efforts don't improve our results—and disappointment in reality is ongoing—our inner tension and unhappiness can become pervasive, with a strongly *disempowering* effect.

Career or relationship difficulties for example, or financial strain, or parenthood—where we've kept at it with effort and hope for change yet haven't achieved the results we've tried so hard for—can move from disappointing to utterly demoralising, as we recognise that what we want is something we may never achieve. We're confronted with the reality that we're 'powerless' to (in this case at least) affect the direction and quality of our own lives.

At this pointy end of disappointment, our lack of agency leads us into struggle with a painful, and existential question:

> "Who am I if I can't shape my world or make my mark upon it?"

Repeated encounters with our own impotence to achieve what we so want to achieve leaves us feeling good for nothing. Self-doubt arrives to sit alongside the sadness of loss, and we may even feel ashamed for not being "successful": *being* more, *doing* more, and *fixing* the problem! Our self-esteem plummets.

We conclude, *I'm* a failure.

Instead of seeing the loss as something simply occurring, the sense of failure is deeply personal, rippling through to the core of our identity.

The loss becomes a reflection of *Who* We Are and our powerlessness in an inhospitable world.

And so disappointment can bring on something of an identity crisis, and a disconnection from Self.

And we lose other vital aspects too: trust and hope.

Worst of all, we lose *trust in Self*.

The reality was that everything I'd tried for was falling over and there was nothing I could do to meaningfully turn things around. Sustained disappointment brought on anxiety and even terror—as I felt my powerlessness!

Regularly I found myself totting up the disappointments; looking at how and where they manifested in my life, and concluding that since the common denominator in all of my results was me—I must be the problem. I was a disappointment!

I TURNED ON MYSELF
Saddled with this deep sense of my own powerlessness, I came to believe that all that lay ahead would be more difficulty. My bone-deep belief was that trying—and trying again—would bring nothing (as usual), because I (rather than the effort or opportunity) was not enough.

I GAVE UP
Unsurprisingly, my low self-worth decimated my motivation, and led to a tendency to give up on things. I wanted to hope, but the possibility that my hopes would be dashed (again) with disappointment (that awful feeling) setting in instead, made me afraid to.

The more let-down I felt, the more I believed that the future would yield only more letdowns—and I felt too fragile to summon up the inner resilience I'd need when yet another thing I tried for, hoped for, and put effort in for, might fall flat. Life was not to be trusted. I was not to be trusted. It seemed saner for me not to try for things that might not work out.

Without hope that I could manifest something for change—there was little to strive for. I had become a leaf, tossed about by my life, with no ability to seize control of it or impose my will on it.

And so disappointment became a life-sapping emotion, instead of being the motivator that gave me the drive to try again.

DISAPPOINTMENT BECAME MY PREVALENT FEELING
I became increasingly disappointed, and disappointed in myself. I was disappointed that I was unable to provide for my children; disappointed that I couldn't show up with more strength, hope and positivity for them! I was disappointed I was couldn't create the opportunities I wished for—like travelling, or splurging on a new lounge suite!—and disappointed I couldn't join friends for a night out because there was little money with which to make that choice.

Not that it mattered: I was no longer myself, and no longer fun to be with.

All of this inclined me to shame, which led me to withdraw, not just from the opportunities (such as they were) and challenges of my life, but from others too.

Shame is poison—poisoning us from the inside.

Our need to hide from life and from others intensifies, and we become isolated, anxious and fearful, despite no specific or direct threat. Things we once considered pleasurable no longer bring interest or joy. We're always stressed, and we may express this in chronic sadness, worry, anxiety, anger and even violence. Physical symptoms—including headaches, sleeplessness, weight gain or loss, and being miserable—arrive.

Prolonged exposure to disappointment can even bring about serious stress-induced disease, including heart disease, digestive disorders and a depressed immune system.

To protect myself from the pain, I began to let go of my aspirations: my Big Picture. I felt I had to give up on it; to no longer invest myself in wanting to do anything or care about outcomes. Apathy now joined with pessimism, creating a vicious cycle in my life, wherein I stopped putting in effort and taking positive action, because I no longer believed in the future. I simply got through my days without trying for anything.

After several years of this, the best part of my day was when I could go to bed and let consciousness fade away.

But in the mornings when I woke, Reality would crash back in. "I am still here." *And my heart would sink.* "This is still my messed-up, awful life, that I never could have imagined I would be living. I will never get my Big Picture; the one that would have had me safe and fulfilled."

It was terrifying. And I suffered because of it.

COMPONENTS OF SUFFERING

PAINFUL EMOTIONS PILE ON...

Often the worst scenes we read in books or see in movies are those of people suffering, rather than (as you'd expect) death itself.

It's the suffering that is so terrifying.

> **Suffering (Verb)**
> —*to undergo or be subjected to or to feel or endure pain, distress, injury, loss, or anything unpleasant. To sustain disadvantage, or loss, to submit to hardship.*[2]

And this definition doesn't come close to describing the actual experience of it, the degree of excruciating pain (that's not always physical), and how debilitating that can be.

There are degrees of suffering of course.

PEOPLE HAVE SUFFERED TERRIBLY OVER THE CENTURIES

Millions of people have experienced unfathomable terror, horror, loss and fear. Being burned at the stake, half starved to death in prisons, tortured to the point of insanity are some extreme examples. Those who survived were left with lives forever changed.

The World Wars and other wars since have brought terror and despair, as bombs have rained down on cities and towns, destroying lives, homes and legacies—and horror, with young people set up to kill or maim other young people in appalling scenarios. Millions of lives have been lost, bringing endless heartache for those left behind. Alongside the grief of loss, thousands of people are ongoingly desperately worried about missing loved ones, tortured by their thoughts about them and what may have befallen them; unable to get closure.

People are wrongfully imprisoned, many are trapped indefinitely in solitary confinement, while others exist in constant fear of cruel beatings, or torture. Many are caught in endlessly abusive relationships, sometimes killed by those who profess to love them. Children suffer beatings, incest and rape at the hands of the adults they most trust.

Citizens who reasonably expect to be able to live a normal life, are trapped in limbo, their governments so corrupt that there isn't any functional infrastructure on which they can build their lives and create possibilities. Countries have instead been hijacked and destroyed by their leaders—leaving families, homes, heirlooms, jobs decimated, fathers, brothers and sons tortured and murdered, women and girl children abducted, raped, sold on—or murdered in turn.

Thousands are starving, homeless, alone. Increasingly we're seeing people sitting on street corners with cardboard signs, having lost everything, including their self-respect. Many people are hungry, not even thinking of the next meal because it's not coming, or in pain with no remedy. In some countries, they're foraging rubbish dumps, looking for stuff to recycle and sell for food. Anything beyond the next meal is unthinkable.

No-one is immune from suffering.

Famous, wealthy, good-looking, talented people try to numb their pain with drugs and alcohol, give up and even kill themselves. Others, with the world at their feet, find themselves battling debilitating diseases from a young age.

Disabled people live in broken bodies, struggling with powerlessness in a world that casts them aside. Accidents break others into quadriplegia, or leave people brain damaged, unable to even breathe for themselves.

Many others are suffering horrifically in some physical sense, and there is terrible emotional and psychological suffering too.

There may be different definitions of suffering, and there may be times in your life past (or life to come) where you have—or will—experience suffering. But everyone knows what it is.

SUFFERING IS A PART OF LIFE FOR ALL LIVING CREATURES

Even while most of us in Western cultures manage to escape these more extreme forms of suffering, every single person at some point in their lives, has to withstand assaults on hope, effort, peace, self-esteem and personal power.

That may be living in times of drought or flood; with physical or emotional abuse. It may be losing all that we have worked for and held dear, including relationships, money, health and prospects. It may simply be having to accept death and parting, in the last moments of life.

Suffering is an elemental and inextricable part of what it means to be alive. As much part of Life as water, air, earth, fire, sunlight and billions of other people. And it has been for all time that sentient and intelligent creatures have lived on the planet.

All we can do is accept that suffering will come to us one way or another, and see it as integral to life.

SUFFERING IS TRIGGERED BY LOSS OF SOME KIND

It may be loss of opportunity, of a relationship, of assets that create a sense of safety for us; loss of our health, or our self-esteem.

Some losses are more devastating and far-reaching than others.

Some people consider themselves to be suffering if they have a fight or fallout with a loved one, or experience the pain of losing their job, or are burgled and lose precious items and heirlooms.

Though these may be everyday disappointments and losses for many, for others (who have not encountered true difficulty before and who don't have large reserves of resilience or much self-esteem for example), the pain, distress, injury, loss, and disadvantage is no less real, and can cause considerable suffering. Because…

Outside of actual physical harm or pain, suffering is essentially an internal experience. The way we think about the things we've experienced and the weight we give to those experiences is what causes our main distress.

Our *thoughts* about our situation compound or alleviate our experience of suffering. We can bear loss more robustly if we know it will come to an end, and/or if we know that we're capable of carrying it for as long as it lasts. We can remain hopeful, tuned to that light within us that still dreams, that strives to make something of ourselves and of this life we have.

However, when we're unable to change things and can see no end to our suffering, that light inside us can get snuffed out by overwhelming grief.

GRIEF IS ONE SIDE OF THE COIN OF SUFFERING

> **'Grief'**—described as *"sharp sorrow; painful regret"*, with synonyms of *"agony, anguish, despair, heartache, heartbreak, and pain"* [3]—is a response to loss.

Grief is the emotional expression of our powerlessness.

As already noted, we've largely confined our 'acceptance' of real grief in our Western culture to the loss of a loved one. Yet the many very painful losses in life outside of bereavement bring on terrible and enduring personal suffering, because while the causes may be very different and hurt terribly, what is always and particularly painful about it, is that we're left feeling powerless.

Losses outside of bereavement can be even more difficult to deal with when we feel personally responsible (and even culpable) for having landed ourselves where we now find ourselves. We're perpetrators, not just victims! We can go through massive grief even though no-one has died. And we don't understand what is going on with us, or why we feel so terrible.

It never occurs to us that the loss we've suffered is very much a bereavement, but one that strikes at the heart of our sense of ourselves.

We are dealing with a death: of the way we see ourselves, of the trust we have in Life, and often of hope too.

We've been cut loose from something that held us (and our sense of ourselves), steady. Without this anchor, and dealing with the fallout (the painful thoughts and feelings) our sense of identity and agency are impacted. Who we were 'before'… disappears. We lose ourselves in pain and sorrow for a time, as we try to remake ourselves in the 'afterwards'.

> *When circumstance stole away the life and future I'd wanted to be creating, I grieved…*
> - *what we'd practically lost*
> - *my sense of feeling safe*
> - *lost opportunities*
> - *my sense of being an enabled creature*
> - *my sense of being understood*

Denied choices I wanted to make, losing hope for the future every week that things didn't change, I was grief-stricken every day from the moment I left my bed in the mornings.

Yet no-one had died.

I wasn't actually homeless and starving on the streets. I wasn't struck down with illness or disability, or in terrible, life-threatening circumstances due to war, inquisition, rape, beatings, abuse or unlawful imprisonment.

But I felt powerless, hapless, and ineffectual overall.

I was suffering disempowerment in a very real sense — and grieving the resultant suffering. And the fact that it was much more my thoughts about things than physical reality, did not make it less painful. —Or less valid. I couldn't see an end to it, I had no tools with which to navigate it, and no power to change any of it. In the face of this powerlessness, a pervading sense of fear arose within me, accompanying me wherever I went.

To be in an ongoing state of uncertainty, pain, grief and anxiety as the constant backdrop to life is incredibly stressful, and ultimately debilitating. Fear rises: a terrible form of suffering in itself—that can become the catalyst for a personal crisis with no sanctuary, and no road out.

WHAT IS FEAR?

Fear: (Noun)
—a distressing emotion aroused by impending danger, evil, pain, etc. The feeling or condition of being afraid.
Synonyms: foreboding, apprehension, consternation, dismay, dread, terror, fright, panic, horror, trepidation, qualm. [4]

Brain biology tells us that complex cognitive behaviour—or thinking—happens in the cerebral cortex (the outer part of the brain). Processing, concentration, planning, memory, judgment, emotion, personality expression, decision making, and moderating social behaviour are all done here.

This is the part of our brains where (hopefully) we spend most of our time!

Deep within the brain though, is the Limbic System with the Reptilian Brain—which is in charge of creating our 'fight, flight or freeze' reactions.

In moments of crisis, this part of the brain has us quickly 'reacting'. In fact, it takes over from normal thinking, takes 'control' of the whole brain—*forcing* us into the reaction that will keep us most safe and surviving. During this time, access to the cerebral cortex is actually disconnected, stopping us from thinking and planning a response, and we simply freeze, flee or fight!

Yet this makes perfect sense: we don't want to be wasting time considering possibilities and probabilities when we *should* be saving our lives! But this reality is significant. Because it means that in moments of great stress, we're not able to think straight!

There are repercussions to this though, when we find ourselves in extended stressful, anxiety-inducing situations that engender insecurity, let alone actual fear. Then and ongoingly, we are less and less able to access our usual resources, responses and even good sense, just at a time when we need them most! We're actually reduced by the fear; closed down by it—and become less and less able to access our 'Selves'. This in part explains that sense of 'losing ourselves' that many experience in traumatic times.

MY GREATEST DEMON WAS FEAR ITSELF

Losing the external supports and programmes that had kept 'me' propped up and my 'identity' intact revealed that more than the discomfort of loss, dislocation and uncertainty (which were awful enough), my greatest demon was the FEAR itself.

The facts—that my husband was dealing with cancer, and that I didn't have a job or might be less skilled than I needed to be—were less of a problem than the *feeling*s I had about it, because they brought paralysing side-effects.

I **cried** a lot. Often unmanageably. On **sleepless** nights I'd lie awake hour after hour in the grip of the *feeling of fear*: an actual physical reaction that felt like a shudder moving through my body, bringing a sudden shortness of breath, the uncontrollable welling of tears. And sobbing.

When I did sleep, the streaming inside me continued, flowing from my adrenals in a tide through my brain, my dreams, my reality—jerking me awake in the middle of night to find myself in the middle of a **panic** attack, bathed in sweat, heart hammering wildly. And sobbing.

And as waking reality reclaimed me from unconsciousness in the morning, the cold hand of **dread** would clamp painfully around my guts.

Fear feelings continued to **overwhelm** me as I carried out daily tasks. I would frequently have to lock myself in the bathroom to cry in private—hyperventilating and trying to stave off another panic attack.

> *Having always been rather afraid of death, I became terrified of life — of the feelings that seemed to define it, and had to be carried every day. —Feelings I could no longer bear. I began to have the ongoing urge to not exist.*

Fear is the other side of the coin of suffering.

FEAR

WHAT IF.....?

I was constantly inside my own head, going regularly over my current reality, tabulating the losses, anxiously considering the prospects for the future, and looking the threats to survival in the eye.

The voice there repeatedly threw all my fears in my face, asking "What if...?" of me, and proposing frightening scenarios. I'd imagine the very worst happening.

> "What if my husband doesn't beat the cancer?"
> "What if I continue to be unable to get a job and earnings?"
> "What if we lose all our assets, our security?"
> "What if I end up failing my children?"
> "What if I lose even more than I've lost already?"
> "What if I fail even more than I already have?"
> "What if I'm actually not good enough, not worthy enough?"
> "What if everyone finds out I'm a fraud (family and friends especially)?"
> "What if I'm too old, too foreign and I've used up all my chances?"
> "What if I really have nothing to offer?"

"What if I don't matter and I'm actually surplus to requirements?"

ORIGINAL FEAR

Our earliest knowledge of our own existence was when we were in the womb: a blissful time of safety and contentment—and probably the most peaceful and happy time of our entire physical existence. We were fed, not too warm, nor too cool. Nothing was needed, or wanted, or missed, or concerning. Even gravity made no demands on us.

All this changed in a heartbeat the moment we were born. We suddenly encountered a world totally different from everything we'd experienced from our earliest moments of awareness. It was too bright, too loud, and we had to breathe! We felt cold—or too much heat—or hunger—for the first time. *It was a shock to the system.*

For the first time we would have felt afraid, and instinctively vulnerable.

Thich Nhat Hanh (the celebrated Vietnamese Buddhist monk) describes this in his book *'Fear'*[5]. He gives a powerful description of this as our first experience of suffering — causing *'Original Fear'* — and explains how Fear becomes one of our earliest drivers in life.

ORIGINAL DESIRE

Then, we worked for our first breaths, and cried out for help if we were too cold, too hot, hungry or thirsty. We would die of course, if we didn't breathe or didn't eat—so instinctively we did what we had to, because we had the desire to survive. Thich calls this 'Original Desire.

Our greatest desire is to survive, and every subsequent desire has its root in this original, fundamental one. Fear becomes our most basic driver *because* we desire to survive: *need* to survive.

As we grow up and age, Original Fear and Original Desire travel with us, Tich says, with both keeping us fighting for life. Fear galvanises us to anticipate what needs to be done to avoid rock bottom, while Desire keeps us motivated to push forward and past uncomfortable circumstances, onto safer ground.

And whenever we're under threat, our desire to survive is triggered, plunging us into fear.

Original Fear and Original Desire partner with each other in push (Fear the driver) and pull (Desire), keeping us moving into avoidance of death for as long as possible.

Fear keeps us in a state that is in direct opposition to our natural state of seeking not just to survive, but to thrive! Being *trapped* in 'fear' makes us feel intolerably powerless. And over time, we lose perspective, become fragile—and may ultimately falter sufficiently to simply give up.

ONGOING 'THREATS' IN LIFE

Life simply is packed with 'threats' that we have to navigate daily. But when they're frequent, unremitting and extended, we can become absolutely triggered into fear, and personal loss, even without losing anything substantial.

Aloneness: Loving connection is the only safety nature offers us. We're physically safer in groups—and more likely to cement our place in the group if we get to 'belong'. This 'need' gives rise to…

- Fear of **not being loved.**
- Fear of **judgement**. This affects all of us, no matter who we are. It's especially hard for younger people who will often take dangerous risks that they know are life-threatening to avoid being judged and labelled by their 'friends' and onlookers, like taking silly dares, drugs, and reckless driving.
- Fear of **failure**: that everything we do or try will come to nothing and we'll 'be' nothing (and rejected) as a consequence.
- **Existential** fear: fear that we don't matter. That we—and our lives are pointless irrelevancies.

- Fear of **rejection**—by others, and by ourselves.

Suffering: the experiences of:

- **Loss**: death of a loved one, bankruptcy, fire, ill health and disability, to name a few.
- **Pain** and discomfort: signalling that our physical bodies are in danger.
- **Lack**: having enough. (This, more than death apparently, is the greatest fear for retirees who, approaching the end of their lives, don't know if they can last on the means they have left).
- **Powerlessness**, or lack of agency: having the means to get what we need.
- **Loss of identity.**

And of course, there is the ever present reality of **Death**: a threat that's always in the future.

Given that life contains so many stressors, it's hardly surprising that that the experience of suffering is so often present in our lives!

We're always wrestling against the feeling of fear and the suffering we feel in it, regardless of who we are, where we come from, what we've achieved, and how much we own.

As we grapple increasingly with a sense of 'lack' in current times, it may be useful to look at the starring role it plays in Suffering, a little more closely next. Because…

LACK BRINGS ON FEAR

At some level we're always aware that Death is ultimately brought on by loss. At the most basic level, this would be loss of air, of food, and of shelter from the elements.

Undersupply brings on a feeling of *lack* (even if total loss can be avoided) and we fear it for the warning that it is:—we're approaching a danger zone around 'survival'.

'Lack', riding uncomfortably close to the finality of 'loss'—is the rumble strip along the edge of our path that alerts us that we're close to 'danger'.

A lack of money will mean we can't pay for a roof over our heads, or feed ourselves, or provide for our kids. Lack of access to proper medical care may lead to loss of health over time. Both eventually could lead to loss of life. And so on.

Actual lack (where we tighten our belts and go without) is the klaxon that signals that our situation is now precarious: danger—terrible danger—is approaching. And may not be staved off.

No-one wants to feel the anxiety and fear that the sense of lack brings! It is debilitating and misery-inducing. And the more we struggle in it, the less able we become to see options for ourselves. The prospect of more suffering looms large, and we retreat from it. We worry that we'll fail to keep bringing what we need into our lives. *So, long before we actually suffer loss, we're already suffering in this fear of lack.*

Of course we encounter again the problem that 'lack' is discounted in our society as *not legitimate.* Only *actual* loss (as personified by poverty, bereavement or violence for example)—is.

Yet the fear of 'lack' is often the genesis of suffering.

(This is why, even when we have 'enough', our instincts to stockpile against possible 'lack' is strong! *"What if...?"* Our brain plays the tape, as we face our difficulties.)

BUT WE WANT MORE THAN JUST TO SURVIVE!

While survival of our 'organism' is primary, our needs aren't just physical. We desire to be as far removed from 'lack' as possible; in other words we desire—to thrive!

And alongside we have our Big Pictures embodying our aspirations, that have us weaving with Possibility, and motivating us all into personal improvement and growth.

Every day though, we get glimpses of our imagined, hoped for worlds that don't fit the real ones we're living in. The sense of 'lack' rises again as we struggle with our *unmet* needs in the *loss of our Big Picture*, and we suffer.

And that's without our 'lacks' in just *living* and experiencing life's often troublesome events!

Some examples include:

- relationship breakdowns
- lack of self-esteem
- too little (or too much) work
- financial limitations and feeling insecure
- constraints in possibilities
- lack of choices
- deteriorating health and independence
- retirement

'Lack' (and loss) constantly triggers thoughts and feelings that bring up doubts about our personal power to withstand these—projecting us into the future. There, lie all those deeply buried fears.

Now, fuelled by "what if"s?" they bloom into unhappy scenarios, that end with more losses:

- loss of happiness
- loss of comfort
- loss of love
- loss of self-esteem
- loss of self-respect
- — and even, loss of our lives.

'LACK' CAN BECOME A SELF-FULFILLING PROPHECY

When we're down to the bone, unable any longer to manage things that are tricky and troublesome with any equanimity, we can become more sensitised, and less tolerant. We become 'defended' and reactive.

This can throw relationships into turmoil, as others' quirks and mistakes hurt and irk us—and these, turning sour, in turn deprive us of other really important survival needs, such as the need for love and connection. And self-esteem.

We can become caught in a downward spiral. Hopelessness descends, putting us just as hard (and just as unexpectedly) onto our knees.

The longer we're caught in this state, the more unable we become to rescue ourselves from life's challenges. Adrenals burn out, exhaustion sets in, and we enter a survival state from where nothing new can be seized on, created and built.

UNREMITTING STRESS MAKES ONE FRAGILE

Now it becomes harder and harder to keep perspective on Self or circumstances.

It may seem logical that suicide would be strongly related to *actual loss* experienced. Yet, through my counselling conversations with Grief clients, I would argue that the fear induced by 'lack' (the 'what if' projections) is often more likely to bring it on.

Because, with loss, one is given a final outcome to carry. It's painful, often terrible. But it's done. Yet with lack (which may come on the back of the loss), the 'what if's' hold one in an open-ended experience of vulnerability and threat—of fear—and of powerlessness against that.

It becomes intolerable. And perhaps ultimately impossible to carry, in the end.

WHO AM I IF I CAN'T…?

OUR SENSE OF IDENTITY UNDER SIEGE

These interrelating things—disappointment, fear, grief and suffering and the anxiety about being a victim of circumstance—affect our ability to function well and normally in the world.

Because each of them can shut us down. Their combination can be soul destroying—and who can function then?

LOSS (PARTICULARLY SUDDEN LOSS) INDUCES A CRISIS OF MEANING

Does what happened make any sense?

We may first blame Life and others for the situation we find ourselves in, becoming bitter, resentful and angry. We can get stuck in one or another of those phases for long times before we finally reach acceptance.

As we noted earlier, we may turn on ourselves, wondering what *we* did to deserve this, blaming ourselves for not being good enough, for our mistakes and oversights, and feeling worthless for having ended up in the cul-de-sac that our life led us into.

How do we incorporate the difficult events into our personal life stories? How do we go on living in a world where such things can occur? What does this event say about who we are? Will other people think less of us?

And what is this that has arisen in us and taken us over as a result of it all?

Our Identity has become caught up and intertwined with the thoughts we have about ourselves, our lives, and our experiences. Our sense of ourselves based on our previous circumstances is gone.

We don't know how to reset, and we don't know who we are anymore.

WHO AM I?

We mix up our Identity with money, power, success, what we own, what we look like, and what we're doing. So what we do, where we live, what we eat, who we spend time with; who we love, what we make space and time for in our lives; how much we travel, our clothes, jewellery and scent; the art we collect, the books we read, the restaurants we eat in — all come to define us, and often inextricably so.

What we think, do and 'have' becomes "who" we are.

And if these things cannot manifest in our lives or occur in the places and way that we choose, then Who are we? (apart from powerless and highly frustrated!) Can we remain intact without them?

In the earlier stages of loss, we certainly feel diminished without all these things. When we fall on hard times and they are actually stripped away, we have little to hold onto to get ourselves out of trouble.

We lose ourselves when we can no longer project the Identity that our means once supported, and can suffer an identity crisis.

As our existence becomes an ongoing experience of painful emotions, the discomfort can leave us stretched very thin, and feeling very fragile.

"I hate my life," I wrote. "I've felt this way for too long now. The 'me' that I once was is already so diminished and suffering, that she has almost disappeared. Certainly is currently unrecognisable. Like a snake that needs to shed its skin but can't—and, all jumpy, is unable to function, move properly or focus on anything for long. Can't relate with the other snakes even: just obsessed with its own, unshakeable skin."

All my life, I'd been told by significant others that I was 'great': wonderful, competent, organised, etc, etc—feedback that was echoed at work and with the results I achieved there.

At the time, I worried about this feedback, and often felt 'fraudulent'—because a part of me knew that the feedback wasn't about who "I" was, but about the results I created. And those were often dependent on variables like luck, or quick thinking—rather than some intrinsic quality of 'me'.

Yet I could believe that there was *some* truth to the feedback. And it became an important part of my Identity.

This false view of myself proved to be the biggest thing I tripped over when *Life As I Knew It* ceased to be.

"I" WAS MY PERFORMANCE

All my life, I'd been told by significant others that I was 'great': wonderful, competent, organised, etc, etc—feedback that was echoed at work and with the results I achieved there.

At the time, I worried about this feedback, and often felt 'fraudulent'—because a part of me knew that the feedback wasn't about who "I" was, but about the results I created. And those were often dependent on variables like luck, or quick thinking, rather than some intrinsic quality of 'me'.

Yet I could believe that there was *some* truth to the feedback. And it became an important part of my Identity.

This false view of myself proved to be the biggest thing I tripped over when *Life As I Knew It* ceased to be.

I am no longer that—that was successful.

Perhaps I never was that. Perhaps it had just been a moment in time where I could pull the wool over everyone's eyes, or make the most of an opportunity that happened to be there then.

So who was I *really* then—on a real note? Was I what I *looked* like? Was I what I'd *done*? Was I a failure? A victim? A no-one?

And could I survive *this*?

How to bust out of my cul-de-sac if effort, positive thinking and trying all the ways I knew how did not transform my painful situation and open up new paths? How could I offer something different, something more—like all those happy souls already ensconced in jobs and lives that work? How could "I" compete?

Not being able to affect the direction of my own life for my own good and in terms of what I'd envisioned for myself left *me* feeling useless; nothing would ever change for me because *I was* 'me'. And wherever I'd go, I'd take myself with me, so it wouldn't matter how hard I'd try. I was never going to get the outcomes I wanted!

WE LOSE OURSELVES

Whether due to unforeseen events and circumstances or simply one's personal journey, this is an experience that most people go through at some point.

We get jolted out of our groove and tossed into the unknown: left uncertain, insecure and questioning everything.

Our 'failure' activates our fears about ourselves and our safety. The more stressed and unhappy we are and become, the more we find that we lose our ability to hold onto clear ideas and thoughts, and even tasks, previous competencies and strengths.

The more disabled, incompetent and despairing we feel in Life, the less likely we are to have the ability to rescue ourselves.

And so we lose ourselves further, and a vicious cycle ensues.

We get stuck in the past, in an idea of ourselves, our lives, and our dreams—because that's all we have left in the bewildering and blocked reality of 'now'. And if we are not able to let go of that past, it can lead to misery, desperation, and an inability to properly *be* in the life we *do* have.

SOON, WE'RE HIDING A BIG SECRET

And because the popular message is that we need to be seen to be successful, or resilient, or to persist and get back to being happy and 'business as usual' we soon lose the courage to let our real selves, our wounded, fallible selves—show. People don't like to be confronted and discomforted, and by instinct, we don't want to generate that in them.

And—at some level, we now believe that we *are* failures (and failures attract judgement, pity and maybe even rejection). So we keep our true situation secret from those in our circles, and pretend.

When we've been an Achiever and have always fallen on our feet and been okay—people assume that we always *will* be okay. Still *are* okay. They think we're strong and able, and can take care of ourselves. They believe that what they see on the outside (as we cover up our pain and shame) is truly where we're at! They don't understand how our identity and belief in ourselves are slowly being decimated by our inability to manifest the usual results and success.

Behind closed doors, I was mentally and emotionally stuck in a place alternating between rage and despair, that was totally debilitating. And it was incredibly burdensome for my family to experience alongside, taking much from them in a situation where we'd all already lost so much.

So with everyone else, whom I only had to see in small 'bites', I showed up with a mask, keeping my armour up to face the world—and pretended. Sometimes I'd 'see' myself and be shocked at how normal I looked to the world! But I knew the game was up and it was just a matter of time before it became obvious to everyone that it was all a lie. I wasn't going to be able to come back to my life or to them as the person I once was, since everything was so impossible and I was the one who'd broken it: by being me.

This sense of a loss of Self and the resulting debilitation is a very real phenomenon that is not well understood by others in our lives. Even professional agencies dedicated to help those of us struggling with this sort of loss underestimate the depth of despair we feel, and the sense of personal culpability.

We're not just depressed. We're disconnected from ourselves, from hope, from possibility—and feeling disabled, and desperate.

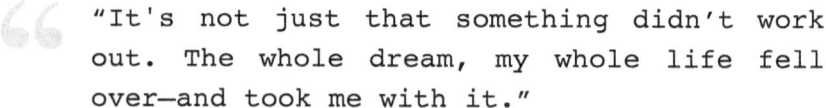
```
"It's not just that something didn't work
out. The whole dream, my whole life fell
over—and took me with it."
```

We begin to shy away from interactions, and then to hide, becoming more and more withdrawn from others, from Life. We're more and more alone with our shame. Even when we're with those we love and trust, our personal dislocation and ongoing 'pretending' come together to make us afraid and tired. It's a really lonely place to be.

Yet this is *where* we are. Not *Who* we are.

DIARY ENTRY...

 iary entry, 2015

"Half the time I feel like just giving up.

Everything seems pointless. So much effort, so much hope, so many affirmations over the months, even faith in Self—have shown me that despite trying, Life doesn't budge.

I remain trapped going nowhere.

How to bust out of here if striving, positive thinking and trying all the ways I know how, haven't transformed my painful situations and opened up new paths?

Effort and care make no difference in opening up doors for me so that I can manifest what I need and what I desire. So that I can actually make some choices!

It makes no difference that I'm here.

I can't affect my direction for my own good or for what I once envisioned for myself. I feel useless, and that nothing will ever change for me.

It seems to me that the easiest thing is simply to give up banging my head on a brick wall, stop reinventing the wheel, and stop the suffering.

Just get off the planet.

Why not?"

∽

PART III
THE SCHOOL OF HARD KNOCKS

WHAT'S GOING ON IN OUR WORLD?

THE STAGE IS SET

THE "EXPERIENCE" OF LIFE

With a deeper understanding now of why and *how* we personally suffer, let's return briefly to the bigger picture that's generated this general increase in suffering in the world, and in the middle class particularly.

Because make no mistake: **we're struggling today with our *experience of ourselves in the modern Context.***

It's not that you've stuffed up badly, or are to blame for your current malaise (although to *some* extent of course you have and are). It's not that you have been given a deficit of resilience (although your reliance muscles may need some serious exercise at this point in time).

The fact is that you are living in volatile times, standing on shifting sands, and having to find new ways of balancing yourself in it . *We all are.*

But to begin to deal meaningfully with this collapse of our lifestyles, possibilities, peace, joy and general mental health, we need first to understand the 'scenario'.

- What exactly is this 'bubble' of abundance we've been living in?
- What have the thoughts, ideas, beliefs, values and understandings on which we've based our whole lives *generated* in our modern lives today?
- What has changed to bring about so much new struggle and suffering in modern Western societies?
- What does that mean for us—now, and going into the future?
- What can we do to reclaim what is truly important, valuable and empowering in a Human life, that cultivates resilience in hard times, and enables us to prevail despite change and loss?

So let's look more closely now—at Life outside of what we *know* about it, to see if we can arrive at something closer to Truth.

CONTEXTS

Everything happens in Context.

'Our' Context begins with the vast, apparently endless Context of Space, in which Earth (and other planets) spin around a vital, life-giving Sun.

Planet Earth—a smaller Context—is the container for the lives we're all living. Inextricably part of and bound to it while we live, we're all the threads that make up a great tapestry of Life that plays out on it—woven together with other people and living creatures, circumstances, beliefs, possibilities, situations, myths, cultures, nations, weathers of all kinds.

This container is the scenario (or stage) on which absolutely everything that we experience in life, plays out.

THE EXTERNAL CONTEXT

The stage is set with the props of our individual Contexts—of countries, nationalities, cultures, friends, families, and homes. *These our our External 'Contexts'.*

And—everyone's Contexts are different.

- There are the particular circumstances we're born into and a prevailing culture (and attitudes and values in them).
- There's specific time in history (holding certain possibilities and not others) when we arrive, and the particular events that occur (locally and more widely)—while we live.
- And there are our family members, our family culture, and the ideas and opportunities embedded within those, that provide a 'script'.

I bring this to reality to your attention as a first point of call. It's important to keep it in view as we think things through here, since we don't get to control Contexts directly—and very often don't even have much influence over them. *Yet we are constantly subject to them.*

THE INTERNAL CONTEXT

On the stage, your lived experiences and perceptions of these; your yearnings and questions, the restorations you want and the improvements you're working on are arising in you all of the time. They immerse you in an inner 'din' that rises constantly to the surface of your attention, holding you in an internal 'silo' of experience and perceptions, creating a 'reality' that you're uniquely living. *This is your Internal Context, and you occupy it uniquely.*

Whatever 'facts' occur, unfold in the *Internal Context of You* and your unique 'gaze': your consciousness/awareness of yourself having an experience. Put the same facts in a different person—and those 'facts' actually aren't the same, or even 'facts at all! They certainly don't have identical impacts or meanings for the other person.

You could even go so far as to say that if 'You' didn't exist, many of those "happenings" and "facts" wouldn't exist either.

IN SUMMARY

These Contexts are the fields on which both existence generally, and personal experience specifically, play out. They are the backdrop to everything that happens outside of us, and *to* us. Against and within these—everything takes place.

The External and Internal Contexts combine in unique mixes to create unique frameworks, that hold very differentiated challenges and opportunities for each of us.

And within these, we must come to know ourselves, make our choices, and try for fulfilling lives.

Whatever our unique Context-combination may be, it is important to strive to see and know it for what it is, since *it* is informing all the time and changeably—and often with a heavy hand.

Let's return now to this bigger, External Context, in which our lives (and possibilities) have been playing out, and take a closer look at how it is currently informing our lives and experience.

What are the disruptive impacts that it's having on the way of life we've come to take almost for granted over the last seven decades?

And what does that mean for us, going forwards?

OUR WESTERN CULTURAL CONTEXT

A 'SET-UP' OF EXPECTATIONS

Traditionally in our Western culture and societies, there have always been 'the poor', 'the working and middle classes', and the 'wealthy'.

By 'poor', I mean that group of people who barely hold it together financially, or who perpetually rely on family help, or on support from the Government, or are homeless.

By wealthy, I mean the wealthy entrepreneurs, C-suite executives, the educated, aristocrat classes with inherited fortunes, and even the despots and dictators—who don't worry about money or where it's coming from. For them, money is assured, it's already theirs, and there's plenty of it. And there are many working class people who've pulled themselves up by their bootstraps, and are happily and wealthily living lives in that category of absolute choice.

And then there's the rest of us. That great group of the 'middle class' who are sandwiched in-between the financially disadvantaged, and the enriched.

OPPORTUNITY RISES...

In the "Previous Normal", the middle classes became the fastest growing demographic, swelling in size over the decades of the long boom time that followed the end of World War II, as our possibilities and skillsets expanded exponentially. Millions of people were able to move upwards in the social hierarchy through new opportunities—into choice.

With our baby boomer parents' achievements, our knowledge that the common man can strike financial luck, and with opportunity as our inspiration—we've looked upwards from here, aspiring to move into the wealthy class to improve our lot and expand our choices. Expecting a rising income over the years and moving progressively up the income scale to create choice-ability has been a vision many of us have carried starting out.

And why not? We were prepared to work hard to get there, and that was always enough. We believe that anyone can achieve, regardless of a disadvantaged start.

Until recently, these times have been referred to as the "best of times". The poor and suffering have had access to substantial help and support when compared to times past. Since the Second World War, levels of poverty have generally declined, access to information has certainly increased, and we're better educated than ever.[6]

We've lived through huge changes in the last twenty years as the internet has become an integral part of our daily lives at work and at home. It's hard to believe now that there was barely email in the early 2000's, when my husband and I were first making our way to Australia! This amazing technology has brought not only a powerful means of communication and the dissemination of information (almost all Human knowledge) to every nation that facilitates it—but also incredible opportunities for work; a whole new industry, along with possibility, for increasing numbers of freelancers and entrepreneurs today.

And during these last twenty to thirty years the ability to buy a house, affordable cars, and cheap but lovely clothing had never been as good, and a long period of low interest rates and rising house prices helped many to build up their wealth.

Many of us enjoyed the benefits from much of this: personal happiness in and satisfaction with life had never been so high for so many. People expected to be able to go out for dinner reasonably often, and to go away on holidays; to have meat and dessert regularly on their dinner tables; to pay for their kids to join sports teams, take music or ballet lessons or receive extra maths tuition—or even go to a private school. People expected to be able to have our teeth done regularly (and even straightened)—as a norm.

Everything was possible if one follows the rules for success, we concluded. *Particularly if one put in effort.*

AND NOW — THE SET UP

In our societies, it's been natural to conclude then, that the route to happiness is via "success".

And it's reasonable, normal, and the most natural thing to want these therefore—both for ourselves and our children. And we talk about happiness and success with a sense of righteousness and pride—as if they're *values,* and good ones at that.

We must get "there".

> **"Success" has become the point and pursuit of our lives, the orientation for all our choices, and even our reason for living!**

We've even bought into the idea that we *deserve* to be happy and successful—particularly when we want this for our kids.

But we've attached certain words to the notion of success. *Wealth. Beauty. Status. Recognition.* These reveal a subtle fold in our thinking that we might not even realise is there: that what we really mean by "success" is that we gain wealth and achievement.

And, if we extrapolate this down, we 'win' by being rich—and coming first.

And we're taught (and teach) to chase this idea from the time we're small: *Life is a race to the top.* We actually come to believe that our worth as a person is tied to the attainment of "success" in this form.

BIG PICTURES

As young people, we have generous, open hearts, and trust life. Generally we're eager to please and do well, and so we absorb this value without question. We begin to construct an idea (or 'Big Picture') of what a "happy" life looks like—which includes the values, ideas and actions we believe will enable us to meet our own expectations, while rising to those of our families and peer groups.

On the other side of school we seek to meet our needs as independent adults. We're future focused and reasonably skilled: doers, achievers, dreamers—and armed with our unique skillset, we're up for just about anything. With our Big Picture ever present, we distill goals from it that we hope will move us in our chosen direction. Of course, embedded deeply within these are our cultural notions of success—not only in our ideas about "success" but also from what others are doing and achieving.

Because everyone we know is posting on social media, giving us glimpses into their wonderful, exciting lives. Clearly it's possible—and we want that too!

Mostly, we assume things will work out well, and expect to figure it out along the way. We know about our rights—clean air, enough food and the right to be happy—and feel confident of our 'claims'.

EXPECTATIONS

So we go into it, blind and enthusiastic, holding fast to the belief that our Picture is the route to the happy life, and *must* be realised; firm in the belief that Life will deliver up the opportunities and possibilities that we can begin to shape to our visions, through our efforts. Though we compare ourselves to our peers, (growing our self-esteem if we do better than them, or perhaps taking a hit if we feel they've outperformed us), once released into our adult lives we don't generally think too much about things going wrong or coming at us out of left field.

We work for our chosen lifestyle—whether we're in college or University still hoping for it, or already in a job and trying to improve our way to a better salary.

These are the rules, this is the Game of Life. We've played by them, and many of us have had the wins we were promised—and more!

Until recently.

A SHIFTING CONTEXT

HOW THE "RULES" CHANGED

*B*y recently, I'm really referring to the last decade or so, beginning soon after the 2008 Global Financial Crisis.

Outside of disasters that derail in an instant, many of us have been waking to a dawning reality that Life is gradually serving us less and less well. We live lives that might *look* okay on the outside—yet inside, it's often a different story.

We don't *win* any more.

Despite living 'good' lives in times of plenty and reasonable peace, we've been finding ourselves increasingly squeezed, and feeling financially stretched and stressed.

These days, we hardly ever go out for dinner, we don't upgrade our car, and we never can afford to go on holiday—much less overseas. Buying our own home is simply out of reach.

We're having to' settle' and be increasingly 'realistic'—letting go of our once dearly held hopes and dreams. We may even be totally *off* the path that we'd set out on so confidently! Instead, we're scrounging around for opportunities to just keep it all together.

Worse, we've lost the sense of Life as a place of possibility. We look at what Life 'promised' and wonder where the path our parents trod—that set our expectations—has gone.

And we've lost the sense of ourselves as empowered. We're estranged, lost and down.

> "Times are tough" the news articles reported when the world wasn't recovering economically in the timeframes expected and predicted after the Global Financial Crisis in 2008.
>
> I shrugged this off as The Usual Sensational Headlines. I was convinced that my struggle to get back on track and re-manifest after our personal disaster was the failure on my part to make the right decisions, to budget properly, to try harder to secure a job (and then a better job). — To be more thoroughly qualified, or to have been more recently employed. Damn that career break to raise children! I couldn't undo my actions and re-grasp my opportunities with more foresight, planning and wisdom.
>
> There had been regular bloodbaths on the International Stock Exchanges over the years that everybody would get in a lather about; a couple of months later, there would be surprise bounce-backs, and it would all have been something of a storm in a teacup.
>
> Yet by 2014, things were still 'down'. And it continued. Month after month—spawning the Greek Economic Crisis for example. Alongside this, millions of people had become displaced, scrambling to get out of the way of the bombs and guns of ISIS and the Syrian civil war with nothing but the clothes on their backs—flooding into Europe along with economic refugees from northern Africa. Now there were massive additional financial pressures on the already stretched and under-par economies there.
>
> Still none of this struck me as remarkable. It was just the usual bad

news fomented by the Press to keep everyone transfixed and anxious. But then, at almost at my lowest point in the aftermath of my husband's illness, something caused me to sit up and take notice.

GLOBAL RUMBLINGS
The unexpected results from the Brexit referendum rolled in, shaking the established order and bringing into sharp focus the economic difficulties that European economies were suffering.

Greece (and Italy's) financial crises suddenly made sense as part of the struggle that has undermined many European citizens who previously enjoyed reasonably stable lives.

And soon after that, Donald Trump—a citizen with no political credentials or experience—was elected the Republican nominee for President of the United States of America.

A BIGGER PICTURE UNFOLDS

Analyses of the 'Brexit' message over the next weeks pointed to the reality that the British middle class were doing it tough. Donald Trump becoming President the next year corroborated that similar difficulties were unfolding in the middle classes in the USA. And, now that I thought about it—seven successive governments with revolving prime ministers in less than ten years in Australia did not tell the tale of a happy and balanced society moving forward, business as usual, either.

Clearly citizens were shaking their metaphorical fists at their Establishments, and trying to change things up.

Commentary and analyses around these events exploded in televised analyses and articles in the online newspapers that I was reading across the USA, the UK, and Australia, over the next few years. Something was up. Everyone researched, discussed and tried to understand the themes and messages that underpinned what had happened. Commoners and experts alike were interviewed.

Story after story about middle class struggles emerged.

People around the globe were finding themselves in extended, reduced circumstances—feeling poorer and less empowered by the day. And they were *stuck* there, with the solutions that used to work in the past either no longer available, or no longer working in the new economic landscape. Trends showed that wage stagnation, unemployment and uncertainty were ongoing issues.

Many were dealing with regular bouts of adversity; having to dig really deep to overcome it (or not, as the case may be), and struggling—practically, psychologically and emotionally.

Suffering was on the rise everywhere.

Headlines about anxiety and depression were becoming everyday ones, and new findings on suicide and its causes resonated with the desperate thoughts and feelings *I'd* been having.

It was clear that millions of ordinary, hard-working, hopeful, middle class people — who were *not* suffering a lack of education, and had *not* been born into poverty, overcrowding or scant opportunity—had been swept up and tossed aside by new economic and political realities.

It was eye-opening. Millions of others were going through the same thing that I was. What I was experiencing had become a worldwide reality for millions of people in the Western World.

Millions are *still* experiencing this. In the aftermath of the Covid-19 global shutdowns, with the loss of thousands of businesses and jobs, and rising inflation and interest rates, millions more likely will.

THE GREAT SQUEEZE

You, may have found yourself under ongoing pressure in this changing cultural milieu. And not just in terms of your values and perceptions.

Costs have been rising, but salaries—not. Many people have stagnant or shrinking incomes, especially when the cost of inflation is taken into account. (And that's about to get worse on the back-end of Covid19).

Many jobs have been merged and disappeared, or become redundant. Those who have lost jobs are finding it increasingly hard to become reemployed. People are struggling to get enough work just to pay their bills, let alone make bigger choices, or treat themselves by going out for dinner occasionally.

Certainly there's not enough spare cash for life insurance, saving for a rainy day, a disaster or a holiday away. Many can't afford to save for retirement—and don't believe that they will ever be able to retire.

For many, life has become a precarious existence with short-term contracts and zero hours, stagnant wages in the face of the ever-rising costs of living. People are actually living those realities I feared, like homelessness.

The 'Baby Boomer' expectations (that so many have held), of getting educated, getting a job, working hard, being rewarded and rising up the career ladder—to buy a house, increase our net wealth, indulge in fun (and maybe even fab) experiences, from simple holidays to overseas trips, eating out, or going to the theatre—are all suddenly (and completely) out of reach.

Improving ourselves from our starting point has not been enough: it's not given us the position we would have liked, the connections we needed, and the opportunities of choice.

It feels unfair, and particularly when we perceive that this isn't happening for others in our peer group or family. It didn't occur to us that *our* future could be all bound up with disaster!

Most of all, we're disappointed.

In our heads we blame circumstances or our relatives, or the government, or the migrants and refugees, or politics, the banks, economics, the environment, or bad luck.

Or—we turn inward and blame ourselves for being useless or unlucky.

Either way we're anxious in the present, fearful of the future, and feeling powerless to change our trajectories. Our trust in the Rules of Life and in ourselves has become eroded.

Why did the rules have to change, and how on earth do we get back to feeling safe and happy again?

ANALYSIS (IF YOU'RE INTERESTED)

Key changes in our wider Context have contributed to these reductive shifts.

Economically we've been ongoingly whiplashed since the 2008 Global Financial Crisis. Yet I see a series of events as linking up across this century that have shifted something fundamental in our Western cultural edifice — perhaps beginning with Al Qaeda's 911 attack on the USA in 2001.

This is my take on it:

1. After 911, the USA invaded Afghanistan and then Iraq, bringing increased instability to the Middle East for some years.
2. Meanwhile the World was becoming a truly global economy with improved trade agreements, and the rise of the internet making global communication easier and giving Western economies more access to the emerging markets in Asia.
3. Manufacturing increasingly began to be moved out of First World economies, to countries where labour was cheaper.
4. And at the same time efficiencies were being vastly improved by exponential developments in technology and robotics. More and more jobs became automated.

Factories in middle class economies began to close down. Once-prosperous low and medium-skilled workers began losing their jobs, and were soon left behind in economic misery. Living standards for these people began to decline. Less income meant less spending, which meant that the economies in the First World began to shrink and struggle. Wages became consequently stagnant.

- This fallout from Globalisation was already negatively impacting millions of people when the GFC arrived into Western economies in 2008, crushing them even further.
- Then, in 2011, Islamic State (ISIL) emerged from the remnants of al Qaeda and the invasion of Iraq—and massively displaced local people in establishing their Caliphate. The Syrian civil war began. Millions of people had to flee the Middle East as a result, flooding into Europe and looking for jobs at a time when Greece and Italy were still on their economic knees, and Spain and Portugal were struggling with record levels of unemployment and inflation.

And in the background, in many Second and Third World countries, wars and ongoing conflicts, widespread corruption, economic mismanagement and power plays were (and still are) massively disrupting the economies and social fabrics there. Millions more people were displaced as a result, and look largely to Western culture for safe haven, further burdening these already unstable economies and disrupting existing social infrastructures. This exodus of people from homes, communities and country is continuing today as Russia now wages war, forcing millions of Ukrainians to flee the bombing of their cities and towns.

A SEISMIC SHIFT

Coming back to back, these different but significant upheavals have been a tsunami of change, combining and building and moving inexorably towards us over the course of the nearly twenty years since the Millennium.

They've literally shifted our known and previously manageable wider Context so massively that teetering economic, political and social systems now permeate our Western First World realities. And so while what's been unfolding is largely outside of us individuals, our societies and communities in the industrialised First World have been *seismically shifted* all the same.

THE OLD ORDER HAS GONE

What I hope I've shown unequivocally here, is that this is not politics and economics as usual. *There has been nothing like it in the Western World in our lifetime.* (There's not been a pandemic in our lifetime either!) The life that we now experience is changing faster than ever — and it's global, rather than just national. Impacts *from* everywhere are *felt* everywhere, even in the furthest reaches of the poles and the Amazon. Simply put, it's volatile!

None of this is just temporary, as we may believe or wish! "Just a little time to recover and 'get back to normal' and it will be business as usual again."

It will not. The global and political economies that massively dislocated industries, jobs and people—can't simply be undone. "Business" has changed permanently.

We've been blind to its scale—and certainly to the significance of much of what has unfolded in front of our very eyes. Our larger Context has in fact changed so significantly in the last two decades, that we're running on a completely different track now—though most haven't realised this.

A small number of people have made vast sums of money in this scenario. But for the majority of us, 'certainty' has gone astray. Opportunity has been smashed, and our strivings and dreams dashed.

Many, many people—with education, valuable skills, ambition and ideas, are finding it impossible to keep on the track they were promised and programmed to follow, and have been forced to revert to something much more basic when it comes to standard of living. Pilots are driving buses these days—if they're lucky enough to have landed the job!

THE "RULES" HAVE CHANGED

Across the world we're increasingly caught in the grip of anxiety, fear, and grief at loss, as things shift.

Millions of us, who have created viable, fulfilling lives on the back of the core Western cultural values of freedom and choice—are now living the painful reality that our ability to continue living and manifesting these values has become eroded. In too many cases, they've become completely lost.

Our social fabric is currently stretched to breaking point, with differences of opinion on what the best way forward for us all is. It's probably not such a surprise that far-right Political parties and affiliations have arisen in countries in Europe, South America and the USA, trying to chart a way forward based on the old rules of 'control'. We simply don't really know how to manage ourselves effectively around all this change and the curved balls that keep coming at us.

We weren't told about and didn't anticipate the vagaries of Life that seem to be an integral aspect of our experience now.

And we've not been raised or trained to carry the suffering that they inevitably bring on.

THE GREATEST RISK IN OUR FUTURE

THE ANGUISH OF THE MIDDLE CLASSES

*O*n the back of all of this, a *phenomenon* has been unfolding across Western middle class groups the world over—and has been for some time.

THE MIDDLE CLASS IS SHRINKING

The "New Normal" is Western societies' public acknowledgment of the massive shifts in the order of things, and the dissolution of the usual patterns we've relied on for the last two generations.

In this "new normal", the middle class and its usual expectations is increasingly experiencing the practical circumstances and lack of choice — that previously were the domain of the poor.

> **For the first time in history, the middle class is shrinking, as people fall into poverty at record rates.** [7]

People have lost their jobs and have never been able to replace their income—and have gradually lost everything.

Many have had to become self-employed; others are forced into long-term situations of working on short-term contracts—often having to provide their own expensive equipment (incurring thousands of dollars of debt) with no guaranteed hours, no holidays or sick pay.

People have put their money, hearts and efforts into enterprises like farms, but are being screwed on price for produce by the big corporates, while still having to pay back thousands of dollars to banks or the government (or risk losing their assets)—when they're already unable to make ends meet. Many have lost everything in these scenarios, including their reputations.

Too many are *under-employed*—paid less and forced to work less hours too: putting terrible strain on cashflow and no longer able to make ends meet. Or—they must work more hours for the same pay, with a reducing quality of life, yet grateful that they do at least still have an income.

War and political conflicts have destroyed lives, families, and middle class hopes, dreams, homes and heirlooms... Over 100 million people[8] are displaced today—more than any time in the last 70 years, many of them from ordinary, stable families across South America, Africa and the Middle East, who've had to leave everything behind and try to start again somewhere else, often far from home and loved ones.

That's one in every 80 people on the planet!

On the other side of these stories, people are left with very little—and even nothing. Carrying instead heartbreak, fear, anxiety, confusion and the sense of having personally fallen over. Many of them are unable to ever get back up again.

There is stress. Terrible stress, and a sense of lack.

WHY IS THIS SIGNIFICANT?

The middle class is that great group of people across the continents who are the engine of both society and the industrial economy. Yes, often it's the poorer, less educated people who are growing the populations, but in so many ways it's the middle classes who *shape* it.

- They're aspirational. They strive to improve their situations, developing themselves and their capacities.
- They innovate on the bigger projects that are to the benefit of all.
- They create momentum as they work their way up into an education and to having the means to make real choices.
- They're cohesive. *They're collaborative.*
- Thus, they 'shape' and 'lift' (see below).

Being collaborative and innovative are the key pieces here.

Generally speaking, people at either of the ends of the 'class' spectrum tend to be less collaborative, less innovative—and more inclined to be preoccupied with their own worlds and issues. On the lower end (and with more existential concerns), the Poor tend to be preoccupied by their lack of means, opportunity and personal power. On the other end, the Wealthy, in situations of plenty and often with a lack of real motivation or purpose—are often caught up in selfish individualism, more preoccupied with themselves and/or the deployment of their considerable power over… well, everything.

I'm generalising of course. There are notable exceptions in both of these categories!*

THE MIDDLE CLASS SHAPES AND LIFTS

My point about the middle classes is that they're drivers of development and change—in positive directions.

In their determination to understand and improve their world, they seek personal upliftment and to want to help their children to truly thrive (grow, flourish, succeed, prosper). They see the benefits of collaboratively pulling in the same direction with supportive others with similar aspirations and values. Their impetus for personal and collective improvement efforts and initiatives ripple into Poor lives, enabling and uplifting them too—paving the way for them to move towards and into middle class aspirational life themselves.

As they achieve their aspirations, many middle class people move into the wealth class. Yet in healthy and functional societies, the middle class ranks are constantly swelling—replenished and expanded as the lot of poor people improves. This is a sign (and has been for thousands of years) that Human *civilisation* is working well in improving (and empowering) itself overall.

THE MIDDLE CLASS IS THE CANARY IN THE COAL MINE

When the middle classes are shrinking—not due to people becoming better off but for the opposite reason—it reflects the general lack of opportunity, and is a reduction for all. Everyone gradually becoming worse off (declining, withering, languishing, pining)—is the absolute opposite of thriving.

'Society ' begins to go backwards.

First, opportunity reduces, and then goes away. Systems that are designed to support and expand possibility and promote thriving become limited or exclusive or bureaucratic, or fall away altogether. The same can be said for services. Investment in public infrastructures falters.

Grappling and failing, people wake up every day to deteriorated Contexts and a reality of derailed aspirations and lives. Their belief that the world is a safe and benevolent place that they just need to step forward into; a place where they can create and thrive—begins to fall under heavy question. They no longer see themselves empowered as they once did. They become disorientated. Mental health begins to deteriorate. They stop believing in possibility (the fuel of the middle classes!)—and in their own personal agency.

Of course it is people who establish, drive and uphold families, friendships, and social fabric. When they are in possibility, in self-empowerment and self-esteem, they bring care and excellence based on hope, to these things, and to their work. When they are disempowered, their anger and disenfranchisement shows up in their outputs.

Because suffering (particularly sustained suffering) has impacts on the Human soul: on a person's outlook, motivation, hope and effort. And when it's widespread, it's a sign of terrible dysfunction in the collaborative systems of society.

That brings consequences.

Collaboration falls away. People lose faith in each other, and hope. With hope dwindling, people no longer trust themselves, each other, or Life itself. It's every man for himself in a dog eat dog world.

Things begin to fall apart. Law and order first shifts into something more sinister, and then often breaks down.

With nothing more to lose, people begin to arc up against the constraints and reductions. In societies where many people own guns—anarchy, lawlessness (and even war) is next.

When it spills over borders—well, in the nuclear age, that can bring on the end of everything.

This is simply dangerous, and must be addressed.

POSSIBILITY IS SUBJUGATED BY OUR CURRENT CONTEXT

The seismic Contextual changes in global economic, political and social structures we're now experiencing are significant because they have so fundamentally and adversely affected (and even changed) Possibility—particularly for the aspirational middle classes.

> `Possibility is that alchemical place that anyone can step into, to create all kinds of magic.`

The middle class is still there, but millions in it can no longer work the Possibilities that were inherent in and available to them, in the "Previous Normal". They can no longer *choose* as they used to, leverage opportunity as they used to, purchase goods and services as they used to—or drive growth and development forward as they used to.

They're simply subject to this Context of the "new normal"—and are 'stuck' there.

They're still aspirational: they want the opportunity to shape themselves and their lives in community, and to be part of something flourishing. They aren't (yet) the poor who can't overcome their vicious cycle of poverty, yet their lives are deteriorating in that direction.

And they can do little about it! In fact, in many cases they find themselves still standing amongst contemporaries who *do* still have "means", who *can* still make choices, and are headed off in directions they can no avail themselves of. Different realities are being lived in the same space!

Outside of being left on the sidelines of their own lives and having their painful experience dismissed (more pain), people take it personally. And not because they are high maintenance, or over-sensitive or entitled (amongst the many dismissive remarks I've heard said). It's that they come to believe that this 'singling out' of them *means* something: something about *them;* something *awful* about them. It takes on a personally 'defining' power—in the negative.

There is ongoing stress and pain.

And Suffering.

RISING ANGER

Currently, there is a widespread feeling that the world in the 21st century is not only robbing ordinary citizens of their possibilities and abandoning them to reduced circumstances (and their fear)—but is actually out of control.

All over the democratic Western World we've seen peoples' anger—and rising anger. It's been expressed in election results, in news articles and blogs. In demonstrations, vigils and even riots.

There is anger at the spread of unemployment, leaving whole regions and generations bereft of choice, and hope.

There is anger at the financiers who brought the global economy to the brink of disaster, yet have continued to take home huge rewards as if nothing had happened!

There is anger at the governments who have presided over the disintegrations and the chaos we're witnessing, and failed to control corruption, the spread of extremism, war, and global chaos.

There is anger at the disproportionate salaries CEOs have been taking home during these times of such hardship and reduced opportunity. Where most people have seen their standards of living stay static or decline, these Executives have been rewarded with bonuses in the millions of dollars, on top of already very high salaries and substantial benefits.

There is anger at the perceived impotence of governments and global institutions to work collaboratively, and to create stable environments of peace and opportunity for all societies.

RED FLAGS ARE FLYING

People try hard for as long as they're able to. They do try generally to be as great as they can be! *No-one sets out to be a failure.*

Yet, with their possibilities, "means" and choices reduced, they become disempowered. Personal disempowerment becomes dangerous for the individual, and to society, as people become increasingly disconnected from possibility, then from others, and lastly from themselves.

I have wanted not just to normalise—but to *legitimise*—this particular experience of suffering. Not just because it's truly painful personally, but because together, we are creating so much of what is happening on this Planet at this time in Human history.

We need to be coming out of our best selves, rather than our most broken selves—not just to get through this, but to create something else: the next act for Humanity and for all life on the planet, to create a sustainable future for all.

This actually matters.

THE MIDDLE CLASSES ARE IN NEW TERRITORY

Where does what's left of the middle classes go, to turn things around for themselves?

Despite all our effort and self-belief, we're NOT validated, increasingly we feel we don't 'belong' and we hardly know who we are any more.

Many parts of our economy are looking awfully fragile right now. With Coronavirus having globally 'paused' many of our societies, Western Governments have handed out massive amounts of money to help beached citizens and keep their economies ticking over. But we don't know the effects of this. How will the money will be repaid? Are massive tax hikes looming in our reduced futures? Wage stagnation continues to be a real problem (it's been ten years or longer now)—only exacerbated now by the long 'pause' of Covid-19. Retail trade has fallen over time, and particularly on the back of the Covid pause, resulting in more reductions in spending, more closures of more businesses, and more job losses—in an ongoing death spiral.

And that's not even counting the ongoing dissipation of jobs that is resulting from continuing automation and development of robotics and other technologies in workplaces.

When I look back at how it was then—and how different it *now* is, it's clear to me that the recent past way of life and 'rules' were actually just a temporary gift to a particular couple of generations, at a particular time in Human civilisation.

And it is no longer being given out for free.

Subtle shifts in our daily lives, our possibilities and choices reducing, uncertainty replacing our once sure footing in our world, the future seeming constrained—are all in direct contrast to the heady years of growth and expansion that marked the lives of the two generations of people since the end of the Second World War.

Life is much, much trickier for many of us now. For most people on this planet, life—is actually about just *getting by,* with a lot of suffering thrown in.

We've taken it for granted that things should roll out as we *think* they should.

We've taken it for granted that each generation will do better than the last —earning more and enjoying a higher standard of living.

Yet the things we've taken for granted, are no longer things we can count on.

Our rights, such as they are, are no longer givens.

—Like having ongoing employment, with a rising salary over time, feeling safe in public places; or even just going out to the shops and rubbing shoulders with other shoppers…

> "I just feel like I'm not going to be able to do and get all the things my parents could, and all the things I've wanted to do since I was younger. They are starting to seem less achievable."

The problems facing our world are real and serious, and we have all felt their effects at home. Many of us look at our kids now and know that unless they strike some kind of crazy luck, they won't have even what we have (little as that feels now)—and certainly they won't be able to afford to buy their own home.

And we're not done yet.

*Note: I don't mean to minimise or even discount the effects of these massive shifts on any other population group. Certainly philosophically, emotionally and socially there have been equally painful impacts on the wealthy — though generally they're not aspirationally impacted by the economic effects (at this stage at least) to nearly the same degree. And the poor are suffering with little to no agency and often low expectations to begin with; are thus perhaps less susceptible to further disempowerment and disappointment (with the same reductive psychological and emotional impacts) than the middle class demographic.

"REAL" VICTIMS

OUR "FIRST WORLD PROBLEM"

Meanwhile, Western society is very reluctant to take seriously the notion that there *is* generalised suffering in our educated Culturescape.

Suffering must be terrible, life-threatening, and/or abusive to be allowed to wear the label.

Yet the fact remains that despite not starving, or living on the streets, or in terror of violence every day, many of us are living lives of quiet desperation!

Just because one isn't a displaced person, or the survivor of terrible war, or born into seriously disadvantaged circumstances, or someone who has experienced adversity, tragedy, or loss on some unbelievable scale— doesn't mean they don't feel legitimately desperate about the fact that their ordinary life and hopes have gone out of the window and been smashed on the ground.

IT FEELS PERSONAL

When we're trapped in our circumstances and mentally suffering in them, spending time with others who are *not* going through what we're going through makes everything feel worse—whether that's hanging out with a group of friends or walking with a crowd down the street. Because *we feel singled out*, as if we're the only person going through this 'reduction'.

And often we carry a lot of shame about that.

No-one else in my circle really seemed to get what it was like to confront my terrifying, difficult situation (and my useless Self in it). —Or to understand how I felt about it.

None of them had to. No-one else I knew had been struck down by difficulty or calamity of this kind. No-one else I knew was having to get back up off the ground. No-one else I knew felt disappointed—and desperate —about their lives.

At the peak of my suffering, I was often given well-meaning advice by those whom I know, love, and care about. Basically, I was told to improve my attitude and be grateful.

> "There are many people in worse situations than you," *I was told.*
> **"Real Victims.** You're not homeless, hungry, or abused; not persecuted, tortured, raped and terrified, or living in a war-torn country. Who are you to complain? You're lucky—look at the all the good things you've got! Stop feeling sorry for yourself. You have a 'First World Problem!'"
>
> *Others said, as the years went by,* "It will be alright, don't worry. Things will work out! Exercise! Be positive!" *Or—*"this too shall pass; things will change!"
>
> *Silently, internally, I seethed.* How do you know things will change? *I*

thought. They haven't so far. Why should I hope for anything different? Their commentary didn't help me to deal with my overwhelming feelings at all (which was surely the intent!)

Unable to recover my 'normal', I was watching friends, colleagues and contemporaries continue to enjoy the successes I'd enjoyed before, without hiccough, impediment, or experience of loss or lack. By contrast, I was feeling keenly how we were falling further behind by the day, by the month, by the year, and living loss, fear and grief as a result. I felt desperate. Their encouraging (yet dismissive) attitudes and advice only served to boost my loss of self-respect, courage and sense of hope.

To have my losses and consequent fear written off as a 'First World Problem' made a mockery of my feelings. And negated my suffering. To be told to be grateful that my situation wasn't much worse — simply shamed me.

DISCONNECTION

It was painful to have to address what I was going through with friends and family, who were obviously saddened to see what was going on but found it hard to identify with, and after a while, didn't know what to say to me about it (other than eventually to admonish me about my attitude and my need for gratitude). I couldn't tell them the one thing they wanted to hear: that things had improved in my life.

That they were enjoying their usual lives and successes ongoingly put us on different tracks, and immersed us in different consciousnesses. As time went on they stopped coming by to visit. Gaps between communications got longer and longer and, eventually, reluctant to reach out, I went into retreat.

In this deepest, darkest moment in my life, I didn't want to be a burden to someone else.

I had an awful experience where I bumped into a parent from my childrens' old school, who suggested we catch up over a cup of coffee. Innocently, I agreed. Once seated, she smiled brightly at me.

'So what's been happening? Is your husband well? Does he have a job yet? And what are you up to?'

I started to talk, and my throat closed up.
Pinching myself on the soft part of my inner arm (hoping the physical pain would override my rising emotions), I tried to speak on.

To no avail. Without further warning, I broke down in the middle of my sentence—but totally. In moments (and to my unfolding horror)— I was sobbing uncontrollably in the middle of the café: the kind of crying that has you choking over your sobs like a small kid, with a huge excess of snot.

I was completely unable to regain any kind of control for several long minutes. And there weren't any tissues! It was awful for both of us, and a reminder that I really did need to keep things on the surface, and deflect all questions back to the asker.

I put myself back together eventually, and resolved to avoid all such situations again.

Which I managed quite successfully.

KNOW THAT YOUR PAIN IS LEGITIMATE

Many people are miserable today because their lives have been shipwrecked, along with their dreams and plans. Often under extreme stress, living in fear, with rock-bottom self esteem, they're suffering terribly. Though this may be dismissed as 'a First World Problem', this kind of suffering is often no easier personally to bear, than suffering is for those at the more extreme end—and too often these days leads to the death of the struggling person.

As said earlier, *bad things happen to good people*. These good people find themselves in situations where they actually need help and support; to be comforted, and to be gently returned to the places within themselves where courage, resilience and hope still dwell.

Yet, not being a "real" victim, not being able to share how miserable and terrified we are in our Life—means that often we're alone with our pain, with no resources for us to turn to.

It's normal to feel overwhelmed and upset by distressing events and circumstances, and the way each individual reacts will be very personal, and dependent on many other factors in their lives and personalities.

- Not being a *'real' victim* does not mean that your suffering should be swept under the rug and minimised.
- It doesn't mean that you should be putting on a brave face and pretending that you're not struggling.
- Nor should you feel ashamed that you're not in an extreme situation and yet have the cheek to suffer.

It's your pain and *it matters* in the scheme of You, your life and your Context. No-one should be telling you how deeply you should feel about it, or whether your grief about your losses is reasonable or not.

I'm not advocating victimhood.

On the contrary. Having the sense of being a victim is ultimately disempowering. But what I am saying is that individual pain can (and should) be taken very seriously, and we don't have to feel bad for struggling in it.

COMMON EXPERIENCE LEVELS THE PLAYING FIELD

People often experience feelings of *guilt* about the situation they find themselves in because they believe (as I did), that they are somehow personally to blame for their 'misfortune': that it's the personal weakness in *them* that has caused them to find themselves so ruined, so lost, and so stuck.

- They feel they've let their loved ones down.
- They're humiliated in front of their friends and peers.
- They hate themselves for their weakness, their pain, their suffering and struggle.

Cut off from the common experience, living with shame and disempowerment, they become a 'literal outsider'.

While legitimising personal suffering is certainly helpful, what is often even more helpful is knowing that we are not alone in our experience. For many of us, the inevitable pain of Life is easier to bear when it is normalised for us.

I've been told by people who were actually there at the time, that in the months after the end of the Second World War, many people expressed some sadness that it was over! They spoke quite nostalgically about the experience of everyone being in the same boat. With the war underway, all the usual external signs of "achievement and success" that set one lot of people apart from another, were gone. People from all walks of life found themselves suddenly sharing a common experience—and with one common purpose: to make it through the disaster and tragedy, and out onto the other side.

Burdened by losses (material and relational), what was left was the business of engaging with one's own and others' humanity. Those hard times in fact often brought out the best in people, revealing strengths, capacities and depths they barely knew they had. People helped and comforted one another, and felt connected through their bigger, shared cultural and ideological values. They found themselves playing valuable roles; bringing unique skills that could make a positive difference to bear in a terrible situation—even if it was just the ability to make someone a cup of tea, or comfort them in their loss.

This truth is no different today, for us.

It goes to show that even when circumstances are disastrous, if we don't feel singled out by them or alone with them, we can actually bear up incredibly well, leaving us with a sense of personal well-being, even while we're suffering hardship and tragedy.

CULTURAL MYTHS

TRAPPED BY OUR "STORIES"

Our "suffering" really begins with 'where' we find ourselves—in Context. (And, as we noted earlier, we quickly extrapolate this into 'Who' we are…)

This Context—the wider one that has morphed into sudden, harsh reality around us—has profoundly affected our experience of lives (despite effort), and of ourselves in it.

In part that has to do with the practical struggles many of us experience in the more challenging circumstances, and the fear and sense of powerlessness that arises in us as a result. The *lack of "success"*, as we've defined it.

But the other part has to do with our cultural expectations of what Life 'should' be, and what we're 'entitled' to in it.

And underpinning these, is one of the most profound myths of our Western culture.

> **Our birthright is HAPPINESS.**
> **We 'should' be Happy.**

That *sounds* wonderful; after all, who doesn't want to be happy? *"Invitation accepted. Thank you very much!"*

But this where we've shot ourselves in the foot, metaphorically speaking. Because we've also concluded that *success* is the path to happiness, to the point that we've based our entire modern day life on "success's" achievement.

Which means that if the heady heights of achievement (as seen in many lives splashed across our media today) becomes unreachable due to Context, then so, apparently, does happiness.

Cue epidemics of depression…

Let's look a little more closely at our ideas around this subject, to understand how they've caused such a phenomenal stumble in the general mental health of our Western societies.

IT BEGINS WITH "MORE"

Our ideas of what will make us successful (and therefore happy) often come from our parents' values and hopes for us. And in many cases, they were raised in less fortunate times, in an era of less available and less affordable "stuff". During the First World War, The Great Depression, and then the Second World War, there was loss, and lack — and even after those were over, there was much rebuilding and restocking to be done before the deeper sense of 'lack' and uncertainty began to alleviate.

Growth and ambition were remedies.

Now—at the beating heart of *success*—lies the concept of *interminable growth*.

It's growth of population (hey new taxpayer!) and of ever increasing consumption. We believe that…

- We need access to and supply of ample and unending amounts of food, treats, alcohol.

- We need lots of money, and several cars, and preferably more than one home—and these should contain multiple bathrooms and garages, butler's pantries adjoining the kitchen, several sitting/entertaining areas, and even a home cinema.
- We must *have stuff* in multiples, like TV's, gadgets, glassware, dinner services, sofas, tables and chairs. Owning vast wardrobes of clothing, collections of shoes and handbags, jewellery and multiple watches is essential.
- And if we're not storing the stuff that we're not using (and probably don't remember that we own) in our spare room cupboards, cellar, attic or garage—we rent storage for all that overflow.
- Undertaking frequent travel and undergoing adventure experiences while staying in luxurious hotels is a norm.
- Having multiple degrees, large amounts of power, social status, and top and multiple connections are expected.

(Growth of our souls, or of kindness and compassion; a sense of personal responsibility or of wisdom—not so much. These 'internal' matters don't add value to either the growth economy or really to our Western ideas of "success").

SELLING THE STORY

'More' and 'growth' are cultural 'values' we've now been handed, at home in our own societies, and internationally. And they're easy to buy into, since the concepts play on our fears of lack (and therefore also of being judged).

This makes Western culture's pervasive marketing of the notion, compelling.

At the coalface of this we're shown a detailed world of opulence and opportunity outside of our own four walls—*a world that has never been so widely visible before*—via a constant supply of photos, videos, newsreels and glitzy advertisements on television, the internet, social media and in publications.

Information about wealthy peoples' lives (like the Royals and celebrities) used to be scant for example, limited to glimpses of rarified lives in the trailers before feature films, or grainy photos, video footage and lame anecdotes at the end of the news snippet on evening television.

Importantly, those lives were clearly understood to *not* be the norm.

Nowadays though, they're on full and regular public display, featuring in specially designed 'celebrity' magazines and newsfeeds, and often with their own websites and Instagram accounts. And, there are exponentially more of them! Looking gorgeous, in sumptuous surroundings and dressed in the best clothing the world has to offer, they present us with a wonderful reality of extraordinary wealth, comfort, and personal freedom —*almost as if the lives they live are those of everyday people. People like us.*

Being exposed to all of this daily, right in our own homes, can make it seem something that even the people next door seem to have!

In fact it has created a certain "normal" in our minds over the last two decades, and set new expectations of Life and of ourselves in the First World environments that we live in today. And the bar has been set—to extraordinary.

Then, Marketing has sold us the idea that this is possible for all of us.

We could be just like them if we diet, extend our hair, or wear *this* brand of makeup or clothing. *We* could live like them—if we copy their investment advice, or buy that look-alike item of furniture from a particular store. *We'll* be the envy of the neighbours if we dress our kids in the same brand of clothing the royal babies wear. We *should* aspire to look like these guys, and live lives as full and rich as they do!

BUYING THE STORY

The ongoing absence of anything like it in our own lives has been fuelling our fears of lack and feelings of frustration and craving, and raising the question of our own "success". Then our kids come home from school and tell us how embarrassing our house or car is and how it makes us look 'poor'—and our fears are confirmed. Uncertain of ourselves in the face of all the extraordinariness everywhere, we may even agree with them (at least internally) because we think it's true—and that it matters.

Painfully aware of the gap between where we are and what's apparently possible, we grasp eagerly onto Marketing's ideas. We allow ourselves to believe that this "normal" might be possible for us too. We're work hard; we deserve extraordinary too!

So we suspend our disbelief, and buy into this 'reality'. After all, people we know (and even know well) are regularly posting evidence of *their* success in this new game, documenting their wonderful and exciting lives on social media. We only need the better body, the prettier face, the blog, the lucky break, the outrageous thing that becomes a meme—or some other fame-inducing action. We know that many of the lucky people *are ordinary folk like us*—doing well, becoming famous, and getting rich precisely *because* they built the better body, got the prettier face, wrote the blog, got the lucky break, or did the outrageous thing that became a meme...

We work for it, for that lifestyle (whether we're in college or University aiming for it, or already in a job, trying to improve our way to a better salary) so we can have this, get that, be more, and become successful and... therefore, become happy.

We should be "there".

GLAMBITION

In the not too distant past, the markers of success were having a job, and perhaps a car; maybe owning one's own home (though not necessarily!)—and having a family.

People went out to dinner, yes, but generally speaking, fancier restaurants weren't everyday fare. Rather, they were enjoyed as 'occasions', or for celebrating: a 'treat'.

Special or expensive wants and wishes tended to show up at Christmas time or on birthdays rather than at any old time, and the annual holiday was only infrequently an overseas 'splurge'.

Clearly over time, this has shifted.

Now, the job should be high-powered, and preferably carries an impressive job title. 'Big Pictures' have become scaled to luxury cars and mansions; clothes should be designer, and eating out (with expensive wines and champagnes) should be regular, even daily occurrences. (Enviable) holidays abroad are seen as quite regular, and we feel we should buy what we want (not just need) — on credit if necessary—without delaying our gratification or being constrained by cashflow. In fact, "going shopping" is now a leisure activity, where the clothes, accessories and other items we come home with are simply outcomes of the activity, rather than useful (and even valued) items to meet our needs!

'Needs' are a big balance of cash in a savings account, an investment portfolio, ownership of our own home (or three), and all the 'toys'.

The projection of what constitutes a 'good life' has become spectacular.

Assets and stuff, and regular, amazing experiences (with 'proof' documented on our Facebook and Instagram accounts, or a range of that)—are now the generally accepted routes to happiness and peace.

Caught in this "growth" mentality we're simply focused on getting more and more into our lives, with our purpose for living being the building of bigger, 'better 'lifestyles.

"More" has become our society norm.

And we don't question it. We just aim to get ourselves onto that treadmill, sure that if we do—"things" and desirable feelings will eventually come our way and fill us up with joy, fulfilment, accomplishment and satisfaction.

The question is, how much *is* 'enough'? When does what we *actually have* bring on the feeling of happiness that it's supposed to?

A VERY PARTICULAR EDUCATION

There is no denying that the ideas, values and beliefs we've been living by in our Western societies have generated powerfully for us. We've proven them to 'work' on our behalves.

And having done so, we've enshrined them in our national cultures as valuable—even precious.

We took them on from trusted others: our parents and teachers, our peers and societies, and from our nations. And we've orientated ourselves (often protectively) around them, with little reason to question them.

In fact, we were given these ideas, beliefs and values when we were too young to think of them as anything but *Truths*. We simply base our thoughts, feelings and actions, and expectations about Life and ourselves on them, and go from there.

Importantly, these drive us: expanding or contracting us, underpinning our self-esteem and personal power, and our embrace of possibility. Embedded in us as they are, they strongly inform how we see both our world and ourselves, the actions we take (or don't take)—and therefore the outcomes we experience. And not always in a positive way—or for empowering outcomes!

Not only are we not discerning here, but we have no real measure of whether they're objective, malevolent, limiting, empowering, total rubbish, or anything else—until we get hurt!

Invested and immersed in them as we are—wishing only for positive outcomes and happiness (and wanting to be on the side of "right")—we've not really thought about their quality.

We're not aware that we've bought into a BS cultural story...

WE MIGHT BE WRONG ABOUT THIS

Yes—we're constantly exposed to a world that seems full of gorgeous people living wonderful lives of wealth, fulfilment and joy. But, in current, ACTUAL, everyday reality—none of this is *normal*.

The statistics suggest strongly that what we see every day on our internet and social media feeds is reality *for less than ten percent of the eight billion people in the world.*

That's a mere number of people.

And many people confess to curating and *presenting* an image that isn't true at all!

The truth is, most of us are struggling in some way all the time, practically and financially—and particularly internally—as we wrestle with confronting emotions, difficult relationships, challenges at work, or with health issues and the effects of ageing.

Many of the 'success-stories' and even celebrities we hear about are struggling deeply in their personal lives too! Serial divorces, stints in prisons for drug and alcohol abuse, self-harm, depression, simply vanishing from the spotlight—and even suicide—pepper their stories. Yes, they get to suffer with a lot more money, yet clearly no amount of money, success or fame erases their pain and suffering.

Painful experiences, to varying degrees, live with us all always, regardless of "success" or plenty.

The idea that we'll be happy if we're in possession of assets and wealth (and particularly "more" of them) is thus deeply flawed.

Many of us actually have so much already—yet are always striving for more of everything: more goods, assets, status, wealth, security, and 'safety'.

And it's only made worse by the reality that, in warped ambition, we're trying to achieve and live up to unrealistic expectations of our lives and of ourselves! Consequently, even though we may be managing (and managing perfectly well), many of us are needlessly in a state of stress and anxiety about where we are in Life, feeling not only uncertain in it—but actually dissatisfied instead.

And those who are unable to achieve glambition—feel a failure (and even become depressed) despite having plenty of success in their lives by ordinary standards!

Ironically, the pursuit of 'more' as the route to happiness (via success)—delivers the opposite of what we imagine it will.

- Despite *having* plenty of success in our lives by ordinary standards, we're unable to truly appreciate it. Instead of experiencing personal satisfaction, happiness, gratitude and peace in our achievements and lifestyles, we're mired in an ongoing mindset of 'lack', and brought into a state of resultant stress.
- Our anxiety about our perceived 'lacks' becomes our present moment reality, as we dwell on the thoughts and feel the pain that these thoughts bring up in us. This destroys not only our everyday quality of life, but leaves us feeling like failures—and even to become depressed!

This is tragic!

A DIAGNOSIS OF MYOPIA

We've become limited in our world views and experience.

CULTURAL MYTHS | 133

Increasingly now, we're seeing our world through screens, heavily curated and edited by algorithms orientated to the growth economy and consumerism.

Many families no longer sit around the dinner table talking about Life in all its many forms, shapes and nuances—expanding awareness and sharing experiences, gaining useful perspectives in the process.

'Informed' and 'cocksure', all too often we don't talk to our grandparents or great-grandparents with a genuine desire to gather for ourselves the insights and wisdoms they've gained, over long decades of life.

Yet we believe 'we know' reality. We think we know what is 'normal'. We believe *this is Life*.

We assume that what we're seeing and experiencing is the same reality that everyone lives. We imagine that that the generally accepted values, norms and behaviours we see and experience in our communities and societies are not only usual, but acceptable.

We all think that our perceptions and resulting thoughts of what we're experiencing are right and true—and importantly, objective.

Yet, if we had to transplant ourselves into places in the Middle East or the African continent for example, where poverty might be the norm, where there might be no internet, where women are not treated as equals to men, or where the caste or religion you're born to may put you at a serious and even life-threatening disadvantage, we'd be shocked and horrified.

And the people living *there* quite probably think *that's* the norm for everyone!

The idea that without external success we are nothing—is founded on a *business* model, in which we're simply consumers: numbers in a particular Game of Life.

And it's become unsustainable, and not just for the planet. We're all paying a high price for this folly and superficiality, and things are only going to get worse if we continue with this particular way of thinking.

The greater truth isn't actually the concept that our Western culture holds so dear, that we've kept in our sights and striven so mightily for: *that "success" is our main goal—and the only means of claiming true happiness.*

This is a created concept of Human life and an idea of ourselves—tying us down in a bubble of unreality that is not just untrue and unrealistic, but is simply unsustainable—no matter what Culturescape we live in.

And it's disempowering us at our core. And this disempowered state is the absolute opposite of what we're striving for!

> **Our achievements don't define us. (Elusive) "success" doesn't define us either.**

Yet, caught in this thinking, we ascribe importance to false things and false meaning to what is happening (or not happening) to us—and are increasingly disappointed, made unhappy (and ongoingly stressed) as we judge our outcomes and ourselves against these.

And as time goes on, we've gradually become less and less aware of how we've created a false idea of the norms against which we measure and value ourselves, and which we think are important.

Our quest for "happiness via success" has, on the one hand, generated entitled attitudes in our society—moving us into being increasingly selfish and disconnected in a 'dog-eat-dog' culture.

And on the other, it has fostered disappointment, contributing to an epidemic of low self-esteem where we believe that not only do we not *have* enough, but *we* are not 'enough'. Psychologically, there is now much generalised and widespread strain in our societies at this perceived "not-enoughness", with consequent reductions in quality of life, and quality of 'personhood'.

Quite the opposite of happiness!

Banish this myth now. It no longer serves us (if it ever did!)

A WORD ON "MENTAL HEALTH"

LABELLED INTO "ILLNESS"

*L*iving with this mindset about *'should be happy'* as our natural state (and even that we have the *right* to be happy) has created generalised anxiety about whether or not we're *actually okay* during the inevitable periods of time where we're miserable about our difficulties!

When the 'should be' and 'right to' be happy isn't manifesting in our lives, tension is heightened. Everyone we know who realises that we're unhappy is instantly concerned that this key aspect of our lives is off track, and exhorts us to *find* things to be happy about: to do whatever we can to get back to happiness as soon as possible. Not just because they care about our suffering—but because this is the way that things are 'supposed' to be!

The burden of being unhappy is then made weightier by unhappiness about being unhappy—and finally we become *ashamed* about being unhappy!

Emphasising 'Happiness' as our goal in life is not only guilty of setting us up for disappointment and

stress, but has gone further by suggesting that unhappiness is a symptom of maladjustment!

Discussions about 'mental health issues' are now a regular part of our dialogue. Unhappy people shouldn't just settle for it, but must do everything they can to overcome it (and quickly), and connotations of dysfunction and even 'abnormality' are soon on the table if sadness persists.

LEGITIMATE SADNESS

In general, an ongoing state of happiness is elusive because we'll experience a gap between reality and our 'Big Picture': between our desires and expectations and what actually arrives, and the disappointment and fear that results.

For many of us, our efforts to become happy don't work, because they don't get to the heart of our problems:

- our relationship difficulties continue
- our financial worries continue
- our self-esteem issues continue
- our loneliness continues
- our lack of 'perfection' continues
- our anxiety continues
- our feeling of being lost or stuck continues
- our grief at loss continues

Because that's Life: a state of existence where the 'rules' aren't really rules, where change (and thus loss) are happening all the time, and where we have limited power. We're constantly grappling with lack, and loss, bringing 'fear' and 'desire' (the opposite of happiness!) to our doors.

Our experience of our resultant pain can bring on *depressive symptoms*: ongoing sadness, tearfulness, low moods, lethargy, a lack of enthusiasm—and even feelings of despair.

Family and friends and our medical professionals don't relate our malaise to our deep disappointments and the meanings we give them. They don't get our anxieties about our life-threatening inability to manifest what we want; they can't understand our fear that we're 'not enough' and powerless as a result—and how very disabling it is to live with all this. Not being 'seen' and understood alone is painful!

And they certainly don't recognise how much of our unhappiness is seated in the unrealistic cultural expectations (which they perpetuate) that we generate ongoingly 'happy' lives.

We're categorised 'depressed' by them, instead.

SADNESS NOW BECOMES "MENTAL ILLNESS"

This, for many people, is deeply disturbing. Far from being a useful 'diagnosis' for dealing constructively with a personal struggle, (as used to be the case) the word 'depressed' now evokes *mental illness*—and disability—and often comes with negative (and sticky) side-effects .

Yet "Depression" become a "catch-all" word. Over the last decade or so, the Mental Health "industry" has come to *own* the word as a concept in it's own silo — to the point that even employers now will think twice about hiring someone who has at some point been diagnosed as "Depressed" and is—or has been—seeing a therapist!

Admitting to having suffered from "Depression" in the past and/or seeing a therapist will almost certainly cause you be declined for Life Insurance.

There are people who do have mental illness of course: psychopaths, paedophiles, neurotics, and schizophrenics for example)—but the line between these folk and people who are 'depressed' has become rather blurred in the public arena.

Nowadays the experience of "depression" has become conflated with 'clinical depression' and the term "mental illness".

Too often now someone is given this 'medicalised' version of the label—which may even be given early on in the piece. And in terms of our wider, general societal understanding of it, they receive a personally defining (and limiting) ball and chain that can come to weigh on them and their life, rather than help them to recover.

Words and concepts have great power in shaping our perspectives, and on our self-esteem. Being labelled with a 'disorder' just when we're feeling vulnerable and overwhelmed can be experienced as an assault on our already very fragile sense of ourselves as 'enough'. People come to doubt themselves. And how much harder might it be to recover if we perceive ourselves as "sick" in the head? Meanwhile the 'diagnosis' may not be true at all!

WHAT IS "DEPRESSION" THEN?

In the past, *depression* (outside of post-natal depression or other hormone changes or imbalances) was understood to be the deeper and longer lasting experience of *sadness*.

It wasn't 'something' that manifested but couldn't be explained and understood.

It was more than having a bad time of it and moving through the sensations of sadness, disappointment and loss until life resumed itself within a matter of days. It was understood to be a deep, personal and extended unhappiness, in which sufferers felt overwhelmed by their own feelings and unable to rally over time, even with support.

It was bad but not life-threatening even while it was debilitating and disorientating, and was usually given time and compassionate support, rather than labels and medication. Generally with results.

Nowadays there's allowance for brief sadness (after which we *should* return to our normal, happy state). Even grief (generally limited to bereavement, but including disenfranchised grief) is treated this way, with the DSM allocating mere weeks for mourning the death of a baby![9]

There seems to be no place for sustained sadness, without the alarm bells going off and the label being given. If we're sad or grieving outside of the allocated time allowances, we're told that we have a mental health illness, and given the label, "Depressed".

What is my beef with this? You may be wondering…

THE PROBLEM WITH THE LABEL OF "DEPRESSION"

When we're so quick to refer to ordinary depression as a "mental illness" we're not only medicalising and making exceptional something that is both a legitimate and normal part of the Human experience, but we label someone into a psychological *disorder*, with connotations of instability and unreliability; someone perhaps less believable—and even *not quite right in the head*!

This is not only categorising and degrading, but makes victims of those of us struggling here. We seek wellbeing as we labour our way out of loss and grief, and find ourselves labelled with mental illness—which goes to the heart of our identity, which has already been so torn asunder!

When I was struggling through my endless days of suffering, I can definitely say with one hundred per cent knowledge that while I was out of balance, miserable, and hopeless, I was not "depressed" in the way that we've come to use the term. It's surely no surprise that I felt so low, and for a long time! My world had collapsed and I'd lost the agency to direct my life and to make choices. I was in a legitimate emotional state, with my anxiety a natural response to a very real situation.

Yet: *"You need to go on medication to manage your sadness,"* I was told.

So I did.

It made no noticeable difference, and even less so after months on it. Even the idea of anti-depressants (with the placebo effect) didn't seem really to make much difference to how I felt.

Because I wasn't suffering from "Depression" even though I was depressed.

Yes, I dwelt on morbid thoughts—but did this mean that I had a mental illness? Or was I simply stuck in corner, filled with despair? And was that not a reasonable reaction to what had happened?

Yet my anguish was boxed up and labelled: "Depression" and "mental illness". Was it right that how I felt about it all and suffered in it—should have me labelled—as mentally ill?

I was not ill.

For me, something more accurate—more truthful—and much more 're-enabling' would have been, *"Despair in the face of a life challenge."* Being labelled 'Depressed" and told I had a mental illness instead, had me feeling even more disabled, and alone!

'BECOMING' THE LABEL

It's my experience through working with grief clients, that many who have been given this label (that they can never quite seem to escape), get *stuck* in their depressive state, and stuck feeling broken (and disempowered) to quite some extent—simply because they're carrying around the stigma of "mental illness" and the 'identity' it gives them.

When in fact they're really going through a very normal response to the sometimes harshness of life.

Our sense of Self is already under siege at this point without this label and it's associations. Being given the idea that we have a mental "illness" takes away from our sense that our "depression" is after all a quite normal response to suffering and not at all uncommon; that we can dig deep, and ask for help, support and understanding to get through it—and come out whole on the other side of it.

Being labelled "Depressed" can instead suggest that we're undergoing something 'abnormal' in our suffering—leading to feelings of shame, and even helplessness.

> **When people *don't* see themselves as 'abnormal' and 'broken' they tend to find inner resilience—and rally, sooner.**

And because the medical profession has a voice of authority and many people are raised to hear its prognoses as "facts and truths", this label can have disastrous effects not only on identity, but on attitude too (which ultimately translates itself into biology via the Placebo Effect.)

I have found that almost as soon as I'm able to normalise my clients' experience for them, they're able to believe in their own abilities to heal, call upon their natural resilience, and begin to find fortitude in the face of struggle.

So it seems absolutely essential to me to create a distinction between the "depression" that has become the territory of the Mental Health Industry and that can be classed as "mental illness"—and the kind of sustained, deep, debilitating depression you may be stuck in now, as you read this book.

A HISTORY OF UNHAPPINESS

In researching this, I found that the Western cultural idea that we are born to *be* happy, that happiness is our natural state, and that it's not normal to be unhappy—is a relatively recent one.

Because embedded in history books, philosophical and religious texts, and in the wisdoms and ideologies of other cultures and societies is that knowledge we've already uncovered: that suffering is ubiquitous in Life and in the lives of all living beings—and in fact is quite normal! Periods of sadness have always been acknowledged and accepted as being an inevitable and unavoidable aspect of the state of being alive, and a normal response to the business of being a Human Being in relationships and of trying to survive.

No part of society can ever be untouched by sorrow; no one person can ever be exempt from the mental and physical aches and heartbreak that life can bring.

A relationship breakdown, losing a job or opportunity, or beloved and important possessions; or home, country, health, liberty or ability to choose—can (and has) turned lives upside down in a moment, bringing feelings of disappointment (that can last for days or months), fear, deep grief and sustained depressive feelings. And this has been going on for centuries!

Being in this state instead of a happy one is not abnormal, nor is it an illness, mental incapacity or character deficit. It is simply the very uncomfortable (and often disorientating) place that one is occupying at a certain point on the journey.

And while it may be prolonged, it does end eventually.

Happiness may be our *natural* state (and a guiding light towards which we're always heading), yet it's not reasonable to see it as a state that can (and should be) be maintained at all times. Stigmatising it as we have done in Western culture over time; pushing the idea that sadness and grief are abnormal states of being that must be overcome as quickly as possible—has ultimately delegitimised an important part of the Human spectrum of emotions.

To our cost. Because the belief that we're not *supposed* to be unhappy is itself stressful, bringing deeper suffering!

UNHAPPINESS PLAYS AN IMPORTANT ROLE

The truth is that if we were never unhappy, we would not know, value or appreciate the state of happiness and equilibrium.

"Without darkness, there cannot be light."

And importantly, if we didn't sometimes have to really strive and work our way out of pain, we'd stay in a comfort zone, perhaps sinking into apathy and general weakness.

The state of unhappiness is actually an opportunity to find and build within ourselves the valuable qualities of character: Resilience, Perspective, and Self-acceptance.

While I'm not advocating it, unhappiness does keep us motivated and striving forward into growth! The trick is to balance it so that it stays motivating, rather than drawing us into inertia and the depression that results from sustained feelings of powerlessness.

It goes without saying that stressful life events outnumber diagnosable mental disorders by a massive factor. And most people affected by such —view themselves as *not* in an abnormal state (that requires professional care) but to be responding in a normal way to an abnormal circumstance!

So let's not divert those of us stuck and suffering and *depressed* about it into the clinical definition of "Depression"—because it perpetuates the experience as disablement, and promotes a sense that there is something 'wrong' with us, rather than that we're processing.

I believe it would be more constructive to normalise depression while encouraging sufferers to be working to get themselves back on track— particularly in this currently challenging and unstable time, as we wrestle with seismic change in our social, economic and political lives, the breakdown of our biosphere, and as Covid-19 ravages the planet.

Our anxiety or even despair over the manageability and worthwhileness of our lives is an existential distress, not a disease or a personal or social failure. Often we need help to pilot our way through this, with personal growth and development work instead.

If we acknowledge that suffering and pain cause a person legitimately to be in a state of grieving and loss (and feeling depressed about that) without labelling this state as an *illness*—it might then be easier for us to be kinder to ourselves about it when we realise we've fallen into a depressive state, and thus more responsive. Maybe even to seek help.

IMPORTANT: WHEN DEPRESSION *IS* A "MENTAL ILLNESS"

When we're depressed, over the short to medium term we can come to terms with what led to those feelings of depression and the depressive symptoms. And with some perspective and encouragement we can find our way back to equilibrium, even while still suffering.

But, as with everything, there are nuances, and distinctions can be very important.

When we're suffering from *Clinical Depression*, we've become almost irreversibly bogged down by it.

∼

For Sufferers

Sometimes we overestimate our capacity to deal with our feelings.

Sometimes we're afraid we'll be labelled. "Mental illness" looms. That doesn't feel helpful, or comforting. It doesn't make us feel seen! It triggers feelings of shame in some of us, and fear in others.

This can cause us we take a step backwards.

And sometimes we don't want to acknowledge that our feelings have become a real problem in order to avoid facing the pain, doing the necessary work to heal or even 'relinquishing' control.

It's vital that you be clear just how close you have come to the line between 'normal depression' (that you can claw your way out of with time and perspective), and the kind of depression that is no longer a stimulus but a burden of unimaginable and impossible proportions and weight. The kind that is so bone deep and long lasting that you just wish for everything to end every day so that you can be put out of your misery.

When the unhappiness catches us in its trap and we can't find a way out again, this is when we need—*when we must*—get professional help.

Warning signs for this are:

> CRYING ISN'T A SIGN OF WEAKNESS
>
> IT'S A SIGN OF HAVING TRIED TOO HARD FOR TOO LONG - TO BE STRONG

- Feelings of hopelessness and despair.
- Regular bouts of uncontrolled crying.
- Everything feels like too much effort. Nothing is exciting, interesting, stirs our mood; there is a loss of engagement or pleasure in everything or almost everything, including relationships and activities.
- Feelings of worthlessness.
- Withdrawal from others, from Life.
- A wish to die.

∼

For Close Contacts

Because onlookers often don't understand the enduring nature of this sadness, the suffering it brings, and don't want to talk about it (or get tired of talking about it)—sufferers end up with a deep sense of disappointment, loneliness and shame. Often that causes them to drive those they love away.

Later, they'll no longer care for connection, no longer care if they're helped or not. In fact, they have no emotional energy left to extend to anyone. They've so strongly disengaged that it's almost too late: they want nothing more than to give up, and feel the sweet relief of 'nothingness'.

Humans do not function well in isolation. We're designed to interact with other people.

Once they get beyond this certain point, intervention is absolutely necessary, and if this isn't done, it becomes very hard to help sufferers.

If you are in a relationship with someone who has pervasive depression, don't let any disappointment in them, or in the change in their personality, demeanour and prospects allow you to abandon them.

Men especially, often try and hide a problem, and sometimes don't even realise how bad their mental state is. The worse it gets, the more they get into the mindset that they don't need friends, family, love, or understanding—and they withdraw to a greater and greater extent. They become less and less able to speak to someone about their feelings because they have become so isolated.

Then it's too late, and they take what they believe is the only option. Their lives.

∼

GRIEVING THE LOSSES

HOW TO PROCESS GRIEF

*T*his is all very interesting," you may say. "*But my unhappiness is soul sucking and debilitating. I'm still completely and utterly stuck. And devastated. Now what?"*

MY LOSSES REALLY HURT

None of what's been said so far is designed to minimise, or to underplay just what you've been through, or how lost and broken you may feel. Your pain and grief remain with you, around the opportunities that have gone along with the beating heart of your old life, things, work and activities.

Most significantly, there may be the devastating loss of your old sense of Self, and the equilibrium, self-esteem and hope you very much need in order to turn your ship around.

I get—and deeply acknowledge—how painful it is to be in this space; how impossible the low that you're trying to come back from might seem, and how broken and disengaged you may be feeling at this point.

This is still your awful now.

Unless we've experienced loss often and on an ongoing basis, most of us don't understand grief, or know how to deal with it: the all consuming emotion that eats one up from the inside, and the suffering that results. It can be overwhelming to be constantly grappling with the feelings—which are only made more difficult when our cultural conditioning says we 'should be happy'.

Because of our general resistance to the condition of 'sadness', it's often hard to give ourselves permission to grieve. And of course it's painful to grieve; very tempting to simply quash the feelings or turn away from them, numbing or distracting ourselves in order to avoid the experience.

Worse, grief doesn't have an ultimate endpoint where we know we'll 'return to normal'.

Yet when we understand it—how it works and what it's role is—we can work *with* it, find ourselves less broken by it as we do, and overcome it more sturdily as a result. When people don't see themselves as 'abnormal' and 'broken', they tend to find inner resilience—and rally—sooner.

WHAT IS GRIEF?

We experience a trigger loss, a profound experience of 'before' and 'after'—and instantly, the old is gone. In this moment, we lose our 'innocence' and the realisation of the extent of our powerlessness is overwhelming.

What *was*, our expectations, and even who we were—are no longer in place, accessible or relevant. It's confronting. We've been thrown onto the sidelines of our own lives with no say in the outcome—which has simply happened *to* us. Lumped with disappointments, we're bound into carrying painful feelings instead.

Then, with a shock, we discover we've been bereaved of more than we first realised: not just our control of events, but our path and direction, our opportunities and our hopes—and even ourselves! The life we were living has gone, along with who we were in it. Now, struggling to manage our feelings, we're disorientated by whom we find ourselves now to be in all of this.

We enter 'grief'.

Grief is the period of time during which we 'digest' the painful experience while adjusting to the 'new normal' we've been given.

It's a *process*. We're having to release what was, what we 'knew' and who we were, and, over time, accept what 'isn't' anymore and what actually 'is' instead. We're forced into seeing aspects of life, others and ourselves that we didn't know about before.

It takes time to move through this process, before we can find our bearings again and reclaim equilibrium.

GRIEF RESHAPES OUR LIVES — AND US

We have to discover who we are now in the new reality. On our knees, we'll begin to develop the inner strength we need to carry 'what is' for as long it takes, calling up out of ourselves who we need to be to manage it. Over time we arrive at new insights, and truths—a process that's as painful as tearing off our own limbs.

Pain lies in the feeling that we're alone with it, despite the presence of loving people in our lives.

> **But perhaps the true discomfort in grief lies in our experience of our own powerlessness.**

—Which engenders fear...

Accepting the awful feelings as part of the process—giving ourselves permission to be with them for as long as it takes is not only healing but is actually taking an active role, even if it doesn't really feel that way to start with!

Ironically… the greatest cause of suffering is having the desperate need to get rid of it!

As our insights grow, we gain acceptance, and even begin to discard what no longer serves us—experiencing more losses! (Every choice and decision is another loss; a road we'll not be travelling). This is all part of coming to accept that this is real and in our life, which, though altered, goes on.

It's endemic to Human nature to try to survive, as we've seen, and generally speaking, people are resilient. Some days will be better and more hopeful than others. Others quite the opposite. We don't put any of it aside. We have to adjust forwards and backwards on a day-to-day basis as we let go of what we must.

Our strength rebuilds over time, until eventually we're able to get back up again, to reclaim 'walking'.

COMING TO ACCEPTANCE

Later, it's helpful to start to externalise our grief, digesting our experience in conversation, with people we trust. This helps to convert it into our own wisdom about life and ourselves, and is infinitely healing.

Gradually something begins to shift in us, without us even realising it. The 'What if's' and the 'If only's' progressively stop being so important; even begin to seem redundant.

We won't even need to force ourselves to stop thinking about them. They will just start to fade away naturally as we begin to accept that regardless of whether we understand how the thing could have come to pass, we will never *really* know why; that what was possible *then* will never happen now—and it truly is what it is. This thing has happened and can't be undone.

Nothing happens overnight. We can't take things back or start again. We have to go from where we are. But we can reclaim ourselves and create a new future.

It will never become less unfair, but it will stop being surprising. We will find ourselves crying less frequently. We will stop waking up in a cold sweat, or with our hearts slamming in our chests, gasping.

Acceptance of "what is" has begun to come upon us.

WE NATURALLY SEEK TO RECOVER

It's important to know about the grief experience, and the general shape it takes. —Because every one of us will experience it at some point in our life, and at the time it's both disorientating and deeply disempowering. And very often, protracted. We can bear up in it more robustly, if we have an idea of the path it will take.

Most of us don't want to be victims any longer than we have to be, and naturally want to take control of our grieving, deal with our losses, and find our way back out there. And if we understand what's happening, and know that it *will* come to an end, we can also know that we're capable of carrying it for as long as it lasts.

After the initial shock has passed and grief has set in, its important to acknowledge (and remember ongoing) that while our grief may be centre stage, there are other things (and good things) that sit alongside it in our lives that we need to touch base with regularly as we journey through our loss.

> We need to be careful to not lose what we have — to what we have lost. —**Lucy Hone**

In other words, we must avoid, as much as we can, making our grief the only thing that exists in our lives. We can manage to grieve *and* live —simultaneously.

We move forward, carrying what happened, finding as time passes that it's more bearable than it was before.

Eventually we come out on the other side, to see that there are new and different possibilities in the here and now.

And we start to bring our attention to those.

PART IV
THE 'ACTUAL' NORMAL

HOW THINGS TRULY ARE

A NEW ORIENTATION TO LIFE

FINDING A NEW WAY FORWARD

I've offered an overview, a birds eye view of the particular struggle we're experiencing at this particular moment in history, in order to depersonalise the experience of pain and bewilderment. *It's not just you...* While we may feel very individual and even alone—we're actually part of a bigger whole that affects *everything* about our lives all the time.

I've shown this because I believe that with an Awareness of the bigger picture and the outside forces pressing upon us, we're both better able to calm ourselves in the face of difficulty, and become strategic with our responses. Perhaps at this very moment you're already experiencing that simply 'seeing' more widely has put you in a more empowered space!

But, while hard times have always been a part of Life, together we're now facing global challenges at a new order of magnitude. Challenges that can't simply be shouldered and ultimately normalised without consequence in the short spans of our individual lives. These are challenges that must be addressed if we're to go on at all.

ALL FALL DOWN

At the coalface, things are very uncomfortable—and downright scary.

Our 'systems' are under pressure and changing, with our lifestyles, choices and freedoms consequently reducing. Seismic shifts in political, social and economic realities across the planet are breaking societies (with millions of people migrating into new societies and cultures en masse)—further changing all the rules of engagement.

These general struggles 'at home' are shifting along the timeline to a shared predicament, and even to existential threat across the board. Rising threats are the unknown outcomes of climate change over the next few years, and the current global expansion of autocracy and national aggression — with nuclear 'posturing' and our own mad ability to extinguish our very planet, as ever-increasing threats. —Not just to our *way* of life, but to Life on this planet overall.

We all know and feel this, despite the many denials we may hear around us. In fact,

We're living through the greatest transformation in the history of civilisation.

BEING SCHOOLED BY HARD KNOCKS

All that we've relied on is increasingly changing, and less and less facilitative of our Western cultural playbook with its focus on outward success.

'Doing' and 'having' is becoming more and more difficult to deploy.

And this is a terrible problem, because for many of us in Western cultures, this is still the template that provides our shield from existential challenges, and moves us towards happiness. As we've seen, our 'rules' of life in Western society have actually set us up to suffer in ways that other cultures (and our previous generations) haven't. Far from establishing us for ongoing "happiness", the "brules"[10] have in fact become a direct cause of our suffering, disabling and disempowering us. And they've blinded us to the long-held wisdom that experiencing sustained difficulty in Life is actually normal, rather than a reflection of 'Who' we are—or are not.

Uncertainty now prevails. Many of us have been left grappling—*with 'being'*. It's become harder and harder to hold onto ourselves as good and competent people, living in a world with trustworthy others, with a future we can be hopeful about. Struggling with our experience of ourselves in this highly disturbed, increasingly challenging Context, we go looking for wellbeing, only to find ourselves labelled with 'mental illness'.

We don't know why, or what to do about it. We're uncertain of what we're even doing here or are meant to do, in fact—or how to prevail in this strange and unknowable existence.

We've not been taught resilience! In some respects, in our coddled cultures and quests for personal gratification, and in our lives of abundance of choice (even leading to excess)—we've not really needed this! We've coped instead with any difficulties by overriding our feelings with medication for depression or anxiety, and giving ourselves plenty more 'doings' to distract ourselves.

Ultimately it hasn't worked.

The epidemic (and record) rates of suicide and depression—particularly in our younger generations—tells the story that we're struggling and miserable, and can't stand it. That we don't want to have to wake up to carry on with it—for another day, another week, another month.

Getting off the planet seems to be a real alternative.

What this really tells us is that too many of us have not been given healthy, helpful perspectives. We've not been asked (or helped) to build the tenacity needed to prevail during hard times and personal disappointments. We've not developed those inner qualities.

> **We're not aware of or connected to our own inner resources in the face of difficulty.**

Many people are even unaware of the *value* of an inner life, and certainly haven't been given the tools at home or at school to cultivate one.

It is time to change this.

TAKING STOCK

We've been given good reasons to survey the damage, in a Life lived with a lack of Awareness and a naïve trust that "everything will work out if we simply put in effort".

Falling down has given us pause—and cause—to investigate, to rethink everything.

To admit that we haven't really had a proper education in how Life and relationships work. That we have no deep understanding of ourselves either, having blundered into adult life half-blind with a bunch of stories about ourselves, about the 'rules' and 'fairness', and about Life in general.

We need to work out what this experience we're having means, and what it's going to *engender in us,* going forward.

It's perfectly normal to want an easy life. To want *things* to change when Life is going badly—without us having to change ourselves. Few people want to engage effort to improve their lives!

But we can't ask Life to be easier. It is what it is, to a greater or lesser degree. And there's no point in continuing to blame our circumstances, losses and mistakes for our hurt feelings—resisting and struggling against them, feeling hopeless, and continuing on in powerlessness. That only perpetuates the suffering.

We have to ask ourselves to be stronger, or braver, or more resourceful. Or all three.

It's time to let go of the identity and character that have brought us to this time and place, and look at who we need to be to deal with the life we currently have, and with what lies ahead in a changed and changing world. We have to think harder about Who We Are, than we have so far.

We have to decide *Who* we will Be.

We need to look at the kind of person we *need* to become—not only to create the life we do want, but to participate in the great collaborative work that is required of us at this unique time in human civilisation—that will bring our societies and biosphere back into balance so that we all *do* have a future.

Perhaps this sounds harsh… We all want easy. We all want magic! But this IS the practical reality.

We are being prodded forward to meet the challenges of our times— whether we go willingly, or not.

SHIFTING

This is not a situation where some people are forced into adapting to the massive transformations going on around us while others simply wait for it to pass, until they can resume their preferred patterns of behaviour based on the self-centred values of personal consumption and 'doing'.

No-one will be able to sit idly by and watch the world transform around them! Everyone will be impacted in this great shift. Everyone—and everything, will be transformed.

There's nothing wrong with outcomes where input leads to output, effort to reward, and practise makes perfect. In fact it's really important to cultivate our strengths and stand tall in them! But we're not going to be better people or, crucially—*more able people* because we *own* this thing, have *done* that experience, or *look* a certain way.

And, with youth suicide and depression at an all time high in the whole history of recorded civilisation, we should absolutely not be modelling to our children that they have to reach the greatest heights to be good people with a chance at happiness!

We can no longer carry on as the Self that strives for and fits itself to the narrow markers of success and happiness of our current culture. We can no longer be the Self that measures itself by external criteria, like achievement, wealth, beauty and constant gain. These disempowering societal values and self-imposed "brules" have come at the expense of a robust and rich inner life!

We can no longer afford to base our sense of Who We Are purely on the externals because we have not developed an internal substance.

Because when we don't actively develop this internal aspect of ourselves —we cede all our power to outside hands, and allow ourselves to be simply subject to market and environmental forces.

The moment we make any circumstance, institution or person outside ourselves more powerful than we are, we're giving all our Power away.

—And not just in our own personal lives. This is particularly problematic in this age we're living through, where the planet and all life and systems upon it are under huge and unprecedented pressure in an environment of unstoppable and escalating change. We Human Beings are the only force in its way!

And we *are* a force. When we pull together, with common values for a common goal.

BECOMING AGENTS OF CREATION AND CHANGE

We have come into dominance of the planet because our unique qualities have enabled us to create supportive systems for our survival, and dominion over other species.

(So it's not surprising that very often our energies go into more of this sort of thing, particularly when we feel threatened and uncertain!) We experience the power and influence we have in the world as our *results*—out there in the world of form—in what we do and have, who we're relating with, and how productive we are.

Yet we have an ability to live well beyond our five external senses. We are unique on this planet in being able to think, and reason; to choose, to create. To be ultra-resourceful. To *be* inspired—and be inspiring, ourselves.

No other creature on this planet can deliberately do these things.

These multi-dimensional, eternal Selves that we are — are intelligent, intuitive, adaptable and creative. And we're capable of incredible wisdom and depth. These skills have made us incredibly powerful as a species, despite our lack of teeth and claws; our lack of speed or poison.

We are powerful on the inside.

Disenfranchised and inhibited though we may *feel*, the truth is that we each carry an enormous power that we're not really even aware of, and thus often don't wield well, or to our benefit. Many of us have underdeveloped capacities.

We're being called to *draw on our full lineage:* to own, develop and integrate these capacities into our existence so that we can operate fully in all our dimensions as the multidimensional beings that we are. —Not just to survive mentally, emotionally and physically intact, but to continue to prevail at all, and healthily at that, as a species.

We need to learn how to fit ourselves for our unique Context at this point in Human evolution. We must go *inwards,* and develop ourselves to be *in* the circumstance or situation, rather than allow ourselves to be defined by it. *Going inwards* means looking at those qualities that hold us up from the inside—that need to be actively developed and ongoingly reinforced: our perspective, our character, our will. These aspects of our

Identity define us *as us,* and act as a vital compass that guides us forward, manifests our value, and distinguishes us in the world.

The state of unhappiness is actually an opportunity to find and build within ourselves the valuable qualities of character: resilience, perspective, and self acceptance!

There's a part of us that's here to be lived that we're not living—yet.

But we need a powerful new understanding of Life and what is true about Human Beings and our power to survive—to thrive.

This next section of the book will guide you towards and into this.

MOVING THE NEEDLE

It's time to let go of what the matrix has told us; of what we were raised to believe about success and happiness, worth and belonging—and allow for new perspectives that enrich our experience of ourselves and of Life!

We're subject, for example, to Laws of Life (like it or not), rather than the "rules" we've invented together and individually. When we understand these, and consciously work in concert with them, we suddenly have access to the precise levers that amplify empowerment and happiness in our lives!

Everything shifts then, from fixed and painful—into exciting possibility.

I'll talk next about aspects of our inner life and how they work together to make us 'generative'—whether we want to be or not! (Knowing this alone means you'll more consciously create outcomes you really *want*, rather than those you don't.)

I've researched what truly drives and motivates us, and offered answers to the deeper questions we ask all the time about meaning and whether or not we matter. *What principles are really at play when it comes to empowerment?* I've asked, and *why does power matter at all? Why do we desperately want Change* (and at the same time find it disempowering), and *what is so special about Choice?*

A NEW ORIENTATION TO LIFE | 165

These essential perspectives will almost certainly get you unstuck, feeling hopeful, and sensing possibilities.

We'll look then at who we *need* to be—so that we're able to face up to what is asked of us in this complicated, tricky Life. What to do that actually serves and grows us, enabling us to step more closely every day towards a joyous, peaceful existence, in which we make our unique contribution.

> Mental health is based on a certain degree of tension; the tension between what one has already achieved, and what one still ought to accomplish, or the gap between what one is, and what one should become. **—V Frankel**[11]

And we'll look at who we *want* to be, and how to vigorously shape ourselves—to create not only the ongoing 'bequest' we wish to be for those we love, but to actively craft lives we really want to live, *despite* challenge!

You'll become resourced to face and step into the future with resilience, courage, and grace—and enabled to create the meaningful, fulfilling life that you so want to live.

TRANSFORMATION

Imagine totally 'getting' the benefits of being Human after all, and brimming once again with energy and passion, and feeling that your potential is unlimited!

Imagine being able to personally maximise the frameworks that create peace, purpose and joy in your life!

Because despite the wrecking ball of change swinging through our lives —despite the losses, the pain, the sense of uncertainty and anxiety—we actually do control much of what happens to us in our lives , and certainly *how we choose to show up* in the circumstances.

Bringing just *this* to awareness—to re-empower everyone who reads it—is one of the key reasons that this book needed to be written.

It's time to forge a new path.

Empower yourself with Truths, not with dogma.

THE SUPERPOWER OF HUMAN BEINGS

THE GIFTS OF THOUGHT AND THINKING

We begin orientating to our inner world by looking first at what is 'uniquely' Human—and why it matters at all.

THE SELF

All living creatures, generally, are collections of energised cells that have resolved themselves into form. The more sophisticated of these include tissue, blood, nerves, and bones.

This collection is animated by some force (that we don't all agree is even there) but that is sometimes called 'Consciousness'—or even 'Spirit'.

It's an awareness of a 'Self'.

Most creatures simply meet their survival needs. They have little to no conscious thought about *why* they're striving to live, let alone why they may be here on the planet in the first place!

They also don't question their place in the world, or their level of their power in the ecological pecking order.

They can't control their thinking.

- Sensing and instinct rule, and growth and reproduction are offshoots of surviving.
- They only have to know "how?" to effectively live their lives. They receive information that is relevant and particular to them that interacts with their instincts, causing them to follow certain actions in certain circumstances, and to take other actions, in others.

Human Beings on the other hand, have been endowed with a greater level of individuated consciousness than any other creature on the planet.

We have an awareness of our Selves as distinct entities—*with identities: we* name our collection of energised cells, "I".

We know ourselves as separate from (although in) Contexts, and are aware—at least to some extent—of the variable nature of our Personal Power in these Contexts. In other words, we are aware that there *is* an ecological pecking order, and that we're somewhere in it.

And we also have the unique ability to control our thinking.

This, is a superpower.

WHAT IS 'THINKING'?

We initially 'experience' sentiently, but our consciousness (or 'I') actively intervenes next—to process and interpret that experience, and decide what to do with the information.

This is an organic process, in which we quickly assemble a puzzle in our minds from a number of pieces.

Information, associations, feelings and ideas flow and combine in different ways, depending on Who we are and our prior experiences. Ultimately the way we uniquely put the puzzle-pieces together leads to the formation of concepts for problem-solving, insights and conclusions —or 'thoughts', which are the outcome of 'thinking'.

'Thinking' is an active, creative, inner processing that takes place in the Human mind (consciousness), during which we interpret and make sense of our experience.

As can be seen, this puzzle construction isn't something that just occurs 'in the brain' as a part of biology—with thoughts generated by biologic processes. The reality of having an Identity with prior experience (consciousness) is always a part of the process. Consciousness 'uses' the brain as a powerful *interpreting* tool.

It's therefore impossible to 'think' without interpreting. But this means that our thinking has a massive Achilles Heel at it's centre.

Because Interpretations are always subjective.

Most often, we don't give this its due significance. We may have *heard* that we're all subjective, yet most of the time we're able to kid ourselves that in *this* instance, *we (uniquely) have the facts!*

Yet the reality is that often in the moment—and very often—we make a subjective mistake in our processing and interpreting somewhere, and trip ourselves up.

I'll break 'thinking' down into it's component parts of 'understanding' and 'interpreting' to unpack where the problem occurs.

UNDERSTANDING

Earlier I said that most creatures *know* 'how' to effectively live their lives.

But this is where Human Beings are next level. In addition to 'knowing' information, we 'understand' it.

'Understanding' is where we see the relationship of one thing to another and how all the parts fit together in the bigger picture. We see the implications in these relationships too, including the consequences and benefits hidden between the lines.

Out of this, concepts and conclusions ('thoughts') are formed. This makes 'understanding' an integral (and the most powerful) part of 'thinking'.

This unique ability allows us to model the world with ourselves as part of it—yet differentiated and separate within it. With this we can deal with ourselves and our experience powerfully—by being responsive, rather than simply reactive. In other words, we're able to choose from a range of options and take unique, considered and specific action.

Simply put, 'understanding' gives us the tool to be strategic.

'Knowing', is particular, compartmentalised information. We store it away—often passively, even forgetfully—and only bring it into the light of day when it seems necessary. We may move automatically through patterns, habits, and rule-breaking while knowing better, for example—without really engaging with the information we have.

In 'understanding', by contrast, the knowledge is not merely activated by circumstances, or specific to them (as with other creatures). It's *active* in us: on, and always on, and always being expanded and updated.

There is a famous saying, that "knowledge is power". Yet it's "understanding"—that truly is.

 "Any fool can know. The point is to understand." —**Albert Einstein**

Unlike learning 'knowledge', we don't gain 'understanding' by passively accepting what we hear, see, read, or are told. We want to know and understand our experience, ourselves, and others—*for* ourselves.

Simply put, things need to make sense to us, via understanding and putting them into our model of the bigger picture.

And we get to 'understanding', via the question "Why?"

TRUTH

With answers to our questions—to our very existence—we can assert control over the information and what we might do with it.

This is because our survival drives and significance needs have us constantly, actively seeking to establish the true extent of our Power (or lack of it) in the situations in which we find ourselves. *Do we have enough of it to stand up to what we've come up against?*

Because ultimately, all that we have to rely on in this massive, relatively unknown Context, is ourselves (and then each other)!

We need to know that no matter what system we find ourselves in, or what has happened or been done to us—that we can self-direct.

So, our first step is to establish if something is 'true' (or close to it!) 'Truth' takes us to a place where we can engage meaningfully with the chaos of the world.

Knowing the Truth gives us clarity, an understanding of where our power might lie in the various situations in which we find ourselves, and some certainty in an unknowable future. With Truth in place, we can work on manipulating the elements around us that will reduce our chances of dying, keep suffering at bay, and bring us the results we value.

So, we constantly weigh everything we experience to figure out how best to deploy our assets and resources to meet our needs, and define, find, or create what we really want.

We need to know what is real, and what can be relied upon: *in other words, what is True.* We actively therefore, are always seeking the Truth of things, via big, unconscious, on-at-all-times background questions:

"What do I need to KNOW that keeps me safe?"

"What do I need to DO to keep and build my Power?"

"Who do I need to BE so I can manifest what I want?"

And we actively seek the answers.

Of course, there are many, and many of them contain 'truth': there isn't just one Truth!

And then we must metabolise the data we've gathered.

INTERPRETING

There are two aspects to this metabolism that are fundamental to gaining 'understanding'.

- Applying and reapplying our question 'why?' to the answers we get: going deep and deeper to get to the bottom of things—so that we can understand the Truth as nearly as possible.
- Interpreting the data by *assigning meaning* to it. We establish for our ourselves what's really important, over what seems to matter. This means that we 'weight' the data — making it more or less important in our scheme of things.

Knowing the value or significance of something helps us to place it appropriately in our model of the world, enabling us to better 'understand' overall what actions would be best to take (or not) as we seek to survive, and thrive.

We're always trying to reveal what is True in order to empower ourselves and meet our needs. We learn Truth, uniquely, through understanding. And then we imbue everything we understand with meaning.

Assigning 'meaning' is thus an integral part of coming to understanding.

In summary, 'thinking' is the process of making sense of the experience we've had by seeking out the truth of it, attaching to it the meaning we make of it—and then giving this its due weight or significance.

This 'understanding' generates 'Thoughts'—or insights and conclusions.

We 'bottle' these, and place our 'bottles' in our 'bank of wisdom': within the bigger picture of our accumulated knowledge.

These 'Thoughts' empower us to be both differentiated from one another as Identities, and self-directed. Generally this means we're able to make a personal choice (which may be an internal or an external one).

We now *actively* choose to act (or not to), in our responses, attitudes and behaviours.

"Reading furnishes the mind only with materials of knowledge; it is thinking that makes what we read—ours."
—John Locke

ACHILLES' HEEL

But now we must return to the Achilles Heel of Thinking.

Flaws arise in 'thinking' because we don't interpret, understand and conclude to a foolproof pattern that will bring *objective* outcomes!

Outside of our level of education, the nurture we've received and the wealth (or paucity) of experience we've gained, there are massive variances in the kinds of thinking we each engage in...

Some of us think more deeply about experience.

Some of us never fully or deeply understand important concepts.

Some of us dismiss thinking as too much work.

Some of us place false or superficial conclusions on information.

These are just some examples.

And *assigning 'meaning' is also not an exact science*—because accurately giving weight or significance to something can only be done in full knowledge of *everything* else in Context. And none of us has access to that!

We can give weight to things and make meaning based on only what we have access to in our very small container of Self—which will have been formed by the (usually) very limited experiences and truths that can be gained in one small life.

We'll therefore assign weight or significance to things based on our own hurts, strengths, interests, value systems and experience, as our personal subjectivity comes willy-nilly to the fore. (This is how our thinking comes to form such a significant part of our identity.)

This means that the outcomes of our thinking are as diverse as we ourselves are!

And—this may distance us from "Truth" rather than reveal it (though of course we don't realise this at the time).

So it's really important to realise that 'thinking' really is the set of spectacles that we personally put on when we're viewing our world and our experience in it.

If there is one truth about reality, it's that we're interpreting it within the limits of our own experience (including emotional wounds, beliefs and personality) at all times.

Remembering this, will grant you the deepest value as you read here. As I said in the Introductions section, *shifting your thinking is the work of this book.*

THE AWESOME POWER OF THINKING

As illustrated, our 'thinking' plays a very important part in the processing of our overall Human experience. It positions us to maximise our chances of surviving and thriving, while also contributing to the ongoing forming of our Identity—via the conclusions we reach about:

Whether we have enough—and ARE enough—to stand up to what we come up against.

How powerfully we deploy our understanding to meet our needs, and find or create what we really want.

But we also use thinking in a powerfully generative way, literally making something—from nothing.

Everything in our Human world begins with a Thought.

That really is the simple truth of it. Thoughts shape not only *our lived realities* but our practical world as well.

Whether that's a chair, or a bomb or an attitude; whether that's the carpenter or the strategist or the ringleader—neither the product nor the actions needed to bring it to Life could have existed without the Thought about them, occurring first.

We don't tend to break down in our minds how brick houses fitted with running water and electricity, or packaged foods, sewerage systems, lightbulbs, aeroplanes or television for example, have come to exist. Yet every aspect of each of these things was merely a Thought—before it was anything else.

Think about that for a moment!

It's incredible to think that *Thoughts* are at the heart of the form and content our entire Human civilisation—and that they're so generative!

Thinking literally is the most powerful and creative thing going on in Human Beings. Our thoughts *become* things, as our every action (or non-action) in terms of them creates effects.

And I highlight this fact because… *everything has a shadow side.*

THE SHADOW SIDE OF THINKING

Thinking generates powerfully (that's an absolute Truth!)—but it doesn't always do so in the positive way described above. Thoughts can be consciously deployed into very destructive attitudes and actions.

—To further 'evil' intentions, for example.

But awful outcomes can also be the result of (innocently) flawed thinking—that ends up inducing terrible, self-inflicted wounding.

Consider that there are around eight billion different sets of spectacles operating—through which we're each seeing the world *we've* modelled. At this very moment, there are massive conflicts going on in societies across the world about which 'spectacle view' is the 'right' one!

Internal perspectives range equally, as one outlook tells the thinker they're 'broken, not good enough, and that things are hopeless'; someone else's perspectives tell them they can function by making excessive claims on resources because they've 'earned' the right to!

Assigning meaning to things on personal subjectivity—may distance us from "Truth" rather than reveal it. And of course, we don't realise any of this at the time—and often don't pick up on it later on, either.

So while every one of us may be uniquely advantaged in being able to generate 'Thoughts', this very faculty can severely disable us with false and even toxic ones, since they unfold in the highly variable environments of our individuality.

We'll look at how this starts and plays out, next.

THE KRYPTONITE OF HUMAN BEINGS

SPECTACULAR ILLUSIONS

Where and how does the 'spectacle'-wearing begin?

WORKINGS IN THE SILO OF 'SELF'

When we're young and impressionable, we're given *information*.

- —'Rules' we're to adhere to at home.
- Beliefs and values we're handed, that come out of parental or family expectations.
- 'Truths' we're told, about the world and others.

We add to these with others, from our peer groups and societies. And, as we've seen, we take on ideas promulgated in the news and social media, from the internet, by television and movies, and from organisations and societies we're members of—such as school and church.

And while all this information is filtering in, we're adding our own doses of 'meaning' to all of it (stories), as we try to make sense of our experiences and put them in a hierarchy of importance to us.

We 'frame' these stories by familiarity (and therefore make assumptions), and by beliefs (and therefore take on prejudices). Our stories, assumptions and prejudices become 'facts'—and our 'facts' become 'rules': both our own 'rules' and what we come to believe are 'the rules of Life'.

Through these we shape our sense of ourselves-in-the world, and our very Identities—and determine the significance of everything to our Power levels.

And then we underpin it all with our personal self esteem.

Essentially this means we tell ourselves stories about what's happening to us in the moment: how it all works and hangs together, and what it means—creating internal narratives of 'how-it-is'-and-'should-be', and Who we are in it.

We buy into the scripts we make from all this, and then act those scripts out as if they're proven truth.

MENTAL MODELS

These narratives or scripts are called 'mental models' (or, using my term, 'spectacles'!)

We may believe, for example, that "To be happy, I have to make a lot of money", or "Real men don't do housework". That "Life is dangerous and out to get me", or 'I pale in comparison to everyone else".

In fact this is not "the way the world is". This is simply OUR model of "the way the world is".

We don't realise that our beliefs are not facts or rules at all, but simply a personal perspective; that there is so much we don't know and aren't factoring into our interpretations.

We're not even aware that that's what we're doing. Interpreting (or 'perceiving') is so easy and automatic that it's usually not even a choice. We get lost in our own assumptions, 'rules' and beliefs, and simply 'conclude'.

And the more we believe in our model—the more invested we become in it, and the more evidence we seem to find that confirms "this is in fact the way the world works!"

"*Let me speak my truth,*" (a statement most of us have probably heard!)—means "let me tell you about my mental model". (And if it's disagreed with, it's quite often taken as personal affront, since our self-esteem is pinned on the 'truth' of it).

We're (innocently) unaware of how we've created a false idea within ourselves, of what our experience really is and how we measure and value ourselves against the norms we think we're seeing. Our inner reality *becomes* "objective life" to us!

And then we live this experience.

This is how we become blinded by our Culturescapes, caught up in our own 'rules', and waylaid by our assumptions and beliefs!

THE AWFUL POWER OF THINKING

Now when, for example, we're struggling with a challenge that has presented itself in our lives—particularly when it's sustained—our mental model will kick in, bringing our limiting beliefs with it.

"This is how Life is. This is how I am."

The *Thoughts* we then have about what's happened and what it means; what it 'says' about Who We Are, and what we *think* we're able to do about it—generates both our particular experience in it, and our response to that experience.

This may be a positive experience, and a resilient and productive response—with self-esteem intact.

—Or, it may be a poor one, in which we feel diminished and disempowered, and turn away, feeling 'less than'.

Whichever it is, it informs *everything* that comes next—because our subsequent decisions and actions will be based on one of those emotional states—shaping our overall experience, and ultimately, our lives.

Generally speaking, Thoughts arising from a mental model bring limiting beliefs to our experience, attitudes and actions—to the point that we can become chronically disabled and disadvantaged by them.

It's in this space of activation of the mental model, we either remain empowered, positive and engaged with our lives and endeavours, or become disempowered, disconnected, and miserable.

FALLING INTO OUR MENTAL MODEL

For an example of how this works in practise, let's return to our Culturescape, where most of us have bought into the idea that Life '*should*' be fair.

—Yet, in reality, it 'shouldn't' be—and it isn't! This is simply our model for "how Life is". Life *doesn't* play fair — and not just because some people come from the 'wrong side of the tracks' or don't make an effort. In the Game of Life some of us are given hands full of matching pairs and jokers, while others don't have a thing that goes with anything else—and are even short changed.

While it is true that some people play their hands more wisely than others, there is no doubt that there is never an even start. Where we're born, whom we are born to, the health of our body, and the cultural mores and infrastructure we're born into—all dictate what's possible for us (at least initially).

And that's before the conditional acceptance, unkindness and selfishness of others (including parents and siblings, 'systems' and employers) put us on the back foot.

Soon we're realising that so much that happens in Life is not only hurtful to us, and disempowering to boot, but largely outside of our control. We may be shocked at the uneven playing field we find ourselves on, which only ripens our mental models of 'fair and unfair'.

Now into this mix, we'll add our cultural goal of "happiness" via "success", where we're always under (at least some) pressure or expectation *to succeed.*

Succeeding brings *judgement* into play (upping the stakes), because generally, 'failure' (the opposite of "success") is frowned upon. Which is problematic, because Failure is a very normal part of *learning what doesn't work.* And Humans, being fallible, inexperienced creatures—are learning 'on the go'. Failures are simply inevitable.

But ideas of right' and 'wrong' have been piled on us from a young age, when our parents wielded these to 'get us to behave' ourselves. So 'Should' and 'shouldn't', and 'failure-is-to-be-avoided' now add their weight to our mental models of 'fair' and 'unfair', truly immersing us in the mentality of 'right' and 'wrong'.

Unsurprisingly then, when things *do* go 'wrong' and we fail to overcome a problem, or when Life becomes difficult (because it often does)—we're anxious to avoid the label of being at fault or having failed! Stress (and suffering) arrive on the back of these thoughts.

That's bad enough. But now, if we're blamed (and it sticks), our mental model of "it's not fair!" is quickly triggered:

"The way that Life is and people are—is Unfair.*"*

We think that what is happening to us and what we think about it—is real and objective. That it's *actual* reality—that carries certain meaning and weight. We feel disempowered and anxious, reducing our quality of life.

Yet what we're really experiencing is our own subjective perspective on what we've decided is going on.

What we're thinking is real—isn't.

OUR THOUGHTS BECOME OUR REALITY

All of this becomes especially potent when we consider the biology in which our Thoughts occur. Because the unconscious parts of our brains don't know the difference between what we're thinking—and reality.

Our bodies register our stressful depressive thoughts as if they are real threats—and respond with the stress hormones, cortisol and adrenaline.

If our Thoughts continue in a negative vein, our body will be consistently signalling that we're in danger—feeding the anxieties we're feeling. As we think constantly about how we can't stand it, and how *"this isn't the way it was supposed to be"*—cortisol and adrenaline are released into our systems ongoingly, fuelling the Thoughts again in a vicious cycle.

We spend large amounts of time in a state of physical stress: miserable about the past, and worrying about something terrible happening in the future. (After all, we tend to only overthink the bad things, dwell on what didn't go well, and worry about the worst-case scenarios that may present themselves.)

As we dwell more on those thoughts and feel intensely the pain that those thoughts bring, our fears intensify, and more and more—anxiety about loss and lack becomes our present moment experience.

We end up spending more time in our heads than in *actual* experience. We *suffer* from our Thoughts!

Over time, we become increasingly orientated to assessing the degree to which we can be hurt and might suffer—and ascribing importance to things that are happening (or not happening) to us against those 'risks'. And naturally, we button down, defend, and play small.

We create a life in which we're constricted by our self-limiting (and even harmful) Thoughts, rather than expanded by what actually is true and possible.

The quality of our thinking is the difference between it being our superpower, or being Kryptonite to us.

Ultimately we become more and more stuck and suffering, and grieving our condition. We can spend months—and even years—feeling anxious and disappointed, angry, resentful, fearful, and immobilised.

Imprisoned by a mindset founded in our perceptions, we eventually become personally and practically disabled. We come to believe that we're not equal to the task of restoring our personal equilibrium (*I have a mental illness*), much less up to actually dealing with and overcoming our problems.

Our thoughts make (and keep) us ill.

This is particularly significant when we encounter major difficulty. If we're stuck in our heads, and in the past—going over and over our wounds—*that is exactly where we'll stay: in the wounded past.*

We become rooted at the level of 'Survival'. Caught there in bitter stasis, feeling disempowered—we'll simply perpetuate more and more of that reality, until nothing else exists for us.

STRUGGLING WITH REALITY

"But—hold on!" you object. *"My losses had nothing to do with my Thoughts! My life fell over because of circumstances provably beyond my control! I* did *get a lousy hand of cards! My pain is real! This is not helpful!"*

I hear you. That was exactly my experience.

The years of unexpected strain my husband and I experienced in shared parenthood (so innocently embarked upon), and the terror later when he lost his health (and then his livelihood)—were two of the really difficult times that were foisted upon us. We got a lousy hand of cards. Life chipped away at our desires, and served up 'losses' instead.

So what were we to practically DO when what we didn't want, couldn't stop, change, or reverse was simply in place of what we chose, worked for and valued?

The practical answer was to simply accept that what *is*—is. Whether what had happened was fair, or not; and whether we were to blame or not. Truly, what else *was* there to do?

But I didn't like this. My thoughts wouldn't stop raging about the rights and wrongs of things, the unfairness of it all, and ultimately how reduced I and my life had become—not by my own hand. Asking the part of me that felt so raw and in pain to simply "Accept"—felt inauthentic and unrealistic.

Our consciousness of our experience is how we experience our Selves. Was I now supposed to put my *Self* aside—that experiential Being that I am, and—*not thinking or feeling anything about the painful losses*—simply... *exist*?

And truly, was I to strive for this— constantly pushing against the flow of my own mind — for the rest of time?

This was where 'I' became diminished.

WANTING FOR TRUTH

I wanted to 'place' the blame' at the source of my losses and pain. Placing blame somewhere felt like speaking out the 'truth'. It felt that this truth would 'preserve' me.

> **I wanted "Truth" and the restoration of myself as a Powerful Being…**

When things go 'wrong', the first question that comes up is about our power. *Who am I in the face of this? Am I enough? Do I matter?*

This is why painful experiences can have us feeling annihilated, as though we're 'not enough'—and ultimately 'falling apart'. It's really hard to emerge still intact and functional (rather than bewildered, demotivated and with a "mental illness") on the other side of difficulty if we can't get our heads around what the powerlessness in our lives 'means'.

At the heart of the powerlessness we feel is the bitter reality that Life has deconstructed what we 'want' in our frame.

Apart from making what we valued unavailable to us, it's removed our power of choice and direction, as though we have no say in things, and don't matter. It's taken something out of our lives (which we don't like) —and it's also added something in: loss, which is deeply uncomfortable, and leaves us feeling deeply anxious and alone.

In response, we'll usually engage resistance. It's not just an objection to not getting what we 'want' but also a demonstration of what remains of our power in the situation. *I do not accept this. I won't accept this.*

Yet there is another concept in this mix that is worth looking at here: expectation.

THE TYRANNY OF EXPECTATIONS

Expectations are couched in our ideas about 'fairness' or merit—which arise from our model of the world. So, we believe we're 'entitled' to get the certain results we want when we've put in effort (any effort) for them, and are 'owed' wanted outcomes—for following the 'rules'.

What is the problem with 'expectation'?

Expectation owns our peace of mind—using the words 'should' and 'deserve'. It sets us up for disappointment. Which, as we know now, is where suffering begins.

Life doesn't play to our rules! And when things go pear-shaped, instead of being philosophical and accepting about the way things have panned out (this is how Life works), our 'should's are in the mix (these are my 'rules' and Life 'should' abide by them).

Something else 'should' have happened. What *did* happen—'shouldn't' have. We got what we didn't want. We didn't get what we do want. Our personal 'rules' have been broken, leaving us disappointed.

We're suddenly standing on the first rung of the ladder of suffering.

Yet it's not the presence of suffering that's so unbearable. It's that we PERCEIVE it as being so.

We believe this 'should' not have happened. Then, we apply 'meaning' to the experience as we metabolise it into 'understanding'—trying to re-empower ourselves with the 'truth'. We try to find meaning in the fact that we have to suffer at all.

If we can't find answers, we may make it about us—being broken.

—Or we *won't* make it about us (having shown up in a particular way, or with unhelpful attitudes and entitlements) and end up stuck in suffering —unable to take useful action.

We remain on our knees, in despair.

The real 'truth' though, is that our ideas about the 'rules and results' paradigm are faulty. And we've been low on information when it comes to understanding what life is about, what our 'entitlements' really are, and where responsibility for our lives, lies.

The pain lies in *the way we think about* what has happened.

Many of us spend decades of our lives not thinking about the meanings we give things at all. We don't tend to think more broadly than our day to day existence. Often we don't ask questions about the deeper meaning of things either—simply taking everything for granted on the one extreme, or drudging on in Life on the other.

Until loss, lack and struggle arrive painfully at our doors…

TAKING CHARGE OF OURSELVES

OWNING AND SCULPTING OUR EXPERIENCE

*A*s must be clear now, the relationship between our inner and our outer worlds is much more significant than we may realise. An inner processing is unfolding in us all of the time, constantly attributing meaning to our experience—keeping 'understanding' active in us.

This *'thinking'* is *actively creative of our experience of Life.*

It forms the basis of our attitudes, of our responses, of our contributions (positive, negative or reductive) on this planet, of most of our challenges and opportunities—and of our very Identities.

Yet we don't know this in the moment, or recognise the enormous influence it has on both this experience, and our sense of our Self.

With all our impact and results occurring in the external world of 'doing' and 'having'—and receiving so much feedback from that place—it's not surprising that we're both naturally more attuned to it, and ready to assume that *that* is where all the action is taking place!

Yet the truth is, ***Experience is an inside job.***

OWNING OUR RESPONSE TO 'EXPERIENCE'

Since our inner world 'creates' our outer world—straightening out our inner world is a pre-requisite to repairing and improving our outer world.

(This is why my mission is to help you overcome your pain, struggle and suffering; your sense of disconnection from yourself, your path, your hopes, and others. *Because this applies at home, and more widely.*)

As 'experiencing' is constantly active in us (even when we're dreaming!) —*we must take charge of it*. We cannot sit passively by as it unfolds in us —and allow ourselves to become victim to any negativity that the experience may contain. No-one is going to come and save us from it: from ourselves!

It's up to us to orchestrate a personal response to experience, including double-checking the meaning and weight we give it. We must take charge of actively seeking Truth and healthy perspectives every single day that we walk our road. Restoring ourselves into a great quality of life that we love to live will only happen if we take this on as our personal responsibility.

Actively investing in and maintaining our equilibrium means that we can always carry suffering without losing ourselves, grow in depth and wisdom, find joy in Life, and remain empowered—regardless of what may happen about us.

The simple act of uncovering empowering Truths and re-orientating ourselves around them, enables us to calm and resource ourselves in any destabilising, changing Context.

Thoughts can be changed when we are able see things differently: to see beyond what is within the Silo of Self.

The secret with all of this is to realise that it's a skill. And because it's a skill, it can first be learned, and then we can learn to get better at it.

CHANGING UP OUR INNER WORLDS

As with anything, it is hard to begin with.

Yet it's like learning to drive a car. We begin being conscious of our 'incompetence'. With practise, we become first 'consciously competent'—deliberately paying attention to the different factors involved (that we now know about)—and ultimately find ourselves 'unconsciously competent'.

A good place to start is by letting go…

- of the resistance
- of the outrage and blame
- of expectations
- of our sense of entitlements
- of our anger and anxiety
- of the sense of being wronged

Not doing these things will keep us trapped in the pain of loss and powerlessness, and stumbling blindly. There's no sense in doing that when we know better. Even though it takes effort. Even though it takes time.

Next, we deploy our curiosity and our will.

This means:

- *Allowing* for the reality that our thinking may be fallible.
- Asking ourselves to step back and become *curious* (rather than be right).
- Questioning our personal grasp of the 'facts'—following the trail of "Why?"
- Committing to find out what is 'true'.
- Scanning ongoingly for Truth, and regularly and *consciously* reviewing our own conclusions!

This takes humility. Not easy for many of us.

But when we *do* see the internal sabotage going on, we can actively engage our Self, and resist our default thinking. We can switch on, and begin to push against the programming we've received over our lifetimes.

We naturally (and unconsciously) process what we think we're seeing in someone else when we interact with them. But now we begin to bring this home to ourselves. *"How am I interpreting?"*—becomes a part of our reflexes.

We'll begin to catch ourselves in our mental models more and more often, questioning our 'rules' for Life, and letting gradually go of those of our beliefs that are myths!

The power of our 'thinking' is returned to us. We're able to take things less personally. We suffer less, and cope better. We begin to feel better about ourselves—an essential foundation for being positively and constructively generative!!

Now, we regularly ask ourselves to find insight and tolerance for people and situations—so that we can naturally work in harmony with 'what is'.

Understanding ourselves and Life better means that going forward, we naturally become more objective when we assign meaning (or weight) to our conclusions.

BUILDING INNER EQUILIBRIUM

It may seem impractical to orientate ourselves to constantly questioning and disciplining our thoughts. It takes such will and Effort to be so Conscious all the time, and to deliberately apply perspective tests to everything we see! Yet we *can* be a little more mindful and diligent in an ongoing quest for the facts: for 'truth'.

It then becomes more and more natural to us to keep ourselves open and curious, challenging our assumptions, and revisiting our conclusions.

When it comes to perceiving reality, the only thing

> that is really real and true about it is that we
> get to decide how we're going to *try* to see it. We
> get to Choose—to be curious and open.

We'll always be subject to the meaning-making flaw in our Thinking design—to a greater or lesser extent. There's nothing to be done about that. Personal 'meaning-making' spectacles are simply a part of our programme. *Yet this specific knowledge also empowers us.*

 To know that we know what we know, and to know that we do not know what we do not know, that is true knowledge. —Nicolaus Copernicus

Just *knowing* about it—enables us to keep upgrading our lenses for ongoingly clearer vision. We'll catch ourselves in our illusions more and more often, and find our Selves working more deeply in concert with what is actually real and true.

Instead of flying in the face of what's perfectly "normal" and trying to stop it because we don't like it—we work on learning to empower ourselves in it, *and despite it.*

We come to know ourselves as distinct and valid creatures, engaging meaningfully with Life.

We find clarity, and some certainty—and the doors to possibility open. What we make of our lives and do in them—now matters.

Coming into deeper *understanding* is at the beginning of this. When we're ongoingly able to make better sense of our experience by interpreting more accurately, we feel less bewildered and upset.

Why would we choose anything less than using our unique Human talent to think — and think well? The knock-on effects are fabulous! This 'self-healing' alone can empower us (even during our lowest moments) to remain effective, even in the face of change and dissolution, by keeping hold of ourselves.

We know now, for example, that we're multi-dimensional Beings living a multi-dimensional experience; that difficulty and suffering are as normal and inevitable as joy and excitement are; and that ongoing change inevitably brings struggle. We've seen how this one insight cancels out the mental model that "life should be fair'. It cancels out the assumption that life 'should' continue on as it has done so far. And it reminds us that we have inner resources to draw on.

These 'truths' alone can move the needle in our life so that we're enabled live rich, fruitful ones.

SETTING OURSELVES UP FOR ASCENDENCY

I had no idea of the realities, illusions, and actual laws of life interweaving with my experience as I first lived my life, and then lived through its breaking down. I was completely blind—though sure that "I knew" what I was doing, and what Life was about!

I disempowered myself by not knowing (let alone understanding) these important things, and tripped over myself in more ways than those I've already described! Yet now that I see things differently; now that I'm clearer about the illusions and realities, I see them not as Fate or the stupidity that tripped me up—but as principles that I can actually use as levers of power, in my life.

And my life has changed exponentially as a result.

We'll look at some of these principles next, building out our understandings of 'perception', and bringing other hard facts of reality onto the table.

When we strive ourselves into better and more able people, improving and growing ourselves, we're actively crafting and shaping ourselves and our lives.

This personal development enables us to understand how to leverage our own strengths and talents—and unleash our potentials.

THIS IS THE WATER

FUNDAMENTAL REALITIES OF HUMAN LIFE

*W*e'll return to the bigger Context (outside of Culturescape) —first.

David Foster Wallace in 2005, told the story of two young fish swimming along, who happen upon an older fish swimming the other way.

> The older fish nods at them. "Morning, boys, how's the water?" he asks, as they pass by him.
>
> The two young fish swim on for a bit. Eventually one of them looks over at the other. "What the hell is water?" he asks.

I like the way this illustrates how unaware we are of Context; blind to the daily actualities of Life outside of our own small worlds! And we are so because we don't know that we're 'swimming'.

The lack of understanding can cause us to become breathless, to flail around, to panic; and sometimes to fail to make it back to the surface. As we've seen.

So, what is the *nature* of this water?

'WATER'

What strikes me first when thinking about the 'water' is—*what is it in the first place?* And what are *we* doing in it, swimming this complex, often painful life—with all this fear and desire, happiness and success, throwing us from one side of the bus to the other?

Outside of religious interpretations and scientific theories and explanations, the reasons for any kind of existence of anything at all are mysterious. —An absolute enigma! The fact of the Human Being, of the Planet itself and the genesis of anything at all, are a mystery so intense that it's like trying to imagine what a trillion dollars looks like stacked up in your bedroom in dollar bills.

And not just 'how' this all happened (like the Big Bang theory for example)—but *why*! The reasons for any of it baffle anyone who has sat down and engaged with the idea.

Yet when the beliefs, frameworks, and the personal comfort zones we feel safe (and even powerful) in are stripped away, we're left with the only truth we know about living things, (on this planet at least).

We are here to GROW.

It's not only a natural impulse, but in fact our true birthright.

Here, on Planet Earth, there is not a living thing that doesn't carry the blueprint and the agenda to GROW—through thriving—to maturity. In fact there is *nothing* that doesn't grow and change from day to day over time, from the simplest amoeba to the most complex living form of mammal; from external cell growth to internally acquired experience, knowledge and wisdom. —Even the rocks and the universe itself are growing!

Outside of reasons and purpose, our man-made interpretations, and the 'rules' we've laid over everything and play by here in 'Human-life-on-

Earth, we can accept that one immutable fact as an absolute component of both 'the water' and our own lives.

And we don't just grow in our physical form. Life is also a journey of *personal* growth, during which we completely transform: the difference between a caterpillar and a butterfly! Our bodies grow in capability and skill—and from not being able to lift our heads or control our bowels at birth, for example, we come to use our bodies as dexterous tools through which we bring our thoughts, ideas and will into physical manifestations in the world. As our bodies mature, our body of experience grows, our awareness expands; our minds become filled with knowledge and wisdom, and we grow in our emotional and psychological intelligence.

'Growing' is the first and most basic 'rule' of Life. And we're either doing so, and moving into the full expansion of Life, or we're atrophying and dying; beginning the process of leaving it, through contraction. There is no stasis. We're simply always going in one direction or the other.

OTHER KEY CERTAINTIES IN LIFE

There are three other (and eye-watering) certainties about Human life that are integral to the *actual* normal.

The FIRST Watery Certainty

We are all going to die.

No-one gets off this planet alive. And that is the harsh truth of it. This one guaranteed event will occur in our lives—and could come any single day! It might be tomorrow, or it maybe only when we've lived closer to one hundred years. If we are born and survive, it is an absolute certainty that we will encounter death at some point, and lose the fight to live.

Even with power, success and insurance policies, outstanding health and fitness and all the opportunity in the world, we could still die tomorrow. —Or this afternoon! Not one of us will be able to escape it, no matter who we are, how well we've done, how much we are loved, how much fear we throw at it, or how much money we have for cryogenics. There is nothing we can do ultimately to withstand Death.

Death is the first great leveller, from which we are always running, and the first great motivator.

WHY WORRY SO MUCH ABOUT DEATH?

Consider this: the uninterrupted passage of air into our lungs is an absolute pre-requisite to our continuation. And the constant threat hanging over our heads every minute of every day—is that *something may bring our breathing to an end*.

We *need* to breathe in nearly eighteen thousand times every twenty four hours, for all the days of our lives! Think about how tenuous our hold on life actually is in those terms: how absolutely our lives depend on the proper functioning of breathing!

This is what we're defending.

Now consider this: for all of us (who are not struggling with asthma or a lung condition or relying on a ventilator,) breathing is something to which we hardly give a second thought. We simply assume it will keep on happening — twelve to thirty times per minute. A malfunction, and we only have four minutes before brain damage sets in, and soon after that, if there is still not enough air, Death takes over.

Much of what we anxiously hold back from and the concerns we hold—is to allay our fear that something may threaten our ability to keep breathing.

Yet we swallow food past our airway, talk through our out-breaths, choke through our tears, laugh until we cry—all actions that could vitally impact our continued breathing if one thing goes wrong! With all these, we give hardly any thought to the fact that we totally depend on breathing to live.

Instead we worry about things that may never happen, and lose quality of life taking things for granted.

> We play small, wasting our precious time. We avoid experiences, pass up opportunities, and turn away from challenges that would improve and expand us, and liberate our potentials.
>
> —All in service of avoidance (and safety) rather than Life (and growing).

When my husband was diagnosed with Stage 4 cancer with only a 20% chance of surviving the next five years, we realised with a shock that we hadn't actually had THE *conversation! What would happen if one of us died—not only to the partner and the children, but in terms of unmet potentials, wishes not fulfilled, affairs not set in order…?*

We were both in our forties and had enjoyed decades together. Yet the subject of inevitable "death" had never come up. It had seemed such a remote possibility—and a long way off—that we hadn't considered it. But of course, after the diagnosis, the stark reality that this WILL HAPPEN (if not now, then definitely at some point in the next few decades) was right there, in our faces.

Though he is fully well again, we're awake to it now. It's on the table — an upcoming reality. Death will part us at some point, and there is no getting away from it. There is only making the most of this short gift of Life we've been given—individually and together—and planning for what might come afterwards.

Ignoring the reality of Death coming ever nearer as the years pass means we take *Life* for granted, as though having an endless supply of Life, days and years is a sure thing.

Yet spending our efforts on avoiding failure, being ultra-cautious, risk averse, and standing on the edges of life (as if doing so will grant us immortality) is surely a waste of opportunity! —Opportunities we're given to *gain* experiences: ones that will grow us as well as the ones we'd love to have.

Given that our death is inevitable, perhaps worse than Death (and even the experience of dying itself) would surely be to die before we've made the most of the life we have?

Make peace with Reality now.

While we breathe, we do need to strive to live truly, fully and bravely. This is the point of Life, of all living things, regardless of what it may bring to us! We need to accept Life, warts and all, and do all that we can to make the most of it. So the first and most powerful thing we can do is embrace the reality that the clock of Life is ticking, and the sands of time in our hourglass are running—and running out.

Even our suffering ultimately, comes to an end.

The SECOND Watery Certainty

We are all being judged.

I don't mean this in some religious sense. 'Judging' is a Human construct, driven by cultural ideas of right and wrong.

Other people tell us about ourselves, and expect us to be what we are not, what we are not *yet*, and what we never will be—yet 'should' be.

Being judged is an ongoing, living suffering for us —as we're told by people we love and value that we're bad, unpleasing, wrong, disappointing, less-than, and even a failure.

There is little doubt that we will find ourselves judged. By those we love, by those whose opinion we care about; by friends, family, colleagues and strangers; by other races and nations, and ultimately by those who come after us and regard the history we've created for them.

More significantly we will judge ourselves. And often, this is the most important judgement: the labels we give ourselves, the censure (sometimes moving into self-hatred) that decimates our self-esteem.

Judgement can be a motivator—or an annihilation of Self and possibility. In managing everyday life, being judged is one of the most significant and tricky certainties, because if it's not constructive or well managed, it can very quickly lead to a loss of a positive sense of Self, to suffering and pain, and even to loss of hope, both of which can lead to death—even if only a living death.

The THIRD Watery Certainty

Suffering is interwoven into Life and living.

Everyone is going through something, no matter how fantastic things appear to be for them on the outside. From the terrible forms of suffering I described earlier, to milder everyday disappointments and losses. Even in the lead-up to the moment of death, suffering is often present.

No-one is immune.

Suffering touches every single one of us again and again as we journey, no matter who we are, where we come from, what we look like, what we've achieved, or who we know.

Someone we love and care about will die; might betray us, manipulate us, judge us, or break our heart. We might lose all we have worked towards or for. We may lose our health. Our country's economy might go up in smoke, or a terrible war might come and trash everything we hold dear. We might make a dreadful mistake and be caught out; a stupid judgement call that costs us precious opportunity, or reputation.

Or—one or all of these things might happen to someone we care deeply about.

No-one on their deathbed can ever honestly say that they didn't suffer at some point on their journey, or experience any pain. It is a condition of Life.

Not all of us will slip quietly away in our sleep.

For some of us, it will be rough. Pain, anguish. Fear. Spending last moments in agony; knowing it's coming as an accident unfolds around us; fighting to breathe; trapped and terrified; hurting as life bleeds away.

Or longer, more tortuous forms of dying? Brain damaged and trapped in a broken body, waiting years for the end to come, unable to even communicate with anyone. Dying of hunger, or of cold over hours or days.

I'm not afraid of death. I just don't want to be there when it happens. —Spike Milligan

These are terrible ways to go (and a current reality for many people). We will fight against suffering with everything we have. In the end though, even that stops, and death does come.

Death, suffering, and judgement are almost always at at the heart of our anguish, as our deepest fears are disconnection, loss, and pain.

- We swim away from death, because we are so programmed to live, to try, to hope. We don't know why, but we are.
- We swim against fear at all times, because we hate how it feels.
- We judge everything to ascertain how hurtful it could be if it comes too close.
- We swim away from suffering, afraid of its pain.
- And then we judge all that swimming, and finding it wanting, we suffer again.

So we search on, continuously, for that which will keep us from hurting and from dying, and will instead—cause us to be accepted.

IN SUMMARY: THE EYE-WATERING CERTAINTIES ABOUT THE WATER:

Our birthright is to grow.

We *will* die.

We will be judged by our peers, and by ourselves.

We will suffer pain, loss and lack.

All of it will hurt.

People are born. They succeed at some things and fail at others; they feel powerful and powerless; feel every feeling you can name (sometimes for longer periods than bearable).

And regardless of who they are and what they have made of themselves and their lives, they have to face their death as everyone does, with a recognition that they, their life and their deeds were worthwhile, and enjoyable—or time and opportunity wasted, and heaped with suffering besides.

No-one is exempt or immune.

This *is* the water.

Life is not what we see out there on our screens or the smokescreens that people put up for public consumption. It's a journey from birth to death with a lot of growth in-between. And much of that growth is provoked by suffering.

Even people who are really well off, or really good-looking, or really well-connected, or really well educated, or really successful, or really well-loved, or really happy with most of what is going on in their lives—wake to the Actual Normal every day.

Understanding the nature of 'water' and the effect it has on us—and the things that weigh us down and half-drown us rather than buoy us up—

enables us to not only to survive, grow and strive effectively, but to actually strike out powerfully across the 'water'.

You're being reminded of the nature of water here, and must learn how to swim it—perhaps better than you currently are. Because... *this is water*.

SO WHAT DOES THIS MEAN?

- It means we're not objective about what is happening to us in the moment, how it might be significant in the grander scheme of things, or how it might turn out in the end.

We should endeavour to remember this at all times.

- It means that we're constantly reactive, pushed into choosing a way of 'being' that feels safe and safeguards us as much as possible: no fear, no pain, no death—so that we don't have to suffer, and feel that we matter.

- It means that the sooner we accept these certainties about our existence, the sooner we can embrace them as realities, adjust our expectations and turn our attention to something else.

We need to walk the line between striving to live aware that we only have so much time, seizing the day—yet keeping the knowledge of our ultimate death on a low burn so that we're not disabled by the reality.

The most powerful way to achieve this is through a sense of thriving. And of gratitude. Of joyful peace in both.

The combination of these create a feeling of personal empowerment together with a sense of having 'arrived', from where it's more possible to consider that we might have to 'leave' at some point! This is what we're aiming for in Life.

So while we're constantly monitoring our environment to make sure that we're not in a life-threatening situation, we're also looking all the time at what we have to *do and be* to create that sense of thriving and abundance—that not only keeps the wolves from our doors, but also actually brings fulfilment and personal empowerment.

In these true states, we're in deep self-acceptance, less susceptible to judgements from others, and thus more internally liberated to strive again—in a beautiful virtuous cycle, for greater thriving, whatever that may mean to us.

How to get to this we will uncover, as we go on here.

SWIMMERS

WHAT PROPELS US THROUGH 'THE WATER'

We've looked at 'Context' from a few points of view so far.

The global Context, currently in a massive state of change—and changing alarmingly—is impacting Human life everywhere.

Within that, our Western Culturescape and the ideas, values and pressures we feel as we strive for fulfilling lives and contend with the messages we're given weighs heavy.

We looked briefly at our inner Context—the Silo of Self—and how our Thinking and tendency to ascribe meanings generates our personal experience.

And within that, we've examined the three key realities in Life (*the water*), that specifically cause us to suffer, particularly when we're in denial or rejection of them.

With all that in place, we'll look next at 'swimming': first at ourselves *as* the swimmers in the *'water'*, and then at the craft of 'swimming' itself.

OUR KEY NEEDS ARE TO SURVIVE, TO FEEL SAFE AND TO MATTER

Arriving into our Lives and growing into Consciousness, we respond to our natural impetus to meet our needs, and answer demands from our deep internal drivers. So, as our Contexts unfold about us (influencing both possibility and us) we spend much of our energy making ourselves as safe as we can. (Original Desire).

Then (at least initially but often for much longer, and certainly when we hit hard times), we work to put money, goods and success in our lives on a regular basis—to create some certainty, and thus a sense of safety.

Next, *we want to matter*. We want to be validated, to be a part of things—even if that's just being important to someone else. We may think we're trying for happiness, but we're really seeking to belong.

This is known as the need for Significance.

We meet this need through *Connection* with others and through our own *Growth*. *V*ia these we increase the *Contribution* we're able to make—both in our own lives and more widely. These three things give us our sense of Significance. 'Recognition' is at the heart of each of these. *We've had an impact* (on others or Context). Recognition speaks of our Personal Power.

So what we're really searching for with our need for Significance—in a world that is a strange combination of terrifying and full of endless possibility—is our Power!

The level or degree of Power we have in it gives us some measure of Control. When power and control collaborate, we are delivered agency, and the possibility of self-actualisation—bolstering our Significance!

This is why we crave recognition and place value on love and belonging. It's why being valued by others leads to vital self-esteem—and why losing love and recognition is so debilitating.

When we're suffering (usually a disconnection from, or rejection by what we're trying to 'belong' to) and wondering why something has happened to us in particular, we're questioning our Personal Power: our ability to have effect, or make things happen. (Original Fear).

Feeling the loss of being 'Significant'—is what causes our true pain, and thus our suffering.

In summary, our Survival needs physically drive us into Life, as a first point of call—and our Significance needs come into play once those are met, to pull us forward relationally and emotionally, and into multilayered Growth.

Between them, these two forces within us—bring about our lives.

ABRAHAM MASLOW'S HIERARCHY OF NEEDS

Maslow posited that Human needs are arranged in a hierarchy:

> It is quite true that man lives by bread alone—when there is no bread. But what happens to man's desires when there is plenty of bread and when his belly is chronically filled?
>
> At once other (and "higher") needs emerge, and these, rather than physiological hungers, dominate the organism. And when these in turn are satisfied, again new (and still "higher") needs emerge and so on. This is what we mean by saying that the basic Human needs are organised into a hierarchy of relative prepotency. [12]

This model[13] demonstrates this nicely (although I would place 'Growth' as a foundational need, and top the pyramid with the word 'Significance' (or Recognition).

Starting at the bottom, our drivers are shown in order of greatest need. The theory is that as each layer of need is met, we are freed to work on meeting our needs on the next level.

SURVIVAL NEEDS

Unsurprisingly, our needs for food, shelter and safety are the foundation upon which everything else depends, because the reality is that we'll die if they're not met. The red danger zone is more than a 'need': it's an *absolute requirement*.

After surviving and feeling 'safe', everything else in our experience in Life is answering the question about our significance, *Where does my power lie, and what is my ability to manifest it?*

SIGNIFICANCE NEEDS

- This happens in Context **(Connection)**.
- From here we strive for things that are about our potential **(Growth)**.
- And we thrive when we can make choices **(Power and Control)**.

A person whose needs are met on every level is thus enabled to manifest what they want in life out of an inner security and sense of personal empowerment — to achieve their Big Picture.

We feel Significant when we manage our power well and insignificant when we don't.

This is important to our understanding when we're suffering, dealing with change, and finding ourselves feeling diminished by the experience. —Because when we lose our base of safety and security (practical and/or emotional), *loss* highlights that we don't have much power, suggesting that in the greater scheme of things, we're terrifyingly insignificant.

Which leads us directly into suffering...

CONSTANT FLOW

It is not a case of a simple, linear flow in an overall (upward) direction of course! We live our lives in a constant flow up and down this hierarchy (to a greater or lesser degree) as our circumstances, needs and values, and ideals change across the course of our lives.

Changes—like being struck down with a long-term health condition, divorce, moving cities or countries, having children, or the consequences of others' actions that ripple into our lives—may cause us to move up and down the levels, depending. Time and time again we may need to re-establish our safety needs before we can work towards self-actualising again in our latest phase of life.

The model works for our many smaller achievements too. So for example, when we get the toy that we nag our parents for as children, or walk down the aisle with our chosen partner, or create a small business—we're 'self-actualising' each time.

With each achievement we set our sights on the next hope.

We don't 'get there', to enjoy ourselves in a fixed or permanent state of self actualisation—because we're growing and changing all the time!

This is all important to keep in mind when we're dealing with difficulty in our lives. We may feel that we're going backwards, yet really, we're feeling the need to reinforce (or even re-establish) our foundations every time because we've been rocked. The 'fear' that can be triggered by this, can keep us focused on meeting safety needs, at the expense of meeting our other important needs.

OUR SAFETY NEEDS CAN ENTRAP US

Our needs are always changing as we grow of course, and sometimes our agenda to stretch ourselves finds itself at war with this impetus to satisfy our more basic needs. An aversion to risk, narrowed perspectives or emotional blocks can keep us in the lower layers of the Hierarchy, eventually entrapping us into meeting only our safety needs.

The simple *perception* that we're 'stuck' can cause us anxiety around lack, turning our focus downwards to shrink back to where we feel safer. Because nothing else can be on our radar until we're 'safe!'

And when life falls over (as it often does) we'll naturally revert to ensuring our safety needs are met—because that's vital!

But also because, here (at least to some degree) we can exert control. This is one of the reasons why people in great distress often become overweight: if food is available and other choices seem limited, well—that's one thing that we can choose, and can be in control of. It meets physiological needs, and also answers one of our safety needs. It's thus soothing and comforting on three different levels! And during ongoingly stressful times, people can get stuck here, on an anxiously neurotic cycle.

UNDERSTANDING THIS IS IMPORTANT!

In the course of a changing life, we are going to face many 'resets', where the feeling of fear might very quickly rise up and disable us.

Expecting this and being primed to recognise it if it arrives, means that we can avoid feeling so threatened in the moment that we become paralysed. This itself is empowering.

When it comes to suffering, the loss of our personal power is the most disorientating, and the most destabilising aspect of it. Having an understanding of what is driving us from within enables us to continue to Choose to strive consciously , despite discomfort and difficulty.

GRAPPLING WITH CHANGE

THE TRANSFORMATIVE OPPORTUNITY

> *... death is very likely the single best invention of life. It is life's change agent. It clears out the old to make way for the new.* —Steve Jobs

Whether we acknowledge the effects of Change in our lives or not, we *are* all constantly moving down the path of life towards an ending. Yet we try to ignore this reality by seeking out states of permanence as far as possible—around our jobs, our looks and fitness, our homes, and our activities and interests, for example.

Many of us have been able to create a bubble of existence within which we live out patterns of working, holidaying, exercising etcetera, for many years at a time. In this status quo our safety needs are met; we know ourselves, feel contained, centred and balanced, and know 'the rules'—which levers to pull and where and how to place ourselves—for empowerment and comfort.

THE COMFORT ZONE

This is the "comfort zone", within which we exist in a not unpleasant state of stasis. In this place we don't have to stretch ourselves, or even question the status quo. We have achieved equilibrium and things 'work'. All we have to do is maintain it. This is how life is, and life is good…

In fact, it would be *uncomfortable* to change anything—and who wants that?!

Yet… stasis is inimical to growth.

So the intelligence within Life has a canny solution to this problem.

While we're happily floating in our little bubbles, another element is constantly present and in the mix: Change.

CHANGE IS A UNIVERSAL LAW

Operating powerfully (and relentlessly) in the background, Change constantly unfolds as the backdrop to every moment that passes—*here and everywhere* in our external Lives.

Change—is both terrible and wonderful!

Often seeing it as desirable (to bring about the manifestation of our choices)—we *want* it and actively pursue it.

And if we are struggling, we have expectations that Change will make our hell stop, bring on the peace and equilibrium we really want, and enable us once more to make our wanted personal choices without too much more discomfort.

And at the very least, we can hold onto the fact, like a lifebuoy, that things *will* change, even if only eventually.

Otherwise we'd like things to stay pretty much the same.

But if things *must* change, then we want to know how it will all turn out! Because whatever happens, we want certainty: *for things not to change to what we don't want or in a way that's out of our control.*

Yet Change is the natural outcome of life being birthed, living, growing and dying. Like a snake shedding its skin, it's vital to accommodate expansion (otherwise known as 'growth') — and necessary to accommodate contraction (as every moment disappears, replaced by the next).

Our Lives change whether we like it or not.

Change is an elemental aspect of the water.

CHANGE IS FOUNDED IN LOSS

Change breaks down, destroys and removes what was. It's the constant death of the 'old' making way for the new.

Outside of personal ambition or passion, Change comes about from one of two things:

- **Loss** (in relationships, Life challenges, and suffering):
  Something happens that is outside of us.

  Something is taken from us—and something else comes in to take up the space—like suffering, for example. Or a person influences us, or a new opportunity, or job comes along, for example.
  *Change happens **to** us.*

- **Creativity:** *Something new comes from within us.*

  Our vision for ourself and our life causes us to generate something. An idea, a new way forward, for example; developing the skills and capabilities we need to realise our vision, or developing our character strengths and working to become the kind of person we need to show up as. Or even simply having to develop inner strength to carry the burden of suffering. *Change happens 'by' us.*

In *either case, we're invited into Growth.*

'Change' swings into our lives and identities, often stretching out our comfort zones (sometimes as a wrecking ball, causing painful and disorientating havoc) leaving us adrift from our previously secure and known moorings, and dealing with aftereffects that we didn't want or ask for.

Yet this discomfort, conflict, hardship and suffering is often necessary to prick us into action! 'Change' forcibly prods us out of the familiar and into the wilderness of growth and improvement—so that we sit up and look around, take stock. We become creative, and move out of stasis and into growth, and real possibility.

We're asked—no, *required*—to step towards something else. And often this is upward and into our best iterations!

But all too often, the walls first have to close in on us.

 The greatest possibility for advancement occurs at the greatest point of negativity. —Buddha

That's of little comfort when we're encountering really hard times, that we're not sure we're up to managing. We're smarting from our losses, and resenting change!

I remember counting up my losses (yet again!) and being suddenly struck by the deep realisation that I'd judged my life harshly before, in wanting to change it so badly. Now I just wanted *that* back!

But when 'what was' is gone, we have no option but to go forward into something else. Which, I did eventually.

But first—and for a long time—I got myself really caught up in resistance, holding out for some kind of reinstatement of the 'known normal' at least.

DEALING WITH CHANGE

When a problem first arrives in our lives, it usually feels really possible to address and overcome using tried and tested methods—both ours and those of our advisors. Perhaps it's even something of an opportunity or an adventure we're keen to make something of.

We start out on the tried and tested route with our set of 'rules' that we believe in—and maybe even with a sense of peace and security in what we know works.

But when it isn't resolved and we keep encountering dead-ends and disappointment, we feel anxious—and increasingly so over time. Our faces are being rubbed in our own powerlessness, with all our ideas about ourselves and the future shaken up, leaving us miserable and hurting.

We go round and round in circles, getting more of the same useless non-results, more and more stuck, and more and more angry and desperate. Others step in with advice to 'help' us: what not to do, what to do instead and what actions and attitudes they think are appropriate for us in the situation.

We begin to feel judged and inadequate, instead of competent, and helped. The continuing difficulties seem like a personal 'failure' we've brought on ourselves, confirming that we aren't 'enough'.

Worse—we feel our lack of Personal Power.

We're confronted by ourselves 'in scenario', and 'become our results'.

RESISTING CHANGE

Since the Human condition motivates us to pursue certainty and feelings of safety, our ego now encourages us to avoid anything that might further expose or embarrass us, or disempower us further.

We become paralysed by doubt and afraid to try any more unknowns. The thoughts and feelings can be so debilitating that we put our defensive shields up. We don't want to put ourselves through any more of the discomfort these fears and feelings bring.

Now the excitement of new ideas, or untried and untested suggestions and stabs in the dark are quickly repulsed with reasons and excuses about why they won't work. We find ourselves resisting sticking our necks out, resisting new ideas, and eventually, resisting trying any new things—and anything at all. We stop sharing our hopes and efforts with friends and relatives. We withdraw into ourselves.

Over time, we find an acceptable pattern of 'being' in this situation. We attempt to explain it to ourselves, sifting through our thoughts to draw conclusions on our experiences. And we find reasons and explanations to put to those who are concerned or care about us, and who want to see us trying and repairing our failed, heartbreaking situations.

In its own way, it becomes comfortable to be in this headspace with this attitude of having given up. We've achieved a new kind of comfort zone; one that's designed to keep the pain of change out. (This at least, is a place we know.) All we have to do now is verbally rail against Life and its unfairness, with our necks firmly pulled in.

> *"We've tried and failed. We don't want to try anymore, or to work on repairs because it's too confronting to have to deal with continually getting knocked back. Knocked down."*

It's a way of existing in an awful situation-not-of-our-choosing, that we feel we can do nothing about.

It's our protest at change that's happened *to* us, that's forced our hand, and is outside of our current control.

It can also serve in perhaps *communicating* something to those we blame for bringing us to this place of pain.

Digging in like this is a form of regaining Power. *"I won't"*.

Something about this works for us (even if only because it is a known thing and thus has a feeling of safety in it). It's perhaps the last real sense of Power that we have in that moment!

We resist any suggestion that we move away from this attitude, from this anger, and from our conviction that there is nothing we can do to rescue ourselves. But the more we do this, the more we get locked into it as a 'position'.

"We didn't want this, or to be driven to that. We want what we wanted, and we want our efforts to bring that on the first or second go."

Letting go can feel like a personal defeat: as if we have been vanquished in not even being able to hold on to our splendid status of victim!

The only remedy that is acceptable is the restoration of a once-enjoyed reality, or something better. NOT the reality of limping injured off the battlefield of Life, and having to find something else.

'Changing' ourselves in any way becomes a kind of climb down.

A COMMON APPROACH TO CHANGE

In a crisis situation, the ordinary person may be able to draw on an unbelievable response from themselves and be hailed a hero afterwards.

Yet they are not then necessarily changed going forward as the newly minted hero. They'll return to their ordinary lives and ordinary ways, and eventually will be found still being shitty to their spouse or neighbour, if that is what they were doing before.

Someone may go on a diet, heroically stick with it, and lose a heap of weight. Yet something like 90% of dieters fail to keep their weight loss, because they eventually return to the patterns that made them overweight in the first place.

This is because our basic drivers don't change that much. It's only the layers of resolution and willpower we lay over the top of them, that do.

Because, when those layers wear thin, we often find ourselves back where we started. After a while, our more natural instincts return to the fore (be that a victim response, or anger, or apathy, or despair, for example), and we revert to 'normal'.

Chasing down 'Change' as the key to Healing is never going to work, because 'Change' is not simply a set of different externals.

I believe this is a reason that a lot of self-help programmes are less helpful than they're designed to be, particularly when 'Change' is deployed as the tool to help us cope with adversity.

In them, we're asked to focus on an external end result, and then to make almost immediate changes to patterns of behaviour, attitudes, ideas and values. And we're expected (exhausted and demoralised as we are) to somehow to maintain that indefinitely—first to get 'there', and then to remain there.

We rally at the beginning—full of hope—for as long and as hard as we're able! But it can't be sustained because it's an external layer of effort or resolution, *rather than some vital inner shift. W*e eventually fall back to where we began, and find ourselves in a hole called 'stuck' or 'despair'.

CHANGE INVITES US INTO GROWTH

What do I mean by a *vital inner shift?*

As Effect follows Cause, when Change shifts our external Context significantly in any way, it's also calling us to find new ways of responding to this, so that we deploy our power creatively and in new ways, in enacting our will on the great uncertainty of Life.

That response is where the shift is.

Because if we don't change how we think about difficulty or how we respond to it in our lives, we will feel terrible about it every time it occurs, and remain disabled by negative thoughts, and stuck too.

> **The definition of insanity is doing the same thing over and over again, yet expecting different results.** —Albert Einstein

We can resist the call, stagnate and eventually atrophy into a static old age. Or we can step forward into growth: emotionally, practically, psychologically—in maturity, in capability, in insight, empathy and wisdom.

We can—and do—have some influence and direction over this, regardless of our station in Life and the opportunities in our environment. Because…

No-one can ever take away our ability to Choose our response.

- *We can Choose* to actively dig in and stop developing ourselves, embracing stasis and atrophy.
- Or we *can Choose personal growth.*

And this is a Choice that I want everyone to wake up to!

Because not taking responsibility for our response to Change's effect on us—is accepting disempowerment as a force in our lives.

We need to learn to think differently about the reality of Change's ongoing presence—everywhere.

Because if we're open to it, we can step into Change's open arms and be enfolded in something that may well turn out to be truly wonderful.

CHANGE THAT HAPPENS *BY* US EMPOWERS US

In the external Context, Change has dominion: in other words, there is only so much control and Effect we can have there. *We are always subject to Change.* It constantly rewrites the rules we play by and clashes with our need to feel that *we* have power over Life and ourselves.

It follows then that when we can't change the externals, we have to change ourselves. And changing ourselves (eventually) is seeking to understand who we are, where we are, and how we got here.

The only place on this planet where we have true dominion, and is over our internal environment.

Things may not change, but we can!

Why would we ever accept disempowerment when there is an alternative? Working *with* Change, making new choices that centre around our responses (including new and different kinds of choices we'll now make) may be all we can do—but those things are powerful indeed.

Ultimately, we get to decide how much power we will give Change over ourselves and our lives—and for how long—before we decide to step in and reclaim as much charge as we can.

The time arrives where we choose to acknowledge the shifts that have occurred in our life, and even in ourselves as a result of the loss that has been sustained.

Our old way—is gone. We allow resistance to give way to simple acceptance.

And then we move into taking responsibility for what we'll do next.

And that starts with seeking new perspectives, insights and knowledge, upgrading our old ones that have been made redundant to us.

To rescue ourselves, we must climb down from where we were, and *actively* point ourselves in a direction.

THE CLIMB-DOWN

Though we probably know we need to let things shift, yet often we're wary and weary, knowing that doing so is desperately uncomfortable, and often seems unrewarding. We're already carrying hurt and feeling jaded by the journey of loss and change so far. And since things are so crappy and personally impossible right here in the now—how can we envisage (and trust in) an end result?

The last thing we want is any *more* change thank you very much!

But this is the trap of resistance. Resistance stops us from starting.

The hardest part is actively letting go of all we've barricaded ourselves up with, that acts as a shield, keeping us safe through *not-trying-and-so-not-getting-hurt*.

We might never feel okay about what has happened to us. We might always carry the pain that Change has brought us. We might not necessarily be able to extricate ourselves from Suffering. We may already be—or become—permanently disabled by it.

Yet Change, like growth, is an integral part of life. There is no point in questioning either of these for being part of everyday reality!

That's simply common sense!

With hindsight after all, we can probably look back on other major changes we've *had* to make, and recognise the great rewards they've brought—even though while it was happening it was a struggle and desperately uncomfortable.

TRANSFORMATION: HOW TO BEGIN

We stop contemplating Change's 'ruinous' effects on our Big Picture. Instead we accept that Change has forcibly carved the space for *something else*, into our lives, and actively work to embrace it as a valuable growth tool.

Armed with the insights we've now achieved, we must choose that something else, and then work with grit and determination to bring it into being.

It's an internal working; a series of shifts.

- First, as we come to terms with Change's inevitable presence in our lives, we do find ways of simply bearing it; living with it—and striving to do so with equanimity.
- We ponder who we are in our changed Context right now—and who we *need* to be. What do we have to call forth from within ourselves (perhaps for the first time), to rise to the occasion? Change can necessitate reinventing ourselves—sometimes even on a daily basis—with no guarantees.
- Gradually we encompass all this in our new awarenesses, newly chosen attitudes, and conscious new patterns of behaviour.

As this all unfolds, something is shifting within us; inexorably creeping over us. *We're working in the flow of Change.*

We become more *able*, we *do* better, we find ourselves *being* more and stronger, wiser and kinder (to ourselves) in the new Context, and then in the following Context… We're more able to sustain ourselves in the unknown, the different and the uncomfortable—and at every milestone.

Change and Growth *require* us to step towards and ultimately *into* our full capacities and potential.

The fact is, that even if we escape it this time, our 'growing' (that works hand in hand with Change) will *keep* calling us forward.

And when the transformation that is being woven in us really takes hold, our externals naturally change.

Ultimately we will find ourselves feeling gratitude for the experience—and for the *opportunity* to grow!

CHOICE

THE FUNDAMENTAL POWER OF HUMAN BEINGS

I said earlier that we pursue wealth and achievement to achieve "success" (Significance).

But what "success" really gives us is Choice.

"Where will I be? Who will I be with? And why?

What will I do with my time and energy?

What do I believe in, and support? Who does that make me?

Who do I wish to become?

How will I earn the income that will enable me to make these choices?"

CHOICE

Choice is freedom—to be, to move, to do, to impact. We 'experience' our personal power through our ability to make self-defining choices. Wielding this power by making Choices meets our need for significance and gives us the freedom to be self-expressed.

Choice is at the heart of manifesting, and manifesting is our Personal Power.

We Human Beings are constantly reinventing ourselves and our world, cutting away old, useless material and replacing it with fresh, relevant stuff as we change from the inside out.

Our Choices create us the unique lives, values, experiences and relationships that suit our unique selves. And what we choose to do, to have in our lives, to *be* in terms of our behaviour, relationships and actions—comes to define *us* uniquely.

I WANT TO BE CHOOSING!

Yes, I will shout it from the rooftops! *We want to be able to choose what is in our lives:* to do certain things, to go places, to buy experiences, to connect with others in those experiences, and to achieve positive outcomes in our work through effort.

Because Life is about development and growth, and in Human Life (which is about so much more than simply *surviving* day to day)—"choosing" is how we do this.

Choice is our instrument of creation. Our Choices are the brushes and paints by which we shape the great artworks that are our Lives.

And it's not just the *things* we Humans create. Our Choices help grow (or contribute to stunting) our Selves, defining *who we choose ourselves to be in every given moment.*

We see this idea in action when we think back to when we were young, unselfconscious, unfettered children (and of children in general) in a constant state of play as we interacted with our world and each other, reinventing ourselves and the 'rules' of the game from moment to moment.

We see it in our personal expressions of Self today, in the unique ways we say things, the words and gestures we use, in our moment by moment interactions with one another, and in our personal actions and interests. It's expressed in our love of things beautiful, functional and delicious; in how we decorate and present our bodies to society and the world every day .

We're constantly creating, inventing, refreshing, growing and changing, one month to the next, one year after another, Choice by Choice by Choice. We thrive on our Choices, learn from them and expand ourselves and our possibilities with them. Without them, we wither away.

> **"Choosing is one of the things that distinguishes us as Human."**

And we get upset when our Choices become diminished and practical constraints close about us, restricting movement and variety—because that lack of Choice closes *us* down.

WHY DO WE NEED TO BE ABLE TO CHOOSE?

Why can't we just settle, and plod? Why are we always striving to find our direction, to manifest our talents and interests, and seeking to generate something? Why do we want to contribute in useful and valuable endeavours at all?

- Personal Power is innate in us: our Choices enable us to manifest and understand it, and they contribute to meeting our need for Significance.
- We're here to grow: our Choices create opportunities for us to liberate our potentials and grow ourselves.
- We're self-defining: our Choices inform us of Who We Are and enable us to find meaning in existing.

Choosing, dare I say it, is not only an essentially Human quality, but in fact, a Human *necessity*. Like breathing is.

Most of us *need* to feel and know that we are improving and progressing —which an increasing ability to choose both reflects, and enhances. — Because we're either developing and growing (as Life intends all living things to do), or we're atrophying and contracting — rather like sharks, that need to be constantly moving forward or they die!

Without Choice, which enables a real ability to progress—it's impossible for us to self-actualise.

> My disappointments were about failing my need to make a Choice.
>
> In the depths of my difficult journey through my husband's diagnosis, lumped with difficulties and personal failures, I was terribly afraid that Life would never again be more than struggling and striving and never quite 'arriving', for the rest of our lives; trying to progress but really standing still—or even going backwards.
>
> That Life would never again be the creative path of self-expression that it once had been.
>
> Outside of the possibility of losing him, my grief was about my loss of Choice. Without it, I'd not be able to give expression to my values and desires, and buy the essential experiences that I craved—like reconnecting in person with loved ones overseas, or undertaking a particular course of study for example.

To be truly self-expressed we need to be able to choose—even if that's only our own values, or attitude! Losing our Choices is one of the hardest things to bear.

OUR CHOICES CREATE OUR REALITY

Choice is a creative act that manifests as a wonderful form of self-expression and creates possibility. It's an incredible tool to wield power and be self-directed: the brush with which to paint the canvas of our lives. BUT (*important note*)—it operates under the Law of Cause and Effect.

In making a choice—we are 'Cause'. The result we get is—'Effect'.

Next to Creation itself (which we don't truly understand) Choosing is the next biggest creative act in the world. *Because every Choice we make has infinite effects.* Some are small, some huge, some felt now, others felt far into the future.

Our Choices ripple out ahead of us into time—creating effects that are shared with those who journey with us; and are handed on to those following behind us.

Our Choices determine the quality of our lives, shaping us into who we are and creating a legacy that we live daily, moment to moment.

Choice is a fundamental power of Human Beings, because *our Choices create our lived reality.*

AS WITH ALL THINGS, CHOICE HAS A SHADOW

Since not all our Choices are conscious ones, good ones or wise ones—many of them result in effects we really don't want.

Instead of Benefits, we find ourselves with Consequences!

We think that they're 'just choices'—like breathing is: that we make them in the privacy of our own lives; that they're reasonably insignificant and don't really matter.

Yet many of them are the most powerful Choices of our lives. Our (un)healthy Choices (made one bite at a time, one missed opportunity for movement at a time!) impact our biology, for example. Maybe not now, or even for the next ten years, but once those Effects arrive, we will suffer in a diminished physiology—or enjoy a full and healthy old age.

They carry incredible weight and fundamentally impact our wellbeing, our positioning to create desired outcomes, our ability to manage our power, our sense of who we are—and our whole map of life.

***Every* Effect *will*, at some point, manifest.**

And not only in our own lives but also in the lives of people we care about—along with those of people we don't even know exist.

Because our Choices are the Law Of Cause And Effect in action, Choice is no small thing.

All our Choices therefore, actually matter.

> *It was early on in my suffering journey that I realised that my Choices had had a part to play in where I found myself.*
>
> *At first I rebelled internally against the idea.*
> *No. It was Life's fault that things hadn't worked out! It was my nationality, my location, the actions of a significant other in my life; my baggage (thanks parents and teachers) or others' misunderstandings…*
>
> *Those things were true in my life, yet regardless, at the end of the day, I had made particular Choices within and around those at every step of the way — pleased when I could do so, playing the Game of Human life to the full. From the time I was little and could say 'NO!' through to what I wore or what and how I communicated on a particular day; to whether I exercised, was kind or selfish; applied myself to my studies, or decided to study further after school: in every case I had been actively choosing—and thus creating my outcomes.*
>
> *Once I realised the truth of this and its significance, I was horrified. It was all on me.*
>
> *My thoughts churned. And for years thereafter as I reflected on how I'd ended up stuck, I dwelt on my mistakes, wondering how things*

might have turned out differently for me if I'd just made this Choice then, that Choice there, hadn't chosen such and such...

I could see the various points at which my whole life became altered irrevocably because of certain Choices, made when I was too blind to know any better. Conscious and unconscious Choices made at key moments had directed my path forward like the inescapable grooves on a dirt track.

The regrets, the self-recrimination—went on and on. Every day I'd wake up and think it all through again, obsessively—because loss had broken my dreams, stripped me of hope, and left me bitter— and I couldn't quite fathom it. People began to occupy my mind: the things they did or did not do that had 'forced' my hand, taken my chances from me, redirected me elsewhere with their agenda. How I'd let them because I'd cared, and loved them. Because I'd chosen, or not chosen...

I examined it from all angles; wondered about it, grieved over it, unsure what to do with the lump it had become.

The Choices and non-Choices I'd made I now wore like a necklace, each a bead on the strand, each additional one weighing me down, stooping me so that my eyes couldn't lift from the floor.

BLIND CHOICES

Often it seems that our life is happening outside of our control: that we're sitting on the sidelines doing our best to direct it while Life simply unfolds itself around us—often into circumstances we loathe. We want to control the outcomes, dominate the situation, get ahead; be cleverer, wealthier, smarter, more powerful, more popular... And we feel bad about ourselves (or others) because this proves difficult to do.

But let's go back in time and postulate what would have happened if we'd stayed in school—or if we hadn't. If we'd decided not to leave home at that particular time, or get together with that particular person, job or other opportunity...

Each time, *we* made a decision (in good faith admittedly, but nevertheless...) We may not have realised what that Choice would generate, or reduce—yet, at the end of the day, *it was our Choice.*

Yet... there is no point in second-guessing our Choices.

 In any moment of decision, the best thing you can do is the right thing. The worst thing you can do is nothing.
—Theodore Roosevelt

Many of our Choices of course are made blindly since we're 'programmed', conditioned, lied to and confused about who we are, what we should do, where we should go, what our possibilities are and what we're capable of.

And then circumstances affect our course, our milestone—and our lives, along with our Choices. We start out in one direction and find ourselves headed in another, and are often made powerless to redirect despite massive effort—because we're mired in the effects of our previous, blind Choices.

The journey of life is about discovering the myths that have directed our Choices, and making new ones, with new Awareness.

- It's about uncovering what is really true about Life that we can rely on. *Our Choices wake us up to what is 'True'.*
- It's about finding what is really true about ourselves—that we can know for sure. We then use Choice to define and sculpt ourselves and our lives.

- It's about discovering how we can be the Cause of better Effects going forward—for ourselves, and more widely. Our Choices create our future, and *the* future.

Yet the truth is, we only really learn to see as we move along the path.

So many of us wish that we could supersede this rule of Life—and consult psychics and fortune tellers, yet in the end there is no way to surely get this information other than to play the Game of Life, and to move forward making our Choices and seeing what they bring.

> **"We are always just one Choice away from a totally different marriage, job, income, or relationship – with our kids or parents, our work, and our self-esteem."**

Some people don't like to hear that. They don't like to admit that *their* Choices—conscious and unconscious, but made one after another in a long chain—put them in exactly the position they find themselves in now. They want to say it happened *to* them, that they are not to blame, not wrong, and didn't fail. And they don't want to take responsibility for their outcomes and their attitudes.

Yet others are excited by this idea—by the realisation that their lives are the outcomes of their Choices, and that out of these they learn and gain the power to make new ones—ones that could change everything.

> *Ultimately I understood that the worst thing I could do was to be bitter about where I was at. I had to accept with compassion and insight that I was young and blindly treading a path that millions before me had trodden. And that millions more will do after me. That's just the way it seems to work.*

The journey has in part been about learning through seeing the Law of Cause and Effect in action—and in part about coming to see and understand that I still hold the greatest power in my hands: the *power* to Choose.

> *With hindsight, I now see that each bead—each Choice I made—is a beautiful addition to the necklace of Life experience that I wear today, that swings around my neck with grace, adding to my wisdom and beauty.*

No matter what else is going on in life…**we are always choosing. And we always have Choice**… (even if only a Choice of attitude).

Choice is about taking responsibility for that reality at least.

ACTIVATING OUR PERSONAL POWER

WIDENING OUR EXISTENTIAL CIRCUMFERENCE

So we find ourselves swimming in 'the water', seeking to meet our survival and Significance needs in an ever-changing life and world (as we must from the moment we're born)—while striving to keep ourselves empowered in all situations and making much wanted Choices.

And we do keep swimming and striving to our last coveted breaths, because we sense that we matter. Seeking Significance (our sense of mattering) is a dominant focus for us.

Yet we want more than just to swim! *We want a sense of agency in our lives, and power over our destiny.*

HOW WE GENERATE OUR POWER

We gain this organically, through being connected (belonging). And we also actively *draw* Power to ourselves.

Drawing power is a two-part process.

The first is **"Power Over"**: how much power we can *claim* for ourselves in relationship to everything we encounter. So we're always testing our power—in relationships, situations and environments—trying to both manifest and amplify it.

- We exert power over ourselves and our bodies via our aversions and desires.
- We work to have power over others (including our relatives) through our moods and actions, via our reputations, through the giving and withholding of connection, co-operation, opportunity and the means to sustenance.
- We retain power over property and nature, at home and in the field via ownership, poison, the deployment of machinery, weaponry and explosives.

The second is via **"Success"**: **Power through influence**, which *builds* our power.

- "Success" brings Power via '*having*' (and having 'more' of as much as possible)—and in particular, 'more than' what many others have. This results in being able to make more and bigger Choices than others.
- "Success" builds influence—through connections, social status, access and job titles, for example. This enables us to weight the balance of things in our favour, and once again bolsters our ability to make powerful Choices: more powerful Choices than others can make. The more "Success" we achieve, the more Power we gain.

The more Power we draw in these ways, the more Power we have over our journey, and the more Significant we feel—leading to even more Power and Significance…in a wonderful self-sustaining cycle of possibility and longevity.

It may seem from this description that Personal Power is an *Outside-In* job. *Dominate the environment and the others in it, accrue stuff and status, and stand in the sense of being empowered.*

Yet these are *manifestations* of Power—rather than what generates it.

In fact there are two essential active ingredients that are necessary for any of this to occur. Both are *Inside-Out* jobs—qualities that arise within us, that we need to actively develop for any of this Power to manifest at all.

We've looked at one of these already: Choice.

The second one (which actually precedes Choice), is Awareness.

It begins with this sobering reality:

We can't do anything about what we can't see.

UNDERSTANDING CREATES AWARENESS

When we're confronted with difficult circumstances or unpleasant feedback about ourselves—suddenly 'surplus to requirements' at work or struggling in relationships, trying to cope again and again with a mysteriously difficult life, we raise our heads from the coalface of existence and survival, and try to understand what's going on.

The pain pricks us into Awareness. We begin searching for answers.

Setbacks looked at and thought about are powerful teachers, *because they grow our Awareness.*

- We notice how we're responding.
- We probe for the Truth, and consider other options that might be possible.
- We review what it really 'means', and gain insights.
- We've learned something really useful.

Our Awareness of 'what is' becomes expanded, and we are brought closer to the 'Truth' we're always seeking.

We've had an Insight—which changes the way we see things, empowering us to make those new (and better) Choices that could change everything.

Now we can stash those Insights in our store of knowledge and experience to be drawn on whenever necessary—empowering us into truly effective responses.

This is the building of wisdom.

Wisdom is a state of expanded Awareness of what we know to be true, and of the complexity of things in relationship to one another.

Wisdom is gained through the amalgamation of our own experience, understanding, internalised knowledge, common sense and insight.

"Awareness" is *the* key (and powerful) agent in this.

THE POWER THAT LIES IN AWARENESS

I'll use the analogy of a flashlight (or torch) to illustrate this.

Light brings things into view.

We could say that our Awareness of ourselves in our Context is equivalent to the beam of a flashlight.

In the beginning, when we're born, our inbuilt flashlight (our Awareness) is capable of emitting only a tiny beam that illuminates only our immediate Context: our sense of hunger, and fear, and the milk that assuages those. We're barely aware of our own extremities, let alone the concept of a room, or a house; a town, or nation.

Later on, these come into our Awareness.

As we grow up and our Awareness grows with us, more of the 'landscape' around us is 'illuminated'. We know that our bodies can run, jump, and do cartwheels, and that we live on a street with other houses.

Over time, our growing Awareness illuminates even more. We know we're 'alive' (and what that means), we intuitively understand others and their needs and wants, and see ourselves generally in a wider Context: we know we're on a path, we 'see' more clearly about us and further ahead—we begin to see both the limitations we might be subject to and the possibilities we could seize.

> `'Awareness' becomes 'goggles' that enable us to see through and navigate 'the water'.`

The 'light' of our growing Awareness brings more and more into our field of vision over time. The options lying about our road and ahead, including other roads branching off (choices), a mountain range (obstacles), and a horizon (a destination or vision). The more we see, the more strongly and purposefully we can 'swim'.

- *Awareness*, powerfully, helps us to see more truthfully and with clarity what is really going on in us and around us—so that we can make powerful and purposeful choices. Depending on our insights (or lack of them) and our conclusions, we may choose to give up, or persevere; to change course, or simply continue banging our heads against a brick wall!
- *Awareness* extends our vision further into the distance so that we can better see what we're aiming for!

Awareness gives us a bird's eye view of ourselves, our life and of Life itself. Thus it's foundational to our wisdom (contributing to resilience in us). And it empowers great choices, so that we can remain in control of ourselves and our direction.

Our level of **Awareness is** exactly what we've been working on since the start of this book. I hope you can see it's power in you, already.

WHAT IS PERSONAL POWER REALLY?

When we consciously and deliberately combine these particular two of our inner endowments (Awareness and Choice)—which we *all* have—we can create almost anything at all!

This is *Internal* Power.

—And I draw attention to this, because unlike domination and "success", they're not dependent on environment or circumstance. They are endlessly available, generative, and restorative.

Which means that no matter what is going on in our lives, we always have these two Power generating attributes always at our disposal.

Distilling Personal Power into these two key elements allows us to see exactly *how* we gain and lose power, and how combining the two can empower us in any situation.

HOW IT WORKS

When we 'see' (Awareness)—and 'see' more broadly—we can deploy Choice (our tool of creation) *proactively and purposefully for powerful results*. The more we 'see', the more strategic and informed our Choices can be, which leverages and amplifies our Power and impact on key points—in the present, and for the future.

Clearly when the Awareness beam is small or low, we can only just see ahead. We can only push forward a few steps at a time in the present moment, making small obvious choices in terms of what's immediately apparent.

The wider and brighter our beam of Awareness, the more we see of our surrounds—and *the more clearly we can see through them*. We see the way ahead, the obstacles (and the way past or over them), and even something of our destination.

With all this in view we can make Choices that take many factors into account, like the current weather, or a vital water reservoir—and even the future, since we can see the horizon in the distance!

`Choices made on a foundation of a wider Awareness are Powerful.`

This is how some people make a fortune on the stock markets!

They put masses of Contextual information together to make strategic Choices. And the more aware they are of how things fit together and what else is out there, happening, and likely to arise—the better their bets are and the stronger the returns.

It benefits us hugely to be constantly and purposefully improving our level of Awareness, because the more we widen and brighten our beam—the more we "see" 'what is'—both in our immediate and personal environments, *and* in the wider one.

Building Awareness keeps us not only connected to the pulse of Life, evolution and change, but allows us to be deeply and powerfully responsive to it. Being more able to see and correctly interpret what is in our Context or Culturescape, allows us to remain centred—and thus empowered, rather than anxious and disempowered.

Our life's journey builds our experience, increasing our knowledge and Awareness, brightening our flashlight beam to illuminate more and more of our Context and possibilities as we progress.

PERSONAL EMPOWERMENT

When our disappointments, failures and suffering signal that something hasn't panned out as expected, we're thrown out of our external orientation, out of our assumptions, out of taking things for granted (for a moment at least)—and into an inward contemplation.

Our Awareness is rising.

As our understanding of 'what happened' and of what we've done deepens, we see what we were blind to, and gain some understanding of the part we've played in the experience or outcome.

Our *Self*-awareness now rises too.

We're able to see ourselves from a different perspective, and perhaps, somewhat more objectively.

SELF-AWARENESS IS DEEPLY SIGNIFICANT TO OUR OUTCOMES!

- What we know about ourselves, and how we feel about ourselves—affects how we put ourselves out there. What we turn towards and care about, how much effort we put into our actions and what we turn away from and discount—are all based on how able we are to gauge ourselves and our abilities accurately.
- Self-awareness also tunes us into what we need to develop within ourselves: what needs attention, and the skills or attributes we need to work on. A lack of self-awareness means we don't improve those aspects of ourselves that are causing us to trip up, and bringing about failures, disappointments and disconnection. We don't 'grow', but remain fixed in a life with outcomes that often don't work out as we'd like them to—and with no means to address this.

With self-awareness though, we're more able to see how we played in the mix, and thus more able to get out of our own way. We're better equipped to know what disempowers us and needs addressing, and how to play to our strengths.

This all nourishes opportunity for us! And we're much more able to make different Choices than we did before Self-Awareness: the kinds that are truly empowering.

Awareness is simply fundamental to personal empowerment.

Because we can't react or respond to—or effectively change — what we don't know about.

We put a stop on 'growing' when we have no self-awareness, because we learn little or nothing about the part we played in causing our outcomes, and remain in the dark about how and why things happened as they did.

Instead, we assume that 'we know' what has happened, and that 'we are right'. We don't doubt our interpretations of our experience, and believe that our thoughts about what we perceive has happened (and the feelings these generate) are true and objective too!

Our lack of self-awareness keeps us blind, limits and even blocks us: undermining our ability to be adaptable, resilient, creative and improving —and so incrementally reduces our Power.

Nothing can be done about what we don't see or realise. *—And not just what is actually going on, but the possibility that it doesn't have to be this way.*

HOW TO GROW OUR POWER

It goes without saying that to brighten our beam of Awarelight, we do need to be constantly, actively and purposefully moving ourselves as near to Truth as we possibly can.

Think of the lioness who misses out on the buck when her cubs are starving. Does she go home gutted by her failure?

No. She doesn't give it a second thought—because she's not Aware in that way. Not Self-Aware, nor aware that there may be another option for getting food, or another way of killing the buck itself.

All she knows is that to survive, she will have to go out and try again in the only way she knows how, when next an opportunity presents itself. She never questions it. She never feels lousy about it.

She doesn't have the Awareness to do so.

She's also not aware that it might be impossible, or that she might fail again. If she did, she possibly wouldn't try, and she and her cubs would definitely die. She has no choice other than simply to go out and try again and again until her life eventually ends.

We're different, because we are Human. We reflect on our experiences—and learn from them—the practise that expands and deepens our Awareness. It enables us to gain in Insight and to find other ways around the obstacles we meet as we work towards our goals and destinies.

Fixed ideas and beliefs, and general ignorance drain the batteries, and keep our flashlight on a low setting.

The important thing is that we *do* reflect, and learn.

PUTTING ON VISION GOGGLES

I've now brought the Power of Awareness to your attention.

Everything I've written about so far (and will still put before you as we go forward)—has been designed to raise your Awareness.

Remember that our Choices create our outcomes and our lives? Awareness is the key ingredient in refining our Choosing—our creative tool in Life and the manifestation of our Personal Power.

Our level of Awareness is the foundation of our response to the world, our lives, and the pain and the difficulties we encounter. Because what we know about ourselves, and how we feel about ourselves—affects how we put ourselves out there, what we care about and what we turn away from; in what we choose to do or not to do.

It therefore deeply informs how we react or respond (Choices in themselves); what we actually choose (or don't choose at all) to do, and how much effort we put into our actions.

The last thing we want is to unknowingly show up in ways that may push away or even sabotage our Power to create very real possibilities. Yet once we 'see' things, we become enabled to deliberately move away from what we don't want, and towards what we do.

Coming up in The Turning Point (the next Part), I'll be pointing to what specifically will be useful, to reach for and grasp.

GOGGLES AND SNORKEL

STOPPING UP OUR POWER LEAKS

*I*n the highly volatile, unpredictable and difficult-to-control context of Life, things often will not go the way we want them to.

That's reality. And it hurts.

Some of the pain we feel lies in the gap between what we envisaged and tried for—and where thought we would be—or actually are: and disappointment floods in.

We could be simply practical about this. We could shrug, gather ourselves, and try again. Yet often the meaning we attach to the cause of our disappointment simply floors us . *Life is unfair. I'm not enough.* —Or thoughts along those lines...

The harsh truth is that if something hasn't worked out as we hoped and tried for, there was probably something off about our analysis of the situation going in.

This doesn't mean we're wrong about our experience of pain of course. —Or that we haven't been handled harshly. But we do need to consciously seek the real truth of it, rather than become defensive and lash out, or fall into a sense of disablement. There's no point in flying in the face of what's perfectly "normal" with ongoing loud or mute objections, because we don't like it.

The longer we stay attached to what we think 'should' be—and feel frustrated, angry and despondent—the less time we spend in mending and healing through actually looking at the circumstances we're in, and the opportunities in those that are right before our eyes. We can't afford to throw our valuable hours away in toxic feelings and immobility! We cannot let anger or hurt or disappointment become our engine through Life. These will never lift us up and out of our difficulties—and can actually make us ill. And they will most certainly keep us from taking advantage of the possibilities that Life always has to offer!

FIRST—LET GO

Rather than being upset about the past, feeling stuck and ranting at the unfairness of the world, we would be better served by asking:

"What does the way that things played out, teach me? What can I learn from this?"

Letting go of our original agenda, our entitlements and the past-that-didn't-work-out enables us to meaningfully begin solving how to get from here to there.

And honestly, that's the only sane way forward. Because we are on a limited timeline.

What is—*is*. We must learn to empower ourselves in it, and despite it.

We must try. We must revisit the situation and our goals with creativity and hope and tenacity (our inner metal)—and take a next step.

FEED AWARENESS: REACH FOR TRUTH

Reviewing can give rise to Insights that can cause us to learn something, shift our assumptions, and make empowering Choices.

Being able to review what happened, adapt our behaviour, and get back up is the very reason we've risen to the top of the food chain as we have.

Yet if it is true that "experience" is simply subjective perception, how *do* we find Truth?

'Correct' perspective is a tricky, slippery customer: sometimes with us, sometimes not. *The first trick is to know this:* to know that often—usually, even—we're travelling through a situation alone and without this 'balancing' friend by our side.

Yet in fact, we have all the attributes we need to keep orientating to the true north of Truth.

When we're in emotional strife or inner turmoil, we experience ourselves in a 'wilderness' where we're unsure of how to interpret the 'landscape' we find ourselves in. We certainly feel triggered, struggle with our feelings, and notice the discomfort.

The feeling is the clue.

If we truly were out in the wilderness, it's likely that it would be a no-brainer to reach into our pocket and get out our trail map or compass!

Our inner attributes of awareness and curiosity that are exactly that. Our Awarelight has been triggered to become brighter at once, to shed "light" on the situation! We stop and review our inner experience of it.

THE BIOLOGY OF GROWING AWARENESS

Our 'Awarelight' will only grow brighter if we're prepared to be open and curious in the face of our losses, and resist our natural instincts to become defended and closed down by them instead.

The "biology" that grows our Awareness comes in the form of "Curiosity". Curiosity is the doorway that enables us to venture nearer to 'Truth'.

We do have a Choice here, but it's one we have to consciously make.

Because without actively seeking Perspective and the 'facts', we fall into (and live in) a misconstrued Context. With "Truth" missing, we're unable to attribute the correct Significance to things—bringing unnecessary experiences of pain and suffering to ourselves. In them, we cannot truly know whether what is happening to us is:

- normal and to be expected, handled and overcome.
- an important dealbreaker that will significantly affect something important, (including our own survival).
- some major inner work we need to embark upon.
- some key practical arrangements we need to review.

These may be huge decisions with great consequences—or simple things that can be handled without undue stress!

Too often, we'll simply veer away from trying for something because we're scared of failing, or being rejected or judged. Or we might turn away and give up resentfully; wallowing, hating ourselves, blaming ourselves—and perhaps even thinking seriously about giving up entirely.

We could instead decide to get back up after we've been knocked down and do things differently altogether: craft ourselves anew.

Or we might release, glad to be clear that whatever it was, it wasn't the right thing for us—free now to turn our precious remaining hours and energy to something else more suitable, inspiring and useful.

These are life-changing decisions and having proper perspectives when making them, is essential.

THROUGH THE DOORWAY

What will we discover in the Room of Curiosity?

- We'll get closer to discovering and understanding our real ideas and perspectives, and whether or not they're helpful or objective.
- We'll be incentivised to engage with our inner capacities of strength, resolve and resilience as we deal with the discomfort.
- We'll actively work on understanding where our Power lies. We'll see where we negotiated it, and how we danced to its tune. We'll know how much of it we (still) have—and what might build it further.
- Our wisdom and maturity will naturally grow as we begin to have Insights. We'll begin to level up our capabilities and creativity.
- Our true values in life begin to distill. Becoming clear on these and what really matters to us begins to override the reflexive drive to meet what we think we 'need' and to 'have more', and the addictive pursuit of external Power.
- Given our experience, we'll become kinder Human Beings as we develop compassion for Self, and others.

HOW TO BEGIN

As soon as we notice the *feeling* we're having, rather than immediately *reacting* to it and allowing the feeling to drive us, we become **curious** about that inner response. Now, aware that we may not necessarily be accurately interpreting what we're experiencing, we need to consciously **pause.**

Acknowledging the possibility that we've got it wrong takes ***Humility***. But we do need to be prepared always to double-check our assumptions, to probe our own assessments, before deciding on 'what is', and embracing it as fact.

Humility leads Curiosity by the hand.

Now is the moment then to step back, and centre ourselves, rather than step forward and tackle. In this centred moment, rather than giving in to feeling attacked, offended, criticised, minimised, or upset—or becoming defensive, we need to be genuinely interested.

When we're prepared to step back from a thing with openness and interest—and look at it again from a point of view other than our own, we're giving ourselves permission to be in learning (and growing) rather than being 'right'.

Learning is a powerful self-investment!

Imagine how different the world would be—how different we would be—if we all approached our failures with great curiosity and our sense of self-esteem intact, rather than constantly shrugging off 'being wrong' and working to place 'blame' elsewhere!

Because, truthfully, even if the outcome we're wrestling with is 90% *not* our fault, 10% *is* ours to own. We should be curious to know how we got the results that we did.

Being Curious opens us up. We now ask "Why?" (Learning by understanding). Ideally, we revisit our interpretations, and perhaps challenge them.

> *"What else could be true that I'm not considering?"*

We need to give ourselves permission to move out of the mindset of 'right' and 'wrong', 'good' and 'bad'.

Asking too, why we feel about it the way that we do, is powerful. Often, those feelings will tell us something about ourselves, rather than about the situation. While problems are inevitable, it's the *meaning we assign* to each problem, especially in relation to Who We Are, that is significant—and can ultimately become problematic.

"What if that failure wasn't really a failure, but the way I look at myself?"

"What if it's just the story I've been telling myself about it—because it clashes with some unthought-out old value that I carry?"

Curiosity stimulates our Awarelight; now it illuminates more than it was able to before. After questioning our assumptions, our perspective, our apparent 'grasp' of the facts and our objectivity, we "see" a bigger picture, and gain insights. We're closer to Truth now!

Since they widen our beam of Awareness, our lows can actually empower us, even while we may still be standing on the doorstep of failure!

ARE WE RESPONDING, OR REACTING?

When *any* 'situation' is unfolding around us, we're almost certainly seeing it through our own eyes rather than objectively. As we've seen, when our feelings bring crisis and pain, we might fall into the grip of our mental model without realising. And when 'danger' is perceived to be present, our fear can hijack our thinking—shutting off rational thought and proper analysis, often for long periods of time!

A chain reaction of events unfolds:

1. Our Silo of Self governs our Interpretations of what is unfolding.
2. Our mental models/anxiety cause us to attribute Significance to our Interpretation.
3. This affects our emotional state—which in turn, colours our Attitude.
4. Together these determine our Response—or—Reaction.

If we're able to pause for just a moment early on in this sequence to add in an extra step—and immediately double-check and even *challenge* our Interpretation, we might be able to hold back an immediate and instinctive *reaction—to* adjust our diagnosis, and *choose a Response instead.*

(And so we return to 'curiosity'.)

This, of course, is the goal! *But it does mean learning how to exercise some control over what and how we think.*

Because tricky Life gives us lots of cause to 'perceive' and if we don't *make a decision* to challenge our conclusions every time—to be conscious of our assumptions, to be more curious than 'right'—we're going to be miserable every time we aren't gratified—and subsequently disempowered.

Adding our new proven truths, facts, and norms into our 'Pictures' enables us to see things in their proper relationship, and in proportion to everything else. Now we're closer to True and enabled to attribute new (and more accurate) meaning to the experience. We can more consciously decide how it really matters to us, and what weight (Significance) to give it in our overall experience.

In turn, our emotional state is much more likely to remain calm and our Attitude more positive (and even optimistic)—putting a useful *Response* (rather than an off-the-cuff reaction) realistically within grasp.

> *During my husband's Cancer battle, the Cause of my painful effects (my misery, my sense of powerlessness) — was my particular view of the situation.* I couldn't shift my thinking away from the labels I'd given everything: 'this is good'; 'this is bad'; 'this is right'; 'this is wrong'. *I saw life through a filter of disappointment, and then later on — shame and worthlessness.*
>
> *I didn't understand at the time that I was thinking in terms of my mental models.*

With hindsight, I could see that the more that I did that, the more resentment (Attitude) I'd shown up with—and the less real effort, resilience, stamina, positivity and hope were there for my use: all things necessary for the situation alone to be less toxic. I felt more or less in control of my problems depending on the meaning I assigned to them; on how I chose to think about them. What was objectively true about my situation was not as important as how I saw the situation.

And how I chose to measure and value it.

It was only when I was actually able to challenge my Thoughts with new perspectives (I'm not the only person experiencing this, my husband is a good man who's getting better, my situation is difficult but manageable, and I'm not entirely the cause of it (shades of grey))—that I was first able to feel differently about everything.

Myself included.

> **If you're distressed by anything external, the pain is not due to the thing itself but to your own estimate of it; and THIS you have the power to revoke at any moment."**—Marcus Aurelius

Once I stopped blaming myself for my life going off the rails and hating myself for 'failing', I was able to look around for the first time and see the situation differently—even though an hour before, it was exactly the same as it was post perspective adjustment! And in that moment of shift, I was suddenly able to show up differently. For the first time.

And then, for the first time in a long time, I was able to begin to deliberately use my Power (of Choice) to recreate myself, and my life.

And all the results I got after that, changed.

Allowing our perceptions and assumptions to masquerade as truth or reality brings an incredible amount of ongoing discomfort and pain to our doors. And when we lose ourselves in this, we become increasingly powerless to change our situations, improve our lives, and grow ourselves.

Once we begin to direct our efforts more purposefully and productively however,

- we make *things* different for ourselves, *consciously* choosing to move deliberately away from what we don't want, and what doesn't serve us
- we purposefully move towards what we do want—by making *ourselves* different, stepping into who we need to be to get the life and outcomes we want.

The quality of our Responses is improved.

Our *Response* is creative—as Cause—and can change the way everything comes at us for the rest of the day, and the rest of our lives. This could be life-changing!

*Thinking with Awareness (*responding rather than simply *reacting)* means becoming conscious and of all that is going on inside us and Aware of how that colours everything—so that we can more correctly Choose how we construct meaning from experience.

This is really significant. Because…

More than anything else, our future is created by what we actually DO in the present moment.

ATTITUDE FLAVOURS PERCEPTIONS

We're all going to experience great difficulties along our way; terrible, regrettable moments in our lives. Sometimes more than moments (and often many of them)—that will throw us into a spin and cause "reality" to tilt on its side. It's essential that we truly strive to find perspective again each time—striving to remain in charge of:

- our labelling of whatever is going on (or not going on) as 'bad' and something that must be eliminated.
- our striving to respond, rather than react.

Not remaining in charge of ourselves in these ways makes getting "unstuck" conditional on something totally outside of our control.

Not doing so poisons our attitude—to ourselves, to others, to possibility, and to Life itself.

You might have heard this story:

> **One day, a little boy visiting at his grandparents' house, was angry and upset.**
>
> **His grandmother drew him onto her lap. "Do you know," she began, "inside each of us, there is a battle going on, between two wolves ."**
>
> **Her grandson looked at her, intrigued.**
>
> **"One is evil," she continued. "It is anger, jealousy, greed, resentment. The other is good. It is joy, love, hope, humility, kindness, empathy and bravery."**
>
> **The boy thought about it and then asked, "Grandmother, which wolf wins?"**

The old woman smiled and replied, "The one you feed."

Ultimately, *How We Show Up* to Context and to Life (regardless of Perspective) is generative—since we are Cause.

Holding onto negative feelings and the regrets that skew our Attitudes is only going to be feeding the evil wolf within us, with judgmental labels and feelings of loss, lack, uncertainty, stress, anger, blame, victimhood, and resistance.

But with a powerfully good attitude, we're already likely to be open, to be curious—and not labelling things "bad" in the first place!

What we focus on—grows. It's really that simple.

How We Show Up is therefore what matters most.

PART V
YOUR TURNING POINT

IGNITING OUR OWN EMPOWERMENT: RECLAIMING OURSELVES AND THE FUTURE

*I see ye visibly, and now believe
That he, the Supreme Good, to whom all things ill
Are but as slavish officers of vengeance,
Would send a glistering guardian, if need were
To keep my life and honour unassailed.
Was I deceived, or did a sable cloud
Turn forth her silver lining on the night?
I did not err; there does a sable cloud
Turn forth her silver lining on the night,
And casts a gleam over this tufted grove.*

—John Milton [14]

HOW I BECAME EMPOWERED

MY RECLAMATION STORY

*A*llow me now to share with you the massive perspective shift I experienced, that enabled me to pivot away from feeling stuck, miserable, disempowered and despairing—and towards the state of personal empowerment and joy that I'd spent all my life chasing 'having' and 'doing'—to achieve.

Being 'privileged' in being Caucasian and a beneficiary of Western culture, I was soft and entitled, in exactly the way I've just described, despite not having 'helicopter' or 'lawnmower'[15] parents!

Of course, at the time, I didn't know it!

MY CONTEXT

My husband's diagnosis arrived into a Context in which I had been struggling for ten years.

I was raising our children full-time and running our home. And this wasn't as easy as it might sound. Mainly, there were difficulties between our children which became divisive in our new family, so that instead of playing 'happy families', there was constant strain at home and, for the first time—in my relationship with my husband.

I was also at the tail end of the devastating twelve-year disintegration of my problematic relationship with my mother.

On top of those griefs, I'd been struggling with lingering regrets at having left my country and extended family when we'd moved overseas, and at having given up my career (and financial independence) when our first child was born.

It had been a lot of disruption and change in a relatively short space of time, all of which had served to erode my sense of Personal Power, reduce my choices, and deeply alter my possibilities. Instead of experiencing the expanded life I'd anticipated in becoming a mother and in changing countries, it felt as though I'd flown into a cage.

I felt a confusing sense of disconnection in every direction I turned. Most of all, a disconnection from my previously-empowered Self.

Because, even after I'd come to Awareness about all that had and was unfolding, I hadn't been able to mitigate any of it. There was simply nothing to be 'undone'. I had effectively shut the door on my past and the opportunities it had held.

And I had chosen all of it. I was having to lie on the bed I'd made.

The cancer disaster brought all of this to the surface: my despair about my sense of powerlessness at home and my personal lack of security and agency in the external world. My deep, deep sadness.

DOING

Now, in the face of my husband's illness, my attention turned to what I could 'do'.

Having always been directed to, and focused on "achieving", (generally successfully) I had little relationship with my own inner resources. In fact—I gave them no thought at all! I didn't recognise that they were there for me. I was only Aware of (and therefore only sought) the 'how' in the practical world.

"Success" in the form of an income stream would mean I could be responding to practical necessity, helping to meet our survival needs while my husband worked on his recovery. Being employed would surely even return me to something of my personal equilibrium—reducing the particular stress I was feeling of being out of control.

So I focused on doing: adding to my lists and keeping busy with nailing down the particular 'how' that would bring me 'there'.

But it was post 911, the workplace was becoming increasingly automated with job applications screened by algorithms—and frankly, the economy in Australia (when compared to the UK for instance) is small. Opportunity was commensurately small. And, as is the case in many Western economies, the Old Boys Club was where much of the job changing action for skilled and educated people was taking place.

I didn't know this of course.

I had no Awareness of behind-the-scenes locally, or of the global shifts that were taking place and the significance of those to my small efforts. I just became increasingly outraged and freaked out that the levers I was pulling to get this particular result weren't delivering.

> *In the depths of despair and overwhelm, I complained to my husband one day—"Why do we do anything? And why should we care? What is the point?"*
>
> *He looked at me, surprised. "We don't know why we're here. But we are—so what's the point of questioning it? The only thing to do is to get up and go into the day, making the most of what you have, and being the best person you can be.*
>
> *That alone would be meaningful."*

It was a good point. Gosh, if only I had been open to hearing it I could have saved us both years of heartache! *Pearls before swine*.... But he was speaking to that something-within-me that was currently closed down: perspective, tenacity, courage. An inner effort of Character!

The advice didn't gel with the cultural "brules" I was so deeply invested in. I wanted nothing less than reinstatement. I wanted a great external alchemical shift from where I was, back to *who* I was when Life was something that worked for me! I wanted restoration—we were good people who worked hard: we *deserved* restoration!

> **I believed that I could only be myself—be this best person I 'could' be—from a certain space: the reinstallation of the Context that had previously enabled me, to be "me". *That* was what had made me functional.**

I was to come to his wisdom after all.

But by my own path. In the writing of this book.

AN INNER GUIDANCE SYSTEM

Much of the information I found during my quest to bring my suffering to an end was useful.

But there is a profound difference between information that's platitude and the kind of meaningful information that creates insights and actually moves the needle in changing what's important to us.

"Happiness and peace are choices," I was told, for example. *"Breathe. Be grateful."*

Wtf?

The statement above does indeed hold deeper truths, but in the moment when it mattered — when I was on my metaphorical knees—it was absolutely meaningless, because it didn't help me cope either mentally or emotionally in the excruciating situation I found myself in.

Nor did it provide anything practically useful by which I could extricate myself from my circumstances. I couldn't begin to embrace the Truths contained in it.

So, through years of dissolution, I grieved my losses, with my perspectives very much stuck on what I'd lost, and how diminished my life and I were as a result.

OPENING TO SHIFTING

Yet, while my 'outside success' voice was reacting with terrible lament to loss and fear—and even asking to quit and die, at the same time I was still lucid enough to pay attention to a dogged little voice within.

This voice seemed quietly determined to resist the idea, never going along with schemes to end things, and trying repeatedly to bring me to another perspective instead. It kept on at me, tugging at my attention; writing up my real values on large placards in black ink, and waiting in a quiet back corner for me to throw it a glance.

When I did, it would hold them up for me to look at:

> *"Do you have the right to be in an ongoingly sad and stressed state about something that is simply your reality?"*

> *"Can you really, in good conscience continue to affect deeply and negatively those whom you love, just because* you're *miserable, and feel powerless to change your life?"*

My answer was 'No!' each time of course.

Yet as I saw it, if I couldn't turn things around practically, how *was* I to manifest any differently than I was? *I was legitimately unhappy!*

Time marched on.

Stubborn as I am, the months came and went. But eventually, I became weary.

"I-Am-Who-I-Am-Because-Of-Where-I-Am-And-What-I-Have-And-Do" — broke.

What I wanted, wasn't going to happen. "I" and my self-flagellation, my stubborn will, and my 'legitimate' grievances were nothing in the face of that implacable truth.

I had no option but to accept that.

SURRENDERING—OR—MY DARK NIGHT OF THE SOUL

It was part practical pragmatism:

> *"My kids need me, and I can't give up on them. I'm on this road. I have to get on with what I can."*

And part petty, self-pitying capitulation:

> *"I'll let go of all my ideas of what makes a good life; let go of my expectations. I won't care about them, or have any personal hopes. I'll put myself aside."*

I reached rock bottom.

> *"I no longer care about what I WANT anymore. It really doesn't matter."*

Perhaps the phrase "The Dark Night Of The Soul" has a particular meaning on the mystical journey—I may be misusing the phrase. But for me, it was when I finally *allowed*—including allowing a kind of personal disappearing, to take place. I let go. Of everything.

> **I gave Life permission to be what it was. I gave myself permission to simply 'Be' in the space of the great force that Life is.**

I surrendered to what was, and importantly—surrendered *feeling* something about it. Surrendered myself to absolute powerlessness, with deep acceptance of that. Allowing… ego to dissipate, and the dissolution of agenda in the presence of this. Simply Being present to the present moment.

Ultimately I was making peace with Life itself.

Accepting my practical limitations now meant I was prepared to undertake things I would not have previously considered. So, some time later, when the possibility of working in Aged Care and Disability came up, I decided it was an Opportunity.

It was nothing like I was used to doing, and I wasn't trained for it, but it was *something*. A start at least.

I put my hand up and stepped forward.

NEW INFORMATION

My clients were all disabled or aged.

One had developed multiple sclerosis during a successful career, and had also suffered a stroke, leaving her paralysed down one side of her body.

Another had developed Parkinson's Disease in the midst of a healthy and happy life. Another was a famous TV person in Australia, struggling in the early stages of Dementia.

Others needed more care than their families were able or prepared to offer, and were living in Aged Care Facilities.

And another (who became my main client) was an intelligent middle-aged gentleman whose Muscular Dystrophy had gradually, over the years, robbed him of the ability to move—and even to breathe for himself. Prone, with his arms and legs permanently bent, he was dependent on a ventilator, and needed 24 hour care. Funding cuts meant that the fully qualified nurses who'd cared for him previously were no longer affordable—and so it was that someone like me was trained up to take care of him with his very complex care needs.

Though I didn't know it to begin with, this work (along with a later insight)—was to be a major turning point for me, that would change my life.

But now, after years of feeling frustrated, angry, alone and worthless, I was suddenly earning something again—not much, but enough to allow me to start making some choices—while making a vital and positive difference in others' lives.

ENCOUNTERING THE QUALITY OF GRACE

The first thing that really struck me, was noticing that these people, who had much less than me—and who had suffered greater losses in their lives than I ever had—*never wallowed in misery or self-pity*, despite having plenty of reason to. —And not because they were too disabled to know their conditions!.

Every one of them rose each day with hope for another chance to be themselves.

Every one of them carried their burdens with grace and good humour, rather than bitterness.

Every one of them showed gratitude for the help and support they were given in general, and by me in particular.

My main client was simply next level in this (though of course he had no awareness of what I was beginning to observe). Despite not being able to move anything but his hands, he simply refused to let his physical limitations dictate his possibilities or how he showed up in his life and relationships.

He'd completed a degree (achieving a First) by the time I started working with him, and had been invited by the University to complete his Doctorate. He'd bought a small home—saving for it from his meagre income over many years. He owned a blog, and was about to marry (one of his Carers).

And he was always pleasant, good humoured, and philosophical about what had happened to him.

I was humbled by all these people, and by him in particular. They put me, in my misery, to shame.

> **I found myself regularly and unexpectedly in the presence of grace. The old and the disabled towered above me with courage in adversity, and in kindness and gratitude.**

I t was a privilege to be helping them.

A LIFE-CHANGING INSIGHT

Then, one day, browsing the web, I came across a quote from Plutarch.

 "What we achieve inwardly will change outer reality."

And the penny finally dropped. *This* was what I was seeing in my clients.

Although we may lose (or not even have, to start with) our ability to manifest certain practical hopes and ideas, there is another part of ourselves that we can make an enormous difference to every single day.

In the way we show up.

All the stories of people who have demonstrated to the rest of us just how magnificent and inspiring a Human Being really can be—sprang to mind then.

Ordinary people who, in the face of adversity—despite suffering through terrible circumstances, pain, loss, and fear—defined themselves through their values and actions.

By their grace.

Nelson Mandela, Mother Theresa, Desmond Doss, Helen Keller and Martin Luther King jnr are just some examples.

And in doing so, they inspired others, and created unbelievable change.

The enormity of Plutarch's truth struck me with the force of a surge of lightning. Life is much more than an *external* self-actualising via the trappings of "success".

We are not our situations or circumstances. Whatever else may be going on around us—we are ourselves first.

I really care about things, and go out of my way to be helpful and a part of the solution.

I work very hard—I'm never lazy.

I try always to be kind. I don't lie. And I strive for excellence always, in all things.

But I was clearly terrible at accepting *"what is"* with grace.

When I compared my own attitude with my client's; with his strivings and the grace with which he accepted his lot—yet *still tried* for something visionary—I saw a rather small effort on my part to be all that I could be, as a Human Being.

I had been asserting (to myself at least) that my negative thoughts, anger, bitterness, sadness, fear, self-flagellation, and wish to give up—were a reflection of *legitimate unhappiness*? It dawned on me that not only was that victim speak, but it was awfully entitled too.

A TURNING POINT

My long derailment and subsequent employment had brought me face to face with my deeper attitudes and relationship with life, confronting me brutally now with an ugly inner landscape:

- A negative attitude.
- Entitlements, and concomitant bitterness.
- My lies to myself.
- Selfishness.

My external efforts were not congruent with my inner values that I thought I swore by. I wasn't living in integrity!

I needed to shift my image of myself and my idea of what a good and worthwhile life was. Instead of looking at everything I lacked, I needed to look at everything I *had*—to see what I could leverage!

I had the *duty* to take control of my life and attitudes.

Instead of allowing myself to be defined by what I had or didn't have, what I looked like, how many qualifications or friends I had, or what assets I had managed to accumulate—I could define myself.

Through the quality of my character, and Choices.

As he had.

My husband's words came back to me now:

 "The only thing to do is to get up and go into the day, making the most of what you have, being the best person you can be."

The wisdom and insights were there all along.

CREATING MY FUTURE

It was time to respond more consciously to my crisis if I didn't want the derailment to assert more authority over the shaping of my future than I could.

If I was going to be all that I could be as a Human Being, I had to take charge of myself, no matter what was going on in my external environment.

I had to become a Creator. *The creator of who I am, what I stand for, how I respond to life, belief, circumstance, and others — as well as what I do 'out there'.*

That meant striving to understand what makes a great Human Being, and how I could Be that, regardless of circumstance, provocation, lack, or inner feelings. I was going to have to discover ways to flesh that out, strengthen and define it, and polish it up so that it would shine brilliantly.

Once my sense of my entitlements fell away, I started to look outwards and beyond them, and wondered if, perhaps… instead of seeing suffering as something repugnant, I could learn to embrace it as part of my experience, honouring it for creating conditions in which I could be stimulated to become the best version of myself that I could muster.

This *was* my road, regardless of the fact that I didn't set out on it, didn't want it, and believed that I should be on some highway, somewhere else! And I'd already spent far too much time going over what had happened to bring us to this point, blaming Self and others, and/or circumstances—and resisting where I'd found myself as a consequence.

Being in a state of resistance had changed nothing at all. It had drained power from me instead—distracting me from using my 'present moments' effectively to move forward out of 'stuckness', and into something else.

CONNECTING THE DOTS

When it came to shifting things, I could see that letting go of my expectations about what "should be"—and accepting "what is" had been key to opening me up to my new possibilities.

Putting 'I' aside and getting out of my own way; being opened then to a whole world of Human existence that I'd never *had* to glimpse before (let alone even see myself as part of)—had been life-changing.

The path I had trodden with all it's obstacles and potholes had brought me to this very place, in the very condition I found myself in.

It all connected up. And these new insights they'd brought me, were a very good thing indeed.

When I look back now at all that has unfolded since my husband's diagnosis—at the regrets over the decisions we made, the disappointments over what happened or didn't happen, or at what we did or did not do or say: at what happened to us—a deep appreciation for all of it has blossomed within me.

The pain became the path.

A NEW 'WHY'

I had finally come through and out the other end of suffering — as a person who now saw possibility in her life.

But most of all, as one who wanted to liberate the potential within herself.

So what was *I* going to do on this new road?

I decided that I would do whatever it took to walk it with my head up; to appreciate the walking, to do it well, and to be open to a new and unknown destination and whatever lay there. I was (and actually always had been) in charge of the direction and speed at which my mind, heart and spirit could travel.

I now wanted not only to travel this road, but to *learn* to travel it, no matter how hard it was. Instead of trying to dictate the options and outcomes I wanted, I promised myself that I would be open to whatever the Universe brought into my life.

And where previously I had used my will to make my life work practically, now I would lean on my resolve, my spirit, and the strength of my character.

My inner strength.

This quest became my meaning.

We think that our life's purpose is to do something special, to be noted as special. We've been trained for this, and think we know how to make this happen.

And we often succeed, wholly or in part.

But we learn when that something special is taken from us, that our concept of a life's purpose has been extremely limited.

> **Our life's purpose is something we're supposed to Be — rather than do, or have.**
> **And we can co-script _everything_ about Who We Are and Become.**

Although at first my rational mind refused to accept the changes in my life, I had come to see everything that had happened—as leading me to find and fulfil my true potential.

To sculpt who I am.

∽

THE VITAL PIVOT

NOTHING CHANGES, UNTIL YOU DO

*P*erhaps, feeling some resonance with what I've been saying here, you're still with me now because you're actively looking for a real way—a useful, sustainable way—out of the shattered remains of what *was* possible for you.

Perhaps, there's a rebellious part of you that, like me, hasn't *wanted* to take the mindfulness advice of turning away from ambition, and letting go of expectations and agendas!

—A part of you that doesn't want to lie down and give up.

—A part that's saying "NO DAMN WAY! I'm unhappy. I'm disappointed. I may be feeling useless and hopeless, *yet there is something in me that could — that should — be expressed, and be manifested!*"

GOOD! I say!

 "Hope is the last thing that dies in man." —Francois de La Rochefoucauld

There is no way you should ever give up striving for a joyful, meaningful Life! To be your best, most thriving Self! There is so much to live for, to try for—*especially* in these rapidly changing times!

And there is so much you *can* do to retrieve your agency in Life, while reaching for joy and peace.

And yes. *I'm speaking directly to you now.*

YOU ARE NOW AT A TURNING POINT

You could decide that this has all been interesting, but that's all. You could put this book down—and get on with whatever you were doing before, (though hopefully you'll find it hard to un-hear and unlearn what you have inadvertently discovered here!).

That might be… harking back to the old days and the old ways. You might spend the next few years in both this wider, ongoingly changing Context we're caught up in and the smaller detail of your own life—looking backwards over your shoulder, and calling for reinstatement.

You might conclude that we're all simply on 'pause' while the 'Powers that Be' sort everything out, and when they do, you'll go back to 'business as usual'—so wait it out, unchanged and unchanging.

Or—you could decide to perform a pivot. A *vital* pivot.

You could settle on something other *than what you've been settled on, up to now.*

You could embrace going forward in a new framework for your existence, on a new path. This would be founded on growing your personal inner power, rather than working mainly to cement your external power in having things and accumulating 'desirable' labels.

Because when you are empowered *within*, there is a lot less that Life can throw at you that will knock you down… That will keep you down.

- —that will keep you down.

- —that will have you scrabbling because you don't know how to be in a world that's inherently unfair and where there are no real rules.
- —that will have you losing faith in your Self, disconnected from your Self; grappling with feelings of misery and hopelessness when you're called to withstand hardship.
- —that will have you feeling so disempowered that you wish for oblivion instead.

Instead, Empowered, you will stand tall in yourself. You will have resilience. You'll be able to maintain your equilibrium, and help others with theirs. You will engage joyfully in what is meaningful to you.

You will make the difference you are here to make.

You will feel peace.

> "It is not the end of the physical body that should worry us. Rather our concern must be to live while we're alive — to release our inner selves from the spiritual death that comes with living behind a facade designed to conform to external definitions of who and what we are." —**Elisabeth Kubler-Ross**[16]

Unlike what you've done in the past, you will be engaging in conscious growth, rather than growth by default.

This takes intention and effort. It means *deciding* to embrace the challenges that come to you, rather than spending all your energy and effort in trying to get away from them!

You'll be focusing on strengthening your "inner musculature" and developing the capacities and resources you already have, to cope with Life's inherent challenges.

ALLOW ME TO PERSUADE YOU

You're on your current trajectory in any case. And there is no going back. There is only going forward. You've not got what you want (or perhaps even what you need)—but you still have to show up until your end actually arrives! You still must rise every day and step into living and breathing: stepping forward into time.

It's desperately uncomfortable to keep enduring what you've been enduring—yes. But while change itself is uncomfortable, *not* changing will be more so. You cannot carry on as you are, with all doors locked against you.

EVERYONE suffers awful luck at some point. (And extra bad luck seems to follow some of us!) EVERYONE makes mistakes, some of which result in difficult and long lasting outcomes. Yet most are recoverable.

The key is to understand what they were, why they happened—what drove them. IS there a pattern? Will we do the same again in a different way but for the same reason?

 "When we deny the story, it defines us. When we own the story, we can write a brave new ending." **—Brené Brown**

Let's not forget. *You are Cause.* The only thing you are in absolute charge of—and truly capable of influencing—is yourself.

Know this:

Nothing Changes Until You Do.

It goes without saying that doing the same thing over and over again, while expecting different results, is only going to result in more of the same—deepening disappointment and disillusionment. More sadness. More dwindling of hope.

Because the law of Cause and Effect is immutable.

If you don't like your 'Effects' you must work on yourself as the Cause. Even if it's just your mindset—in which you *interpret* the Effects as 'bad'.

You need to take *responsibility* for this.

What else *is* there to do but look forward, now resolved to impact the places where you *do* have influence, and determine to grow yourself into the capable, wise, balanced and engaged person you need to be, to better and more widely impact what is truly valuable and important to you?

BECOMING CONSCIOUS OF YOUR UNCONSCIOUS

Think on this: while you're well able to look around you with discernment at what others are doing, at the attitudes and values they embody and the patterns they are following—more often than not *you've* been living by default and functioning on autopilot. Not *consciously* choosing.

Often not deciding at all.

And you've *liked* living this way! Whether that's simply following the line of people off the aeroplane to the baggage claim, or driving with unconscious competence while your mind freely roams elsewhere. You don't really think about *what* you do, or *why* you do it. Or even how it defines you! It's been comfortable to just 'be'. Maybe you even regularly deploy sayings, like—"no brainer"—to express this as a value: something you don't have to waste time thinking about.

You've done what you've done because:

• that's how its 'done'.

• that's what you were taught.

• that's how your family has always done it.

Most of us don't decide consciously what would be empowering to believe. We get stuck with the ideas and stories our families have bequeathed us, by our Culturescape—and by our lived experiences that have become *belief* about ourselves and our lives.

And since most of these beliefs are subjective stories and generalisations based on painful experiences and a lack of success in our pasts, they're limiting — and actually disempowering.

Yet they run us.

As Carl Jung once said:

 "Until you make the unconscious conscious, it will direct your Life and you will call it fate.".

If we don't look for the patterns in our behaviour; if we don't think about what went before and why, we get stuck in unconsciously creating and repeating patterns and outcomes—and in the consequences of these, some of which are very hard to undo. We then become mired in an unsatisfying life with unproductive relationships, while feeling miserable and powerless, and often with low self-esteem to boot.

This was what Socrates meant when he said, 'The unexamined Life is not worth living".

Because we're then not *responding*, but waking every day to a constantly reactive existence—rather than a crafted life that brings the unique joys and fulfillments that we each crave.

The truth is, this situation you're now experiencing is an invitation to examine the assumptions that have propelled you to this place in time: your assumptions about Life and about yourself.

And these might need to change.

Actively taking on the habitual patterns and limiting beliefs you live by, and exchanging them for Choices aligned with Awareness — that are consequently expansive—is a simple shift that will have you showing up with more powerful actions in every day that's 'gifted'* to you.

LIFE INVITES YOU DAILY—TO LEVEL UP

While we're not definite about what 'Life' here on Planet Earth is all about, hopefully you see that our purpose here in this strange Life is to grow ourselves; that, as *living* creatures, Growth is the one thing we are *supposed* to do.

Change and Growth are your birthright …

…rather than Happiness (which is a side-effect of Attitudes and Choices).

Growth is about Change. Handling this, at the very least, will be asked of you during your life—from the moment you were born to the moment you pass away. Relentlessly and ongoingly—whether it's growing up, carrying out a job, raising a baby, developing your capabilities and skills, or simply managing internal perspective shifts—you must find the way to accomplish Change.

Since Change and Growth mean breaking down and doing away with what often matters terribly to you—from daily disappointment to the deaths of loved ones—you'll suffer. Your experience has shown you this truth already.

You'll regularly be grappling with the reality of 'I have what I don't want,' and ' I don't have what I do want'—finding yourself striving for what may remain elusive, and often feeling disappointed.

Resistance to Change and dissatisfaction with 'what is' will keep you in a state of lack, disconnected from opportunity and your own sense of power and possibility—and even from the people you love most. Resistance will keep you feeling depressed, demoralised and profoundly unhappy.

You want certainty; to know how it will all turn out. But to be truly empowered, you need instead to embrace Change, accepting the inevitability of its shifts and the difficulties and Possibilities that come with those—which include both suffering and joy. In empowerment, you come to see all of this as 'normal'—and trust that not only will you get through it and to the other side at some point, but that you are *capable* of doing so: capable of bearing the discomfort for as long as it takes, without breaking into pieces.

This may sound unlikely, but if you allow it, the interventions of Life can be a catalyst for something even bigger than your original Picture, ultimately deepening and empowering you beyond what you could ever have imagined for yourself.

Instead of seeing your 'disaster' as something that happened *to* you, you need to come to see it as something that has happened *for* you. For your growth.

And when you do step back and adjust your perspective, you may also come to accept that suffering absolutely has caused you to grow and develop, by forcing you out of what feels comfortable—was both limited and limiting.

And you may welcome not only the Change that was wrought, but also the way it was done.

Finding peace (and therefore happiness) is accomplished by consciously becoming ourselves. It is exactly that simple, and exactly that difficult.

But this is what you need to do next.

SEIZE THE DAY

You are where you are now—and this is your Life. You're here, in the School of Hard Knocks, consolidating the lessons that have brought you to this point in your life.

All is not lost. **And everything is still possible.**

You've simply reached the point where you absolutely have to review, and make clear, informed choices to create your next act.

You simply have to level up your personal characteristics, capabilities and skills—to get 'there'.

The healthy plant that you are, remains, brimming with the seeds of your own potential. It's time to meet them—perhaps for the first time—to liberate them, and then to learn to nourish and grow them!

I invite you now, to level up, with me.

---

* See "*Make Peace With Your Pain*" in the next chapter.

YOUR EMPOWERMENT PATH

PUTTING PERSONAL POWER INTO PRACTISE

*B*ut what to do with what I've been given to carry?

The first thing to do is to believe in yourself as a person who matters, and to believe in your life as full of potential—regardless of what is going on around you, or how tough your challenges and circumstances are.

Here's a reminder:

> **I am not my health, situation or circumstances. I am myself first.**

In other words, you are more than the results of your environment or the conditions (including health) in which you find yourself.

When you hold to that truth, you can accept that there are events and circumstances in your life that are not a result of "Who You Are" or even "What You Did Or Didn't Do". There simply *are* things you cannot change. *And you are whole and valid regardless of them.* However…

 "When we are no longer able to change a situation, we are challenged to change ourselves…" **—Viktor Frankel**

Whatever freedoms are taken away from you, Frankel says, you always retain the power to choose what becomes of you mentally, emotionally and spiritually.

Under any circumstances. (Frankel would know.)

Yes, situation and environment hugely influence whether a person comes from 'the wrong side of the tracks' and behaves accordingly. Yet there are also those (*many* of those in fact) who have seen "Who They Could Be" *despite* the side of the tracks they find themselves on — and have pulled themselves up by their bootstraps.

Don't make excuses for what you're like. Decide who you want to be, and then reach for that Self.

The person You are is the result of an inner decision, not the result of your situation.

This is a freedom—that can't be taken away from you—and is ultimately what makes life meaningful.

LET'S BEGIN: WHAT TO ACTUALLY DO

Decide to try.

You will only get somewhere if you decide to try. You know from past experience that it will be challenging, and yet, made newly aware with the Insights and perspectives you've found here, and armed with resolves and the strength of your character—you can choose to move forward nonetheless.

Make this your initial Choice. Decide to live every day with as much courage and powerful striving as you can muster.

Next—re-evaluate your 'Purpose'. Give yourself a new 'Why'.

Remember, we're really here to grow, so setting your sights on becoming the kind of person you intend *and need yourself to be*—is the first step in a useful direction.

Placing your efforts on growing and developing yourself rather than always only working to change your circumstances or others is an active decision, that changes your life as you go forward.

You don't need "stuff" to try for something, to be loving to those you care about, or to show up as an amazing person.

Which you are. But it does take effort, and then—perseverance.

This initial 'purposeful' endeavour brings a sense of Meaning. Meaning gives you the 'means' (see 1. *INNER MUSCULATURE* below) to *strive* your way out of difficulty—or at least find the resilience to carry it while things are in transition.

—And they *are* in transition! Everything is changing all the time. Nothing stays the same forever. This is a hugely important truth to hold onto in times of difficulty.

The first step is always the hardest (beginnings often are)—and this isn't even hard! You are alive right now. You can make changes in your life starting this very minute! Simply *decide* to try.

Why? *Because of who you will become in the process.*

This is the purpose of all our lives: to become Who and what we can Become.

Who You Are, over what you do, what you have, and even what others do.

And there is only one way to do that.

You 'create' yourself by working on your specific character-istics, developing personal traits that are self-defining, positive and strong, that enable you either to handle and overcome your problems, or to live with them with grace, remaining balanced and intact in the face of them.

1. INNER MUSCULATURE

Feelings of defeat, fear, despair and hopelessness are nihilistic, and if you allow them to *inhabit* you, you'll be left with nothing but a sense of the pointlessness of loss, struggle and suffering—and little reason to go on enduring it. They need to be *actively* pushed back, from the 'means' within you.

The 'means' refer to drawing on your inner qualities, first to manage—and then to prevail in difficult circumstances.

Resilience and *resourcefulness* are examples. Holding onto the sense of possibility is another.

Those inner qualities *are* there, but you may have to develop them. While you *are* growing and changing all the time, *you need to take an active part in sculpting yourself,* into not only Who You need To Be to create and realise the life you want—but the Self you *aspire* to be.

Because our inner world 'creates' our outer world—straightening out our inner world is a prerequisite to working on our outer world.

This means that you need to become crystal clear with—*Who You Really Are.*

- How do you show up in Life—and what effect does that have on others, and on you?
- What are your attitudes? Are you negative? Do you find yourself wondering *what's in it for me?*—when you show up? Or does the room light up when you walk in as people feel seen and appreciated by you?

- Are you generous—or entitled when it comes to 'what you can get'?
- Are you honest? Or do white lies and exaggerations often creep in?
- Are you honest with *yourself*? What do you admit to?
- Do you do what you say you'll do: do you keep your word? Sometimes, or all the time?
- Do you hold yourself to the same standards of behaviour and attitude you hold others to?
- Do you take responsibility for yourself and your actions? —Or do you tend to blame others or circumstances when things go 'wrong'?
- What are your ethical values? Do you live in terms of them?
- Do you work hard or are you somewhat lazy? Do you give of your best? Are you part of the solution, or might you be part of the problem?
- How do you contribute to (or take away from) people and places?

With all this, what qualities of Choice are coming out of the person you currently are? What *could* come out of the person you believe yourself to be, or when you're wiser, braver, better, kinder—more powerful?

Remember: **Nothing changes—until we do.**

2. CHECK ATTITUDE

In stories, poems, wise sayings and scriptures, there are many analogies for Life as a "road we travel". Behind us lies what was; ahead of us lies what is yet to come.

We travel it in present time, journeying forward with no idea of what we may encounter. How smooth or bumpy, exposed or shaded the road may be. We have no idea how long ours is—or truly where it leads! All we do know is that at some point, we will be done and off it; that the full-stop of Death will end our journey—whether that leads off a cliff or into Nirvana.

How we do the journey though, is our Choice. Running forwards, face to the wind. A slow, hesitant progress, holding back somewhat; head down. Or, turning away, looking backwards over our shoulder. —With a smile of optimism, or with a frown of doubt and mistrust!

A renowned scientist (and also a *great* philosopher) once said—

> "The most important question you're ever going to ask is, Is the Universe friendly?" **—Albert Einstein**

This may seem an odd question from a brilliant scientist, who offered answers to other, deeply important questions about Life! But it speaks of something vitally important in Human life that we often don't think about, much less give weight to.

Because your answer reveals something about your Attitude to Life. And why is Attitude important? Because...

How you see your world is how you speak to yourself about it—and about yourself.

Your interpretations determine how you feel—about Yourself, your relationships, your work, the events of life, the opportunities that present themselves, and your Power in all of it. These feelings shape your attitudes—and therefore your Responses. And attitude is generative! As Einstein knew, your attitude determines everything about how You show up, what you strive for, what kinds of Choices you make, and how your Life plays out overall.

Most people believe that the Universe is indifferent to us. Sometimes it seems to be working with us; at other times it's at cross purposes. None of it really matters, because we're just here, in random, unknowable space-time, for random, unknowable reasons. We don't really matter either.

Many others believe that the Universe is unfriendly and makes things difficult for us. Bad luck is thus always in potential, ready to rush in at the slightest opportunity. Naturally of course, then they feel helpless at some level, and afraid! *What will happen to us next? How next will we be disappointed, abandoned, betrayed, annihilated, eviscerated?*

What kinds of Choices can you make in the face of fear, if you're already fearful? —When you feel powerless, and like everything else on the planet—pointless?

And, if you think the Universe is malevolent, cruel and out to get you, how do you possibly maintain *hope*?

Certainly there can be no trust in anyone or anything! You must be on guard at all times, careful not to make mistakes—expecting always the worst to avoid disappointment. All you really can do is be on the lookout for the next hit—and duck when it comes, fingers crossed (or pray if that's a value for you).

A BENEVOLENT UNIVERSE

Many people though, assume that the Universe is actually friendly.

So, if something happens that could be 'bad'—they're reluctant to put the label on it or allow themselves to feel diminished by it. Perhaps the thing wasn't bad! Perhaps things happen for one, rather than to one. Thus, when a door is shut against them or they didn't get that thing they desperately wanted, they allow that the Universe may be giving them exactly what they need at that precise moment for their learning and growth. Perhaps good things will come their way (even if only eventually)! Perhaps good can (and will) arise from the ashes, given time.

The point is, *they're prepared to remain open to the experience.*

When you think about things in this way, regardless of whether the Universe is actually friendly or not, it's obvious that this Attitude is probably a good thing— certainly a better thing—over the cynical, pessimistic and negative one!

It's the difference between being hopeless and hopeful: a victim or a participant.

Believing in a friendly Universe means you're more likely to travel your road with acceptance and resilience when things go wrong. —More prepared to invest yourself in trying a new way (or a new thing altogether) with a sense of ongoing possibility, with trust in your next move and the likelihood that it will bring some reward. In this space you'll have a positive attitude, enthusiasm, determination, motivation, patience and a great work ethic, for example.

NOTE THIS: None of these positive qualities have much to do with a person's genetic makeup or physical, emotional or mental abilities. None of them are talents or aptitudes. They all are the 'Effects' of self-chosen Attitudes that translate into effective behaviours, including personal resilience and equanimity.

Attitude is the foundation for the building and sustaining of Inner Musculature.

This outcome isn't just the conclusion of the late, great scientist and philosopher Einstein, though. Dr. Martin Seligman actually proved this— in his monumental, ground-breaking book, *Learned Optimism*[17] where he found that negative people become sick more often, divorce more frequently, and raise kids who get into more trouble.

Clearly, out of these different models of reality, one is more empowering than either of the others—and one actually puts us down! Does it really serve you to believe that you're in a pointless, hostile Universe? Does it even make sense to impose such an idea on Life, which is all about thriving and abundance?!

What if the Universe IS ACTUALLY friendly?

We can't know of course, but it simply makes sense to choose an attitude that serves us; an attitude that has been proven to bring better results to those who employ it—over one that closes us down.

Make your Second Choice now. Decide to adopt the positive, trusting Attitude that will truly serve you on your new path.

What is the point of anything less?

3. BRING THE LOCUS OF CONTROL BACK TO SELF

Hopefully you're Aware of it now, if you've vested much of your Power in the external approval levers of what you do, have, look like and in who you know. If—when your Context changes or has changed—your Power (and even your identity) has gone with them, know that, without realising it you've moved your *locus of control outside of yourself.*

It's important to work on breaking the default thinking that has fogged you up with seductive cultural "brules". Know that even just becoming Aware of them enables you to begin shifting away from living out *patterns* of thought, belief and behaviour—to consciously Choosing more useful actions and habits, that you can sustain.

This alone orientates you to an internal driver.

Shifting from the external to the internal is another Choice. Doing so will mean that Context (including environment and others) no longer controls you through being available—or not. You'll be empowered from within instead: in your Attitude (to everything!) and by your inner qualities of patience, effort, acceptance (including self-acceptance!), self-discipline and courage, for example.

You'll be *generating* great responses to Life, rather than reactively trying only to fix your Context (environment and others). *You* are the Powerhouse/Creator at the centre of your own life.

Your values and attitudes are sculpting your Choices and actions, and these are creating results for you. This inner Sanctum (and the qualities you develop there) is the only thing you can truly control.
—In other words, your Self.
***This* is the nucleus of your Power.**

Again—the only environment you are *truly* in control of, is your inner one. So the energy you've been expending managing outcomes outside of yourself, is more powerful when directed inwards now, to grow your mindset, your habits, your efforts, your competency and skills.

4. MAKE PEACE WITH YOUR PAIN

You've probably heard the proverbial saying "Every cloud has a silver lining"—handed out by someone being 'wise' in a moment of disappointment for you.

Well, the word 'gift' carries a hidden meaning in it too, that can offer an even more powerful and empowering perspective in these painful moments.

May I explain?

PRESENT

A word used in place of 'gift' sometimes, is 'present'. John Ayto writes in his Dictionary of Word Origins[18] "The use of the related word 'present' for 'gift' originated in Old French, in the concept of 'bringing something into someone's presence,' and hence of giving it to them."

Gifts are given to express love, or to uplift people in times of sadness or loss as symbols of care and concern. Many would say that the purpose of a gift is to bring joy or happiness into the life of someone else.

Life itself is even often referred to as a gift.

THE GIFT

The etymology of this word arose out of the English word 'give'. It's use was later influenced by the Greek-Late Latin word 'dosis'—which meant both 'gift' and a certain amount of medicine. Too much of the dosage could make it poisonous instead of stimulating healing (in other words, it became 'giftig').

So 'Gift' was increasingly related to a "deadly dose" colloquially. It surely comes as no surprise then, that the word 'gift' is also the German word for 'poison'.

We still see this idea in play today in Medicine. We vaccinate someone to stimulate a response from the immune system, by giving them a micro-dose of that particular pathogen. The immune system, now triggered, learns something about what is foreign to it, and then develops a resource within itself that is now able to keep the body safe from future incursions of that particular pathogen! Homeopathic remedies work on a similar theory.

PUTTING THESE TWO IDEAS TOGETHER

Something that stimulates your Awareness—is brought into your Presence. This stimulation is uncomfortable, even painful. 'Giftig'—or Poisonous—it kills off 'what was'.

The parallel with immunisation lies in that you now have a deepened experience of Life, and so have become wiser. You will not be caught out in the same way again; you will not make the same foolish Choices, or go down the same dark paths.

Your hardships and the pain they bring are a Gift in your life; bringing into your Presence and Awareness the 'something' that can stimulate you into a stronger, wiser, and ultimately more powerful Self.

As we've seen, when your Awareness is expanded, you see further and more broadly, and are more able to improve the quality of your Choices so that they're more positively generative, powerful ones.

Look for the 'gifts' you've been given in your pain. They are there. There will be expanded *Awareness* at the very least. Greater *self-awareness* too —leading to improved personal capacities like deeper *compassion*, more *wisdom*. And if you Choose it, *self-discipline* in efforting towards something new to step into, and increased *resilience*, and *courage*—in carrying your burdens with *grace*.

And when your capacities are expanded, you can show up more effectively—more present to what is going on, while regulating your internal equilibrium and Personal Power more effectively.

You become refocused on what truly matters to you.

These things can actually change the course of your life for the better in the long run!

EMBRACING YOUR ROAD

LIVE, WHILE YOU ARE ALIVE

*I*n Western culture's orientation to 'get' this, 'have' that, and 'do' the other in order to get 'there', the emphasis is very much on the destination, rather than on the journey.

Once we're 'there', we'll be happy—we think. *We'll have 'arrived'. We'll feel safe.*

Ever in anticipation of that 'destination' materialising on our timeline, we work on the 'doing and getting'. It's the idea or value at the heart of our externally placed 'power'.

You could easily do the same with this book.

Having read it, you 'know' what to do now. It's just a matter of creating a 'to-do list' and managing your timeline as you tick the boxes, while anticipating the arrival of the transformations you seek.

But a list of goals that you must now achieve becomes another set of 'should's'—with the destination still off in the distance!

This is only going to put you back on the same path you were on before you began with me here; likely only to bring more of the kind of results you've probably experienced in so many other 'self-help' situations. —

You'll set the book aside, and then, as the distance between you and this reading experience increases, the familiar patterns of thinking and being in your life and the world will begin to crowd out your new insights. All you need is one trigger—and an old set of thoughts and reactions will play themselves out before you even realise it's happening.

That's not a lack on your part. It's the way we're wired.

It takes great internal effort to hold ourselves in newly created patterns of thinking and being until they're embedded and have replaced our default wiring.

And that sounds like too much hard work!

I promised at the start of the book that you wouldn't have to go that route. I promised you reconnection with yourself and your Power in life, and said that working with your inner game would change everything for you.

So I'd like to support you now, in setting yourself firmly upon your Empowerment Path in an easy and practical way.

THE TWO LEVERS OF PIVOT

As with everything, it's the *beginnings* that matter. We can't go full out from nothing and expect to maintain that. Muscles, habits, mindsets for example, all begin to shift into new forms when pressure is applied to the existing structures—but the evolution in them is gradual.

So it is with your vital, life-saving pivot.

You can't simply disengage from the patterns of your life and the business of being in the world! (And you do still have practical aspirations!)

At the same time you need to get momentum going, to see tangible results quickly.

Simply put, this pivot is about orientating yourself differently: towards your inner game. **And you can begin the process immediately, by**

pulling on just two key levers. (And as you go with these, you can adjust both pace and degree.)

1. The first is being prepared to let go of destination, to embrace an *experiential* journey.
2. The second part, is by engaging with *the power of intention* — as a "North Star" that will keep pulling you forwards, even when you experience setbacks along the way.

We'll tackle the journey first, and then bring intention into powerful play.

What if you were to commit to seeing this place you now find yourself in—this road you're on—as something *more* than an interim path to a 'destination'?

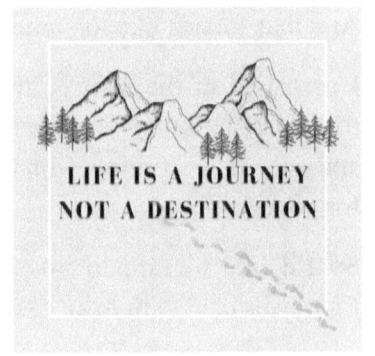

Because it is an absolute truth that no extra days are guaranteed us by Life. The journey could end tomorrow! Taking our focus off the horizon and allowing it to spend more time with us in our moment by moment experience gives us not only a better qualitative experience of our lives every single day, but also brings an ongoing immediacy to our generative Power and its Effects.

Distant (and ephemeral) goals in a future that may never materialise (for whatever reason) now give way to *every single day of our journey being the 'result'* we're aiming for.

- Each day showcases the *results of a crafted You* as you hone yourself in Life.
- Each day brings *results of your daily* Choices, creating your tomorrow and the future generally.

This means your results aren't revealed in the future on the back of a set of goals and a to-do list—but today and every day, on a step by step journey. Daily, you get to meet your latest best, most evolved Self! How wonderful.

So, could you regard at least *this* currently difficult part of your journey —as a Pilgrimage?

PILGRIMAGE

Millions of people of all faiths have undertaken pilgrimages across the ages. In times past, they were difficult and dangerous journeys, so the reasons for undertaking such a perilous trip had to be compelling!

—And they were. These journeys were acts of devotion: paying homage to the inspirational and exemplary life and qualities of a founder or saint, or a revered location. They were also understood to be a valuable spiritual exercise—where Pilgrims were immersed symbolically in the reality of the challenging nature of our journey on this Earth and our short stay here while fostering personal transformation, as the Pilgrims struggled through many hardships to complete their journeys.

Today (and increasingly) many secular people too, have seen the value of stepping off their normal path to go on a journey of self-discovery.

Many of us know someone who has walked the Camino de Santiago (or Way of St James) for example. Modern pilgrims mix with tourists on the Camino, not just for personal gratification, but undertaking a more *sacred* journey. —Knowing that the journey will shape them and shape them for the better, they quest for meaning, truth, values and purpose, seeing the walk as an opportunity to re-evaluate their own life and Self.

But, more than seeking resolution or absolution, they're seeking personal transformation: to become all they can be and become.

You now, have been directed by Life away from the road you *were* travelling on (with the milestones and destinations you imagined you'd find there). You've been put on *this* path instead—where you've been offered a new perspective of reality. If you think about it, this new road may be offering you the opportunity to live another way—as did the Pilgrims while they journeyed.

ELEVATING YOUR ROAD

When you treat your journey as 'pilgrimage', you drop the mantel of 'sacred' onto it. And by 'sacred', I mean something that is considered worthy of a very special kind of respect or devotion.

Treating this phase of your Life where you're so challenged and feel so much personal stress and pain as a pilgrimage—*elevates* your experience, and you. *The journey itself becomes as important as the outcomes you're trying to reach*—and everything encountered on the road is given new and extra purpose and significance.

Can you imagine your experience as a quest for the truth of Who You Are instead of a 'rush-around-and-gather' exercise? It becomes devotion to liberating your potentials, while developing your capacities and sculpting your character.

You're *worth honouring* in this way!

DAILY SHIFTING

On the road, you're gradually letting go of the limiting "brules" that have run your life up to now and decimated your self-esteem. You're living a new purpose. You're striving to recognise and know the higher truths of your life and yourself.

In this space, you're undertaking daily personal development, living strongly from your personal principles. The challenges you encounter call something new out of you with which to respond—calling the best of you forth! You engage, you persevere, you develop your resilience, and you retrieve your ingenuity and out-of-the-box thinking.

More and more often you'll find yourself accepting what is and where you are without bitterness or resentment, without giving up on yourself or your vision, and without judging others—or yourself. *Living in a state of grace.*

It all leads to a personal transformation over time.

Now this may sound like something of a 'to-do' that ultimately will be ticked off the list: *"Pilgrimage—done!"* But remember, this pivot is not about reaching a 'destination' at this time, but about an unfolding journey through Growth, into the Changes that have been forced upon you.

It needs a different 'energy'—that is seated in 'intention'.

INTENTION...

While 'being intentional' does orientate itself around 'result'—it's a much more nuanced approach than simply being 'productive'.

Resolutions and Goals are very much in our faces because they're located in external reality—yet really, they're expressing Intention in the world. Intentions are internal and 'softer, arising from a deeper source within us, often very much as a result of (and therefore aligned with) our values.

Intention is the beating heart of Resolution (and the goals that derive from it). It's the engine that pushes Resolution forwards in the desired direction. Even when a specific Resolution isn't achieved, Intention keeps pulling, directing, and informing our way forwards—towards completion.

> **Intention represents *commitment*—without the "need to deliver" a result.**

Intentions therefore have longevity—keeping us orientated to and tracking towards our North Star.

INTENTION ENGAGES WITH LONGEVITY

Now this is important here. Because, after a long stint of feeling defeated by Life (and even by ourselves), finding the motivation to begin at something (and then keep at it) can be nigh impossible, particularly if we're somewhat jaded about whether or not we really will get results this time.

And usually, this *is* where we begin: with some concrete goal.

But this is where Intention comes into its own.

When we need to get practical and manifest something on the other side of loss, grief and being 'stuck', we need to have something to shoot for. *Intention* can live within us, as that.

An Intention may *feel* something like a goal—but it's much less hard and fixed. It's really our 'why'—keeping us consciously engaged and persevering, *even when things don't work out*. It informs our actions as it keeps us inspired as we step forward into each new day, and strive in our interactions and tasks.

As you now know, having a 'why'—like feeling connected to someone or something worthwhile—makes it possible to carry and push through as necessary (including through difficulty and suffering) as you strive to achieve what is meaningful to you.

It's so important to remember that you're a work-in-progress, rather than a productivity-rat. If you 'fail', reconnect to 'Intention', rather than sinking into a sense of being a failure for not crossing something off your list. *This is one of the most incredibly powerful self-guiding mechanisms you can employ.*

Living intentionally *is thus incredibly powerful, particularly during changing, challenging times*

THE SECRET IS THAT 'INTENTION' IS MARRIED TO 'ALLOWING'.

Intention and Allowing are two sides of the same coin.

Moving through life with Intention keeps you focused, yet 'allows' you to be flexible around 'what is'—without losing sight of where you're going.

In the physical form you need to give effort—and often a lot of it—to your work to see your vision and goals realised. You have to be practical, engage with tasks, and push forward.

When you get to the point where you're overwhelmed or it seems impossible, you need to be able to let go if things get stuck. You have to be able to step back with grace, trust and patience—and let things unfold, while still deeply connected to your Intentions. (And this is easier to do than hanging onto a goal, because it's values-based, and attached to your 'Why').

This lack of rigidity will keep you focused in your chosen direction without becoming demoralised by setbacks. It's dancing with Life, allowing Life to deliver (often unasked for) outcomes, and flowing with them within your structure of 'Intention'.

> *"I will go forward into every day with intention, rather than agenda."*
> *"I set intentions for myself to engage my 'Why' and my inner drivers."*
> *"My Intentions have longevity — and keep me tracking towards my North Star."*

∼

RESOLVING SOMETHING ELSE

Nothing is going to change until you start taking action: inner action, as well as the actual things you do each day.

Your overall intention on this Pilgrimage will be to define yourself (personally and to the world)—as the person you're proud to be.

You'll be making a **contribution** simply by Who You Are, rather than creating for personal gain in a silo.

You'll need **determination** on this journey. You will need to **resolve** to stick with your quest, engaging with your **tenacity** in order to keep going, for as long as it takes.

You'll need to strive to remain **positive** and **motivated** in dealing with whatever the day brings, in order to survive and then thrive again.

It won't be easy and you'll be tested again and again. So you'll need **resilience**, and to be prepared to push through hard times and challenges, even when they're unrelenting.

And you'll need **grace**. You'll have to draw on and develop all your inner qualities to keep going with dignity and with kindness, no matter how challenging things may continue to be.

You always need to remain **connected** with and lovely to those around you whom you care about. They will buoy you on this journey, and become inspired and energised by your example too!

EMBRACING YOUR ROAD

Now, it's time to commit.

> *"This has happened to me. I deeply accept that I'm on this path now."*

Don't be right. Don't be fixed in your views, your vision or your current values. Be open. Be curious. Keep your eyes open for possibility without fixed agendas and inner cravings, like —"I *must* do/have/this!"—or aversions—"I *cannot* do/have that!"

Allow.

> *"I can trust, I can be open to this journey, knowing that Life WANTS to thrive through me—as all Life does."*

And then see what happens.

You have a new direction now. Set your intentions, and walk the road — in that new direction, holding yourself upright through the storms.

> *"I'm going to go forward—doing all I can to ALLOW this road to bring changes in me and shift my Life in an incredible (and positive) way!"*

You will find it easy to remain resolute when you truly believe in the value of this. You understand why it's important, and you're excited to see Who you will become *because* of the journey.

> *"I CHOOSE this new path!"*

You'll live with hope, and find therefore that you can take more courageous action, more often. —More adventurous, outside-the-box action!

> *"I conspire with Life to hone me on the outside, as I sculpt myself from the inside—gradually as is necessary and possible for me—collaborating with Life, in trust, to evolve me for the better."*

You'll choose this because you know, somewhere deep inside you, that you need it. That the moment has come, to level up. The call to shift out of pain and stuckness, out of feelings of powerlessness and the inaction they generate, has become loud in your ears.

The desire to change and grow is the root and foundation of your pilgrimage. This is the ultimate shift into your new approach to life.

Flow begins. Take it from me. This works.

You will find yourself returning to this inner place (the one place where you *are* in control) time and time again, to reorientate to your Intentions and to Choose again, consciously developing and sculpting yourself — to allow growth to take place in you, and through you.

It may be helpful to set some clear Resolutions for yourself—Resolutions that direct your intentionality as you begin this walk. They'll keep you true to your new way of seeing yourself, grounded in your Context, and realistic about Life itself.

I've created a 'Resolutions' Reference/Guide that summarises the ideas I've shared here. If you'd like to use this as a handy Resource to keep you tracking on challenging days (that you could also customise to your own Vision), you're welcome to contact me on my website www.petraspaige.com and I will send on the pdf to you.

RETURNING HOME

For now—allow yourself to be on this pilgrimage. You're *choosing* to go on the journey. *You choose to be changed when you recognise the need for it.*

Eventually though, as all pilgrims do, you will return—to a daily path that becomes a new normal for you.

This return 'home' has its place within the pilgrimage and is just as important as the journey. Because as the journey onto the Pilgrim's path and the destination (the truth of Who You Are) are opportunities for spiritual growth and understanding—so the return 'home' will be about integrating and putting into practise those insights you have gained whilst on this road of pilgrimage.

There will be both superficial and enduring changes in you. But you are beginning to create your personal legacy.

This *is* your pilgrimage.

GO FORTH INSPIRED

STEP INTO THE FUTURE — EMPOWERED BEING THAT YOU ARE

*S*howing up well is one of our deepest yearnings. I know this as an absolute Truth about each of us.

Yet we can easily recoil from this natural impulse when we get hurt, or when the challenges we encounter on our journeys seem overwhelming. Diverted from this yearning as Purpose and from our naturally chosen paths, we get lost in the messages that come *at* us, that seem to be about us and asserting Who We Are: *not enough*. We become disconnected from our internal source of Power, from our sense of wholeness and wellbeing, from Possibility, and worst of all—from our true selves. We lose ourselves.

So what I have wanted to create for you in writing this book is 'Awareness'. Not just of 'what is' (apparently at least)—but also of 'what isn't'.

I have wanted to reconnect you to your Self: to your own goodness and potency, to your own self-generated Power, and to what is truly possible in the face of your sense that all doors are closed against you.

I have wanted to highlight your Self as separate from Context (though stimulated by it) and awaken you to the Choices you always have to define yourself—both because of it, and despite it.

If I have done my work well, bringing this 'Awareness' into your field will already have begun to shift your Thinking, Attitudes and Perspectives on Life in general, on your life in particular, on You-in-Context—and on Who You Are.

Armed with this, **Who might You now become?**

EVERYTHING HAPPENS *BECAUSE* OF CONTEXT

Context is the overall field of Life on this planet: a great treasure box of stage and curtains, costume and masks; where experience is offered, consumed and shared in connection, stories, drama, laughter and tears —*for our own growth and enlightenment.*

Context is, quite simply—Possibility.

Closer to home, Context is environment and relationships: the 'containers' in which our lives takes place, where actions are made possible (or they are not).

Yet we are not our Contexts.

This distinction is so important. On stage, costumed up, we are not the actors we seem to be on stage, nor the play. We are *expressions* of Possibility in the moment! Beyond these, we always Ourselves, looking out into the room at this moment in time.

Context gives *us* the Opportunity—to Be.

But only if we're prepared to engage.

Thanks to Context, we get to find out Who We Are, where our Power is, and how best to use it. —Though of course, we must encounter our fears, our weaknesses, what pains us, and what disempowers us, to discover those things!

A NEW STAGE FOR NEW CHARACTERS

Our Context has shifted massively since the beginning of the Millennium. We've been handed (and are handling) heavy challenges—and all while working under and into uncertainty. These last few years in particular have been a wild ride, with Covid-19 upending our usual patterns, trashing our assumptions of 'business-as-usual', and upending both personal and global equilibriums.

Meanwhile, large and long term changes continue to unfold in the background:

- in climate change and the ongoing destruction of the biosphere on which we depend for Life.
- through ongoing population explosion and migration.
- in the global shift in the balance of power.
- in our changed personal agency in the practical world, given new and extreme economic challenges for billions of us.

These things alone are more than likely to keep us on our toes and grappling with Change for quite some time to come — while many of us continue to struggle with what feels like reduced Opportunity.

Yet it's much bigger than that.

The truth is that since our Context is changing *permanently*, the Opportunities are changing too. Grappling with what's different in the field (almost all of which *we've* created)—requires a new expression *of* us.

BUT DON'T QUAIL AT THIS REALITY!

We remain undiminished all the same. Empowered all the same.

DIFFERENTIATING OURSELVES FROM CONTEXT

The Actor on the Stage receives feedback from the audience (Context) about how their acting has engaged, moved, inspired and shaped *it*. This feedback can engage, move, inspire and ultimately shape the Actor's craft in turn: Insight, leading to growth, leading to upleveling.

Yet clearly the audience, in giving feedback, does not hold either the Actor's real identity, nor their decision to act on the insights it gives. That Power remains with the Actor, regardless of the play or the audience.

Actors who give too much weight to their audiences' responses aren't balancing this with an Awareness of the variability of their own performance or mood, the zeitgeist of the play, or the fickleness of the audience itself. The Actors then aren't seeing the audience simply as a mirror that reflects something about the moment back to them—for their growth and enlightenment. The feedback instead becomes Fact and Truth—about them.

This is handing personal Power over to the audience to define Who the Actor Is: not enough. This is handing over self-esteem at the same time. And that is giving Self away.

Up to now, similarly, we've over-identified ourselves with our Contexts —even merged ourselves with it—giving all our Power over to it in the process.

It is time to take our Power back from Context. No matter what Context does, we are Ourselves. And we are enough.

And in a Context that's permanently changed and changing, where the old 'rules' no longer apply; where our lives have often become more uncomfortable and anxiety-inducing than stable and happy—there are also massive Opportunities now to change and improve all sorts of things!

—Starting with Ourselves. Ourselves as Cause.

Yet we must be prepared to engage.

CHOICE — AND ACTION

To navigate our turbulent global waters and move forward from wherever we are—particularly within, but practically as well—we must Choose to do so. Whatever it takes. —And not because it means our suffering must (or will) end and we'll be enabled to 'return to normal' or even 'excel'.

But because we've been called by Life to move forward: to define ourselves and our way newly—if not practically, then at least personally.

It's not someone else's job to save us. We're not powerless victims of Life. We can expect something of ourselves—called up from within us—rather than always from our environment, or other people.

We can be part of our own solution. Of others' solutions. And of the wider solution. As the unique species that we are, we can overcome instinct, default behaviour, and Choose.

All we need is within Ourselves.

We do this from a clear sense of Who We Are, of what we're personally trying to achieve—and Why. We can Choose to do our most to show up as the best person we can be, regardless of what comes at us. To be our own hero.

All it needs is Intention. And to take up our Choices with resolve.

What we must not choose—is to quit. To give up. Because it's not over. Not yet.

The future is only as bleak as we allow it to become. At worst, we can always Choose to be gracious and accepting of circumstances we can't control or change.

And then we can Choose to be great people within these. And we can take the view that life happens *for* us, and through us. Not *to* us.

There isn't just something to grieve in the pain of our losses.

> **We each have the Possibility and potential to be magnificent—even off the back of disaster and despair.**

There's *always* something to powerfully and passionately fight for. Our growth. Our best iteration yet.

We are *Cause*.

WONDER

If we take a step back from our tiny existences just for a moment, it's hard not to see that we are slap bang in the middle of a miracle!

—Not just of nature and the amazing Life we see in it: an incredible diversity of complex, beautiful plants and creatures; stunning landscapes. It's an amazing variety—all in perfect and interconnected balance on and of our planet, as it spins in its place in the unknowable vastnesses of space and time, amongst other, massive planets and ancient stars.

But also of other Human Beings.

Think of the astonishing contributions of those who have gifted us the amazing things we enjoy today.

The internet, stuffed with all Human knowledge, shared freely and available globally to anyone with a computer and an Internet Service Provider.

The iPhone (and its derivatives), connecting us to one other in ten or twenty different ways, and giving access to all of that knowledge and information at our fingertips.

Aeroplanes that have opened up the world, its wonders, and each other — to so many of us!

The magic of a symphony, written and then played by talented musicians.

Television! Electricity! (Absolute wizardry in my opinion…).

The ability to save lives and heal others — even hauling them back from the brink of death—through complex research, knowledge, expertise and detailed procedures.

Connection: friendship, love, laughter, kindness and compassion; people who love each other. Just go to the arrivals hall in an airport to see what that looks like.

Teamwork. Nothing more needs to be said on this! The dedication of so many to collaboratively lift so many others up with care, for the common good, is breathtaking.

The gifts of eduction, water on tap, furniture and appliances, blankets and shoes; the installation of sewerage systems, the provision of rubbish disposal services…

And then there is the magnificence of the Human spirit: people who have stood for something, demonstrating personal qualities and noble ideals that are inspiring, personally defining—heroic even—who created amazing outcomes that have shifted and lifted us all up in some way.

All—are the awe-inspiring outcomes of Human endeavour, presence, aspiration, and vision.

And engagement.

> 'Life' is truly breathtaking in all its forms. It is truly an honour and a privilege to *be* a part of it—and to be able to *take part* in it.

OUR POWER TRULY LIES WITHIN US

What do the extraordinary people who have realised their immense potential, like Mandela, or Oprah Winfrey for example—icons of empowerment—have in common?

They became powerful inside before they became powerful externally.

They developed their inner strength.

They summoned courage in the face of fear, and persevered when they were exhausted and couldn't contemplate taking another step forward.

It's likely that they would speak about having such strong purpose and connections that they were *pulled* forward, even when they seemed (and felt) defeated.

Their ability to handle adversity, their willingness to tolerate pain or sleepless nights, or to make some sacrifices—and even the importance of developing a thick skin sometimes—were likely all key traits that kept them upright.

No-one who has achieved anything extraordinary in life doesn't possess a healthy dose of inner strength.

Though we may be deprived of our freedoms and have little sense of personal power over our circumstances or situation, it is what's going on internally in our thoughts and attitudes that really moves us towards, or away from—suffering. **Meaning** is located in our interior: in our sense of Identity, in our connection to others, in a vision, or a sense of purpose.

When we come from this internal source of Self and experience, it's possible to prevail—even when it's painful; even in incredibly difficult circumstances; even over time.

Awareness connects you to your Inner Power.

It helps you leverage your hard-won experience and insights into *powerful* Choices, so that you're increasingly able to make new and better decisions about how most effectively to empower yourself.

With Awareness it becomes easier and easier to engage with and step up to the challenge that Life burdens you with. —It helps you see the Opportunities inherent within your challenges!

Awareness brings equilibrium to you. Aligning yourself to a relentless search for greater Awareness enables you to constantly build and replenish yourself and your ability to be truly Powerful.

REMEMBER ALWAYS THAT 'WE ARE CAUSE'

Now here you are. And you are here, until you leave Life on this planet behind. And being here, you will wake up each morning, and must decide what to do with your time and your Choices.

You can be part of the consuming, cockroach approach in this amazing Picture, lurching from accident to annihilation, telling yourself that none of it matters anyway because *you* can't see the point and you feel low and despondent about everything; because you believe that we're all too weak and flawed to be able to make any difference to anything anyway.

Or—you can decide to try for luminary.

To be the best Human Being you can be, engaging meaningfully with your life and others.

Taking responsibility for yourself and the Effects you Cause.

Deciding to bravely step forward into *whatever it takes* to develop your insight, courage, resourcefulness and personal depth.

Striving for resilience, and a fine character. Standing for something, even if that's just being relentlessly kind, or honest.

Creating something, to shift (or help shift) something important into a new direction. To step up, and shape up.

We each have *the Choice, to be part of the problem, or to strive to be contributing—and a part of the solution.*

Your Contract with Life, so long as you breathe, is that you will Grow, through Change.

This tasks you to stretch your thinking and your capabilities beyond where they're currently set—and to keep pushing at the boundaries set by your Perceiving and assumptions—with Curiosity and open-mindedness.

Choose deep values that reflect your Identity, and, supported by a developing Inner Musculature, show up with character traits, attitudes and behaviour that accurately reflect Your Expression into the world.

Bring personal grace and resilience to the table in your circumstances. Particularly in challenging ones. Your strong inner Self will support you, and maximise your chance of achieving a fulfilling and peaceful life, even when circumstances are challenging.

YOUR PURPOSEFUL LIFE

Remember that Context is Possibility and you are the expression of it! Engage meaningfully with it. Be grateful for the Opportunity that it is after all, and keep trying creatively, tenaciously. *You can **trust** that things will shift*, both in yourself and in circumstances: because Change is *always* happening!

I invite you to step forward now, to improve not only your Life, but Yourself in the main.

You are here, with new and healthier perspectives on Life, on Yourself, and on the Human condition.

Take *charge* of your Self in your unexpectedly difficult Life. Resolve to Step Up—*despite* your circumstance

Evolve your Self. *Answer that yearning to show up well.*

Grow.

Sculpt your inner Self—into the most amazing, kind, resilient and purposeful person you can be, regardless of (or despite)—your circumstances. In doing so, you *will* reconnect purposefully to possibility and hope, despite all the ugliness, fear and loss. Because…

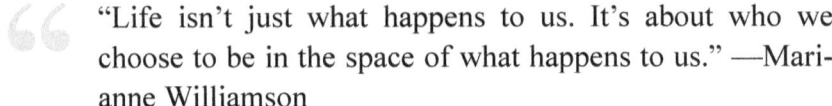 "Life isn't just what happens to us. It's about who we choose to be in the space of what happens to us." —Marianne Williamson

You matter. Not just to those who love you, but simply because you *are*, and are here on this planet with the mission to grow yourself.

The present moment is the future in the making.

Now is your Opportunity, to create your future—and ours.

CLOSING VERSE

Live while you are alive.
Learn the ways of silence and wisdom
Learn to act, learn a new speech
Learn to be what you are in the seed of your spirit
Learn to free yourself from all the things
That have moulded you
And which limit your secret and undiscovered road.

Remember that all things which happen
To you are raw materials
endlessly fertile
Endlessly yielding of thoughts that could change
Your life and go on doing so forever.

Never forget to pray and be thankful
For all things good or bad on the rich road;
For everything is changeable
So long as you live while you are alive.

—**Ben Okri** [19]

GLOSSARY OF TERMS

These definitions are my own understandings of the concepts inherent in these Words.

INTRODUCTIONS

Suffering

1. The feelings of ongoing sadness, distress, anguish and hopelessness that take hold in an experience of powerlessness, when hardships seem insurmountable.
2. When this experience is ongoing, and particularly when it's seemingly without end, Suffering can become unendurable - and lethal.

life: The period during which a person or creature is alive or exists, with a beginning, a journey, and an ending in death.

Self: Who you are inside of your physicality — who 'experiences' in the inner world of thoughts and feelings, is aware, and makes choices. This inner You is always in a state of potential: can be actively, endlessly developed regardless of circumstances — improving/sculpting/shaping your qualities and capacities.

Consciousness: An awareness of Self in Context: responsive to it, yet separate from it.

Hand of (Life) cards: The opportunities you're born with or create as you grow, that open the doors to certain possibilities and enable you to step into opportunity.

Life: The 'intelligent' force that ties all living creatures together in a great interconnected reality, and moves them inexorably forward into time and the Effects arising there.

Personal Power: Our ability to influence our survival, meet our needs, and make things happen. Our Personal Power enables us to actively *shape* our lives in the vast scope of our existence.

Identity: The "I" part of the Self you reveal to the outside world through the expression of personality and demonstration of character.

WHY THIS BOOK WAS WRITTEN

"New" Normal: The state of the society, economy or political climate following a crisis, when this differs noticeably from the situation that prevailed prior to the start of the crisis.

Change: A process or an act by which something undergoes transition and becomes different than it was — from tiny variations to complete transformation.

Culturescape: Essentially the complexity of thoughts, beliefs and myths prevalent in a community or society that form a 'constructed' world of understandings and assumptions — that all buy into.

Ongoingly: A word not yet officially in existence (therefore not found in any dictionary!) but usefully denoting "currently, continuously, and open-endedly — in one single word.

Possibility: The chance that something may or may not happen or exist. Much more than happenstance, it's pure, creative potential, and an ever-present, generative wellspring.

Insight: An accurate understanding or intuitive vision that penetrates deeply into the true inner nature and complexity of someone or something, resulting in new perspective or empowering knowledge.

SELF HELP THAT ACTUALLY WORKS

Wisdom: A composite of our stored knowledge, of what we know to be true, of our insights and common sense, and of the complexity of things in relationship to one another — as held in an ongoing state of expanded Awareness.

Thinking: Existing in the mind, Thinking is the flow of ideas and associations in Humans, whereby they make sense of and interpret their experience, and manipulate information to form concepts and problem solve. A creative process that ultimately leads to Insights, Thoughts and conclusions, which generate feelings and actions.

Grace: A condition that is free of anger, blame, uncertainty and fear, but suffused with thankfulness, willingness, acceptance and kindness. Brings equilibrium that enables us to reach for resilience, and creativity even in the face of hardship.

THINGS FALL APART

Big Picture: Our personal, utopic Vision of our happy, successful, engaged selves living our idyllic lives. Always seeking to realise it despite setbacks and difficulties, we hold to this as a North Star of sorts.

Narrative: A personal account of a connected sequence of events that becomes a 'story', revealing our perspective.

A "FIRST WORLD PROBLEM"

A First World Problem: A problem or frustration experienced by a 'privileged' Westerner, that's dismissed as relatively trivial or minor when contrasted with the challenges often experienced by those in cultures in the developing world.

Applied to oneself, it's a comic apology for trivial moaning. When directed at someone else, it's typically to shame the complainer.

THE SCHOOL OF THE SOFT TOUCH

Tough Love: A person in authority sets clear boundaries and limits and is prepared to treat someone sternly (or even what seems to be harshly) to teach them life lessons that are helpful in the long run. The someone experiences the consequences of their behaviour rather than receiving extra chances, or being protected or rescued.

Rights: Not 'granted' by any authority, Rights are Human ideas of entitlements and freedoms seen as inherent to all Humans purely by virtue of having been born and existing — regardless of gender, ethnic origin, national affiliation, religion, or any other status. Not 'recognised' by all nations, they range from the fundamental 'right to life' to rights which make life worth living, eg. food, education, work, health, and liberty.

Learned helplessness: When a person experiences a stressful situation repeatedly, they may come to believe in their own powerlessness to control or change the situation. Believing that nothing they do matters, they give up trying — even when opportunities for change become available. They avoid challenges, turn negative and don't engage in problem-solving.

COMPONENTS OF SUFFERING

Victim: A person who has been hurt, damaged, injured or made to suffer as a result of an event or action, accident or crime.

FEAR

Original Fear: The fear we felt when we were first born is our first experience of suffering. Avoiding or getting free of this feeling is one of our earliest drivers in Life

Original Desire: This is the desire to survive, and the source of all future desires; the desire to thrive, in particular.

Lack: The sense of something missing, or something unrealised. The sense can leave one feeling vulnerable or exposed, and the inability to address it is disempowering.

WHO AM I IF I CAN'T?

A Crisis Of Identity: A state in which we lose touch with our sense of Self: we're uncertain of who we are, of our place in the world and of our value.

Achiever: A person who 'gets things done', and in terms of our understanding of "success" is seen to be "successful".

Failure: Something —anything — that goes 'wrong'. This includes *public* failures and mistakes, *personal* failures like making friends or getting recognition or in marriage, and *private* failures like moral failure.

THE STAGE IS SET

Context: The field in which everything — all existence and experience — takes place. It thus underpins/informs/influences everything all the time. Contexts are multi-layered and experienced as such and concurrently.

- The Internal Context is our personal experience of events, and the only place where we have real control.
- The External Context is environment and relationships — where actions take place and where experience is generated. We have little to no control here: Context may facilitate or deny us).

A WESTERN CULTURAL CONTEXT

"Previous" Normal: The economic expansion followed by a long-run of unprecedented growth, prosperity and opportunity in First World economies, that followed the end of the Second World War.

The Game of Life: We're born into circumstances (our hand of cards) and must play the cards we're given. Accepting that, we must play with our best effort, while trying pick up better cards and create better options for ourselves as we go along.

A SHIFTING CONTEXT

"Rules" of Life: Our interpretation of what we should do, the requirements we need to meet and 'hoops' we should jump through — to achieve "success".

"REAL" VICTIMS

Victimhood: The condition of a person who has come to feel helpless and passive as a result of misfortune, damage, suffering or ill-treatment. S/he feels personally diminished by anything that goes wrong, even when such wasn't directed at them, and is unlikely to be open to other explanations or possible solutions.

GLOSSARY OF TERMS | 325

It can be claimed to get people to feel sorry for one, or be used as an excuse for something.
It can integrate with someone's Identity, informing their attitudes and actions in life.

CULTURAL MYTHS

Happiness: Feeling deeply at ease within ourselves, and experiencing and enjoying an overall feeling of wellbeing and peace. At the surface there is "no-pain". Deeper, there is the absence of fear and desire that once we experienced in the comfort and safety of the womb. (My definition)

Glambition: The uplevelled, luxury version of Ambition: the outcomes that drive the strong desire for success or achievement are high quality, attractive and/or exciting — as conceptualised by Glamour.

Perspective: Existing in the mind, it's *one* way of looking at something, generating feelings and very often actions. This point of view is biased by personality, values, life experience and feelings etc. rather than rationally based.

Truth: Made up of properties in accord with Fundamental Reality, actuality and proven Facts.
* Absolute Truth — is true in all possible contexts, and is inviolable and eternal.
* Relative Truth — is subject to time, place and perception.

A WORD ON "MENTAL ILLNESS"

Depression: A deeper experience and longer-lasting experience of sadness, that may include one or all of these: ongoing sadness, tearfulness, low moods, lethargy, a lack of enthusiasm and feelings of despair.

Disenfranchised Grief: Describes grief that is not acknowledged as legitimate by society. A loss may be seen as too small or the relationship too distant to justify grieving, so the resulting grief experience is dismissed or not supported.

Clinical Depression: A depressed mood that meets the DSM-V criteria for a depressive disorder: 5 or more symptoms of the illness must have been present during the same two-week period and represent a change from previous functioning, with at least one of the symptoms being either depressed mood, or loss of interest or pleasure.

Also known as "major depression," and "major depressive disorder" different types include persistent depressive disorder (a depressed mood that lasts for at least two years); postpartum depression (experienced after childbirth); seasonal affective disorder, or SAD (triggered by reduced sunlight during winter months); and psychotic depression (triggered by a co-occurring psychosis).

Is characterised by more severe, persistent or chronic symptoms that manifest regardless of whether a person has experienced a traumatic event or major change.

GRIEVING THE LOSSES

Grief: Both the emotional expression of our powerlessness, and the process of releasing the past by 'digesting' painful realities, and adjusting to a 'new normal'.

A NEW ORIENTATION TO LIFE

Awareness: The state of being conscious of something. Specifically, the ability to directly know, perceive, feel, or be cognisant of events and their relationship to one another in the greater whole.

Brules: Vishen Lakhiani coined this term for the limiting cultural rules we buy into, otherwise known as "bullshit rules."

THE SUPERPOWER OF HUMAN BEINGS

Knowledge: Familiarity with the composite of facts, information and skills acquired through experience, education and internalised understandings. The concepts and conclusions that are the outcome of thinking, is packaged as 'knowledge.'

Understanding
1) the mechanism where we gain 'comprehension' of something
2) the deeper level of knowing something, in its complexity.

Meaning: Combining content, context and effect, and adding weight (significance) imbues something with 'meaning'. Meaning furnishes a thing with values or standards by which to judge it.

THE KRYPTONITE OF HUMAN BEINGS

Silo of Self: The interior Context of a person, in which experience and thinking take place, leading to perceptions and resulting feelings.

Mental Model: Personal, internal thinking that explains (to Self) how something works in the real world. People use them to make sense of and interact with the world around them. A constructed idea of external reality (based on an person's unique perceptions, understandings and life experiences) it does not necessarily reflect reality.

GLOSSARY OF TERMS | 327

THIS IS THE WATER

Reality: The state of things that are real and true, as they actually exist, unfold and develop, regardless of Human knowledge, understandings, perceptions, projections, expectations, and experience — including the Laws of Nature.

Water: The developmental journey of Life for living creatures, encompassing the totality of all things, structures and phenomena, (actual and conceptual, observable and not). For Humans, this includes the realities of judgement, suffering and ultimately death.

Grow: To come into existence from a source, followed by a process of natural development, by which something increases in size or substance and changes physically — to become more advanced or developed. Progressing towards maturity

"Actual" Normal: Every individual (regardless of who or where they are) is subject to the 'rules' of 'The Water' (thus often painful circumstances and relationships) in everyday life.

SWIMMERS

Significance: The need to matter — by belonging, by growing, by contributing. Recognition reflects this, suggesting we have impact. Significance is thus is a measure of our power.

CHOICE: CREATION

Choice: Choice is Cause — a response or course of action selected from a range of options that generates (thus 'creates') an Effect or result.

The Law of Cause and Effect: A universal law, and the "law of laws", which states that every single Cause (action) produces an Effect (reaction), which in turn produces another reaction... without fail and with a ripple effect — so that every Effect becomes the cause of something else. *Everything* we do impacts the whole. This law suggests that the universe is always in motion, having progressed from a chain of events.

ACTIVATING PERSONAL POWER

External Power: Meeting the need for Significance is dependent on external factors. Power is 'drawn' via "power over Context" (relationships, environment) and "success" (weight of influence in Context), both of which are variable and dependent on the Context itself. Power is often short term as a result.

Internal Power: Meeting the need for Significance is independent of external factors. Power is generated by combining Awareness with Choice to consciously and actively shape outcomes. Even if external factors reduce the facility to make Choices, an ongoing sense of self-esteem and personal empowerment maintains a sense of Significance.

Self-Awareness: The ability to objectively evaluate ourselves including observing and accurately identifying personal thoughts, feelings and impulses (responses), determining whether they are grounded in reality or not, and managing our resulting emotions. Understanding correctly how others perceive us, and aligning our behaviour with our internal standards and values.

Awarelight: Expanded Awareness. This enables more accurate interpretation of our surroundings, enabling us to make good choices and maintain some control — even in circumstances of discomfort and difficulty.

GOGGLES AND SNORKEL

Reaction: A result of emotion or instinct, Reactions are *stimulated* — often as a 'reverse' movement or impulse — not tied to reason, and with no consideration of the effect of this on the end result.

Response: A Response is a *considered* reaction: time has been taken to think, reason and *choose* an action for a considered end result.

EMBRACING YOUR ROAD

Pilgrimage: A sacred journey for something valuable. An evolution occurs along the way of the journey.

Sacred: Something 'sacred's is regarded as important and inviolable, treated with reverence, respect and even awe, and is thus protected.

Resolutions: Strong determinations to do something in particular about important ideas, values, attitudes, and actions, privately held, or publicly shared.

Goals: Deriving from Resolutions — goals are the calculated steps and fixed points on the delivery line that are needed to achieve Resolutions. They offer a trajectory to get things done.

ACKNOWLEDGMENTS

With this work, I stand on the shoulders of the thought giants who've come before me. So many of the ideas in this book, and the wisdoms and insights it contains have their genesis in the work of other wonderful, intelligent, wise people. I've brought many of them to these pages, and mixed them with my own, or paired them in unique ways with the insights I've gained in my own painful, wonderful, shattering and joyous life.

This work is my own though, born of my difficult journey through the death of many of my treasured hopes for my life and relationships, and the insights that were distilled on the way. Some of the ideas I've shared here, arriving through my own experience—were corroborated over the years as I came across (usually by chance) the work of other teachers—eliciting great internal shouts of joy as their insights confirmed that I was on the right track.

Caroline Myss's work on Personal Power has been foundational in my understanding of how our Power really works, how we lose it, and what to do to maximise it in our lives. Her descriptions of us as a 'huge unit of power' and 'everything you do, think, wear... is a power transaction' were enlightening, and try as I might to talk about this concept in words that are not hers — these were the only ones that could adequately describe it. When you come across them in my work, know that they are hers.

Marianne Williamson spoke in an interview on Youtube about 'inner musculature'. I was electrified by the concept, and went on to work out what that might encompass, and how to develop it with the same kind of care and attention to detail that so many people put into sculpting their bodies in the gym. She's also deeply informed my concept of being responsible for self.

Marie Forleo's many illuminating interviews with thought leaders including Mark Manson, Simon Sinek, Kris Karr and Glennon Doyle, for example, were deeply informative. Van Jones, Brendan Burchard, Seth Godin, Vishen Lakiani and Mindvalley, Robin Sharma and Michael Bernard Beckwith have also all inspired me as I've gone along, and contributed insights and hope.

How lucky are we all that these people are working in the world!

I don't know just how much of my work crosses over into theirs, but naturally a lot does. We're all in this together, talking about similar things—in the spirit of transformation for all, for the upliftment of all—so I offer acknowledgement and gratitude that though sharing their ideas and wisdoms, they have all shaped mine, cast out many of my assumptions and made me into a better, wiser person who could ultimately offer her own insights alongside theirs, and for the same reasons.

Dion, who offered me an opportunity, expanded my mind with hours of absorbing conversations, and brought me to the doors of my deepest insights. My writing partner An facilitated me to show up at my desk and write, and look forward to it! Louise, dearest of friends, whose excellent insights lifted much of this work, and whose enthusiasm for its message has been so valuably affirmative and encouraging!

And last (but not least) I must acknowledge Ric, my husband, who's terrifying brush with cancer and the incredible bruising he received from his employers as a result, was the genesis of this work.

Yet despite his unwavering support through the writing of this book, believing in the work, encouraging me to keep going — and giving me practical permission to take the time out to do it—it's his inner musculature that I most want to pay tribute to here.

He's been a living example of how to engage those muscles no matter what comes at you: to be true to oneself and to unfailingly honour both values and ideals.

Never ever did he lose sight of those things, doubt himself, feel bitter at life, or tell himself that he was disempowered.

He made a decision that he wasn't going to let this thing beat him, though so much was taken from him: his health, his income, and the close and loving relationship we had enjoyed up to that point.

He stood up and invested in his education, showed up loving and loyal in the face of my despair every single day, and went out and found a way to make an income and create possibilities for us.

He's been the steady hand in everything in our lives, and lives the wisdom that I've talked about a lot here, yet struggled to put into practise myself—and is a person of such deep integrity that I've been left breathless by him on too many occasions.

Oh, he's not perfect! But he's inspiring, and it's been a both a masterclass and an honour to learn about the Human spirit and Life—at his side.

SOURCES

START (Verse)
[1] **Okri, Ben**: The Famished Road (1991)
Published Jonathan Cape Ltd, London, a division of Penguin Random House
URL:https://www.penguin.co.uk/books/1038348/an-african-elegy/9780099736011.html

COMPONENTS OF SUFFERING
[2] Definition of **Suffering**
Dictionary.com
URL: https://www.dictionary.com/browse/suffer

[3] Definition of **Grief**
Dictionary.com
URL: https://www.dictionary.com/browse/grief

[4] Definition of **Fear**
Dictionary.com
URL: https://www.dictionary.com/browse/fear

FEAR
[5] **Nhat Hanh, Thich**: *Fear: Essential Wisdom For Getting Through The Storm* (2012)
Published by HarperOne (an imprint of Harper Collins Publishers)
https://harperone.com/9780062004734/fear/

A WESTERN CULTURAL CONTEXT
[6] **Max Roser**: *The Short History Of Global Living Conditions And Why It Matters That We Know It (2020)*
URL: a-history-of-global-living-conditions-in-5-charts

THE GREATEST RISK IN OUR FUTURE

[7] **Pew Research Center**: Social and Demographic Trends *The American Middle Class Is Losing Ground* (09/12/2015)
URL: the-american-middle-class-is-losing-ground

OECD
Under Pressure: The Squeezed Middle Class (2019)
URL: OECD-middle-class-2019-main-findings.pdf

Eustance Huang
Japan's Middle Class Is 'Disappearing' As Poverty Rises (28/09/2020)
URL: japans-middle-class-is-disappearing-as-poverty-rises-warns-economist.html

Andrea Willige, World Economic Forum
5 Charts That Show What Is Happening To The Middle Class Around The World (12/01/2017)
URL: 5-charts-which-show-what-is-happening-to-the-middle-class-around-the-world

Nancy Birdsall, Centre for Global Development
Middle Class: Winners or Losers in a Globalized World? (03/08/2017)
URL: middle-class-winners-or-losers-globalized-world

*[8] **UNHCR**: Ukraine, other conflicts push forcibly displaced total over 100 million for first time(2022)URL: https://www.unhcr.org/en-us/news/*

press/2022/5/628a389e4/unhcr-ukraine-other-conflicts-push-forcibly-displaced-total-100-million.html

https://www.unhcr.org/refugee-statistics/

A WORD ON "MENTAL HEALTH"
[9] **Hari, Johann**: Lost Connections (2019) p.51
Published by Bloomsbury Publishing, London
URL: https://www.bloomsbury.com/au/lost-connections-9781408878729/

A NEW ORIENTATION TO LIFE
[10] **Lakhiani Vishen:** The Code of the Extraordinary Mind (2019) — 'Brules'
Published by Rodale Books, an imprint of Random House,, a division of Penguin Random House, New York
URL: https://www.google.com.au/books/edition/The_Code_of_the_Extraordinary_Mind/hNnOCwAAQBAJ?hl=en&gbpv=1&printsec=frontcover

[11] **Frankel, Victor**: Man's Search for Meaning (1946)
Published by RIDER, an imprint of Ebury Publishing; 1st edition (1 April 2008)
URL: https://www.worldcat.org/title/mans-search-for-meaning/oclc/1239779065&referer=brief_results

SWIMMERS
[12] **Maslow, AH**: A Theory of Human Motivation (1943). p.375
Published by Martino Fine Books (2013 - reprint of 1943 edition)
URL: https://www.bookdepository.com/Theory-Human-Motivation-Abraham-H-Maslow/9781614274377?ref=grid-view&qid=1618266321535&sr=1-18

[13] **Image**: Shutterstock.com
URL: https://www.maslows-hierarchy-needs-scalable-vector-illustration-603660668

VERSE
[14] **Milton, John Comus**: A Maske Presented at Ludlow Castle, 1634: On Michaelmasse night, before the Right Honourable John Earl of Bridgewater (1634)
Published 1637, London. Held by The British Library
URL: https://www.bl.uk/collection-items/john-milton-a-maske-presented-at-ludlow-castle

Credited with the origins of the proverbial saying 'every cloud has a silver lining' — to convey the notion that, no matter how bad a situation might seem, there always is some good aspect to it.

HOW I BECAME EMPOWERED
[15] **'Helicopter' Parent:** A parent who pays extremely close attention to a child's or children's experiences and problems, particularly at educational institutions. So named because, like helicopters, they "hover overhead", overseeing every aspect of their child's life constantly. Definition from URL: https://en.wikipedia.org/wiki/Helicopter_parent

'Lawnmower' Parent: Also referred to as "snowplow" parents or "bulldozer" parents, lawnmower parents have a strong desire to protect their child from any type of struggle or obstacle. And as a result, they're said to "mow over" any problem their child faces, as well as prevent problems from occurring in the first place. Definition from URL: https://www.healthline.com

THE VITAL PIVOT
[16] **Kübler-Ross, Elisabeth**: Death: The Final Stage Of Growth (1975)
Published by Englewood Cliffs, N.J.: Prentice-Hall
URL:https://www.worldcat.org/title/death-the-final-stage-of-growth/oclc/1273611

YOUR EMPOWERMENT PATH
[17] **Seligman, Martin:** Learned Optimism (2006)
Published by RIDER, an imprint of Ebury Publishing; 1st edition (1 April 2008)
https://www.penguin.com.au/books/learned-optimism-9781864713039

[18] **Ayto, John**: Dictionary of Word Origins (2009)
Published by Bloomsburg. Imprint A&C Black Publishers; London. 1st edition (17 October 1990)
https://www.bloomsbury.com/au/word-origins-9781408101605/

END (Verse)
[19] **Okri, Ben**: An African Elegy: To an English Friend in Africa. (excerpt) (1991)
Published Jonathan Cape Ltd, London (1992)
https://www.penguin.co.uk/books/1038348/an-african-elegy/9780099736011.html

www.ingramcontent.com/pod-product-compliance
Lightning Source LLC
Chambersburg PA
CBHW022029290426
44109CB00014B/805